T0071955

SCANDAL

A MANUAL

GEORGE RUSH
WITH JOANNA MOLLOY

SKYHORSE PUBLISHING

Skyhorse Publishing books may be purchased in bulk at special discounts for sales promotion, corporate gifts, fund-raising, or educational purposes. Special editions can also be created to specifications. For details, contact the Special Sales Department, Skyhorse Publishing, 307 West 36th Street, 11th Floor, New York, NY 10018 or info@skyhorsepublishing.com.

Skyhorse® and Skyhorse Publishing® are registered trademarks of Skyhorse Publishing, Inc.®, a Delaware corporation.

Visit our website at www.skyhorsepublishing.com.

10 9 8 7 6 5 4 3 2 1

Library of Congress Cataloging-in-Publication Data is available on file.

Cover design by Owen Corrigan
Cover photo credit © AP Images except middle right photo © Selma Fonseca

Print ISBN: 978-1-63220-677-0
Ebook ISBN: 978-1-62873-533-8

Printed in the United States of America

Nosey Parkers

I f the bodies of George Rush and Joanna Molloy should ever be found floating in the East River, the lineup of suspects could rival any red carpet. Which celeb had finally gotten fed up with reading the swill those two wrote in the *New York Daily News*? Russell Crowe? Sean Penn? Robert De Niro? Perhaps even Police Commissioner Ray Kelly should be asked about his whereabouts on the night in question. But if we could speak from the morgue, we might advise detectives to check first for blood on the spiked heels of Sarah Jessica Parker.

We had a little history with SJP, to put it mildly. Years before it became a life-support system for fashionable women (and the gay men who love them), we witnessed the conception of her show, *Sex and the City*. In 1993, our pal, Candace Bushnell, started doing a column for the *New York Observer*. It was a thinly veiled diary of her life. Everybody knew that Mr. Big was Candace's boyfriend, leather pants–wearing *Vogue* publisher Ron Galotti. Stanford Blatch was her manager Clifford Streit, who'd drop droll asides when we'd all be out at Nell's or The Odeon or Bowery Bar. The following week, his bon mots would show up in Candace's column. Clifford used to say, "I don't mind if my friends use my lines, as long as they let me know in advance."

Carrie Bradshaw, *Sex and the City*'s narrator, was, of course, Candace—only a tamer version of Candace. We never saw Carrie light up a joint in a restaurant while a police sergeant sat a few booths away. We never saw Carrie pee into a men's urinal because she didn't want to wait in line for the ladies' room. Candace could drink Carrie under the table. But Candace also got up the next morning and wrote. Give her credit: she worked hard and almost single-handedly created modern chick lit.

Candace could be touchy. Once, we were checking out a tip about a guy her producer and friend, Darren Star, was dating. Candace was afraid the item would blow Darren's deal to turn her "Sex and the City" columns into a TV show. We ran the item. Happily, HBO still green-lit Darren's show.

Flash forward. Five years into the show, we kept hearing that all was not kissy-kissy on the *Sex and the City* set. After poking around for a few weeks, we ran a column headlined "'Sex' Without Love: A Four-way Feud?"

> "They play the best of friends on HBO's *Sex and the City*. But off-camera, we hear that relations among Sarah Jessica Parker and costars Kim Cattrall, Cynthia Nixon, and Kristin Davis have grown as chilly as those Cosmopolitans they're always guzzling.
>
> 'When they sit down to shoot a scene in the coffee shop or a bar, they can barely look at each other,' claims a source. 'They never go anywhere together, unless they have to promote the show. They barely talk.'
>
> Several sources claim Parker is at the root of the frostiness.
>
> 'She makes about $3 million from the show—more than double what the others make,' says a source. Though she now oversees the show as an executive producer, according to some, Parker is threatened by the popularity of Cattrall's character, saucy bed-hopping Samantha.
>
> 'Sarah is jealous that Kim has got so big,' says another source. "

We included several paragraphs of denials from spokespeople, who insisted there was no friction. Nevertheless, SJP did not let this assault go unanswered. She went to Liz Smith, who handed her entire *Newsday* column to the actress as a hankie:

"It was horrible to wake up after working twenty-hour days, as we all do, and have to read such nonsense," Sarah [told Liz]. "Kim, Cynthia, Kristin, and I are all friends, personally and professionally, and

I know we will go on being friends forever after. . . . I find the report has the old sexist overtone, about women cat-fighting. . . . Do James Gandolfini and Michael Imperioli fall in each other's arms when they aren't working on *The Sopranos*?"

When the column ran, the *Daily News*'s editor in chief, Ed Kosner, messaged us: "Given the vehemence of Sarah Jessica Parker's blast in Liz today, are we comfortable with our sourcing?"

We had to go into Ed's office. We told him we had four good sources who personally knew the cast members. In our next column, we ran a response to SJP's response. We called her a "talented and hardworking actress." We also observed that "the lady sounded as if she were protesting too much." We noted that the *Sopranos* cast actually did hang out together after work.

Two years later, Parker still hadn't forgotten. One night, HBO pulled out all the stops for a gala celebrating the final season of *Sex and the City*. The dinner was at the American Museum of Natural History in the Hall of Ocean Life, where a giant blue whale hung overhead. Parker was wearing fishnets, aquamarine pendant earrings, and a magenta dress that beautifully served up her cleavage. I spied her standing by a diorama of Polynesian pearl divers. Ignoring my instincts for self-preservation, I swam through the crowd and introduced myself.

"Mr. Rush," she said sternly. "You've been very hard on me over the years."

"Well not lately," I said. "Correct me if I'm wrong, but . . ."

"You indicted my professional reputation," she went on. "Let me tell you something, Mr. Rush. I love [my costars and crew]. . . . You should spend a few moments with me before you write something that's not really based on anything but made-up allegations. . . . I've never lied about my personal life, my work, the way I've cared for three hundred people. Your article was one of the most painful things that ever happened to me. For thirty years I've been working and no one has said I've done anything bad."

Every so often, I tried to slip in a word. Then she started getting personal.

"It's a very peculiar job you have," she said. "Why don't you write longer pieces about people? You're so much more dignified. You're better than this, I'm certain. You must want better."

I said, "We're actually regarded as one of the more fair columns. . . ."

"My driver reads the *Daily News* every day," she said (lest anyone mistake her for a subscriber to our working-class rag). "He couldn't believe it. I care so deeply about my relationship with people I work with. You can ask a million people. I work harder than anybody. I work ninety hours a week. My reputation means the world to me. Always remember that! Because I couldn't lie to you. I couldn't face myself."

It was a self-righteous rant that kind of corroborated the original story. But it had a touch of playfulness. After she got all that off her chest, she handed me an "olive branch." It was invisible, but I ceremoniously put it in my pocket.

A few days later, Parker went on a radio show and talked about the caning she'd given me.

"I will say that he was really lovely about it," she said. "He was dignified. He took it like a man. . . . And—who knows—perhaps we'll be dining together one day. You never know."

SJP gave Joanna a similar lecture one night when she covered a play Parker was in. "Why do you do what you do?" the actress had said, as though Joanna were an orphan she must rescue from the streets. Parker's play dealt with the late, great fashion magazine, *Flair*. It was published in 1950, for just one year. Joanna sent a copy to her with a note telling her some of what we're about to tell you here. SJP called and left a nice message, so maybe she "got it."

SJP came to see more of us—probably more than she wanted. She and her husband, Matthew Broderick, enrolled their son, James, in the school where our son, Eamon, was a student. So we'd bump into them at drop-off. One morning, we were taking Eamon to school when we noticed that the *New York Post* had Parker's picture on the front page. Our former assistant, Michael Riedel, who now wrote a much-feared column about Broadway, had reported that Sarah Jessica Parker hoped to star in a play about a husband-and-wife gossip-columnist team. The story said Broderick might play the husband.

After we dropped off our son, we ran into none other than Sarah Jessica Parker.

I said, "So we hear you and Matthew are playing us on Broadway?"

She looked baffled. We showed her the story in the *Post*.

"Well, it's always nice to find out what I'm doing next," she said.

She confirmed that she had done a reading with Alan Cumming of a play in progress by Douglas Carter Beane. He was calling it *Mr. and Mrs. Fitch*. She said nothing was set. But apparently the life of a gossip columnist had a "peculiar" appeal for her.

Working with your spouse is a good way to find out if you're capable of homicide. Somehow, though, our marriage survived longer than those of many star couples we chronicled. In the course of writing almost four thousand columns, we watched America's celebrity culture grow morbidly obese. Of course, we were partly to blame, having fattened readers with scoops about everybody from Lady Gaga to Moammar Khadafy. We'd walked into the paper's art deco building on Forty-Second Street in time to catch the last whiff of its *Sweet Smell of Success* newsroom. As the news cycle spun faster and faster, the job invaded our home to the point where our five-year-old son was suggesting blind items. We wrote our last item in a blogosphere shrill with tweets from *Jersey Shore*. Along the way, we turned down some bribes, made some impressive enemies, and became unlikely relationship counselors to star-crossed lovers. We also came away with a few tales that we've kept to ourselves—until now.

What follows is a collection of case studies—a personal handbook that illustrates how reputations are smeared and scrubbed clean. It demonstrates how scandals are started and how they can be, if not stopped, slowed down. Our education in infamy may provide a little guidance in how the famous will ignore you, bully you, bludgeon you, and, occasionally, try to seduce you. This is a cautionary tale for any reporter who might face off with slippery public figures who possess money, fame, and power. Those who protect such public figures may see it as a manual for taking advantage of reporters. Readers who don't fall into either category may just enjoy watching the fight—and learning a few things that your favorite stars would rather you not find out.

No Experience Necessary

Neither of us set out to write a celebrity column. And yet, we can see now how our families planted the seeds—and, dare we say, spread the fertilizer—for our future crops of gossip.

As Joanna tells it:

My family didn't have a lot of money. But the stories they told about New York were like gold to me. Most of them had lived in Manhattan since the 1840s, since fleeing the Great Famine in Ireland. They had names like Baby Rosaleen, Chickie, Patsy, and Zahbelle. During Prohibition, my grandfather, Ray Molloy, saw some gangsters riddle "Mad Dog" Coll with Tommy gun bullets while he made a phone call at London Chemists in Chelsea.

One of my aunts would note, "Yeah, it was the last straw for Dutch Schultz and Owney Madden when Mad Dog kidnapped Frenchy."

That would be Big Frenchy DeMange, Madden's estranged partner in Harlem's Cotton Club. Mad Dog had kept French hostage in the Cornish Arms Hotel on West Twenty-Third across the street from our family business, the Molloy Funeral Home.

"You know, they say Mad Dog sent Frenchy's private parts to his mother in a box," said one of my aunts.

Another aunt yelled, "How did she know they were his?!"

Laughter and much clinking of ice in glasses filled the room. I was about twelve and glad they hadn't banished me from the room.

One of my cousins, Georgie Rooney, was a cop who walked the beat in Hell's Kitchen. One day a teenager threw a rock that knocked his cap off. The kid's name was Mickey Featherstone. He was a repeat offender. Cousin Georgie saw him again a couple of weeks later, sitting as calm as clams on a milkbox at a gas station. Georgie asked him, "Which hand did you throw the rock with?" With a smirk, he held out his right hand. Georgie grabbed it and crushed his fingers against the curb, breaking some. "He didn't even flinch," Georgie said. "He showed no feeling of pain whatsoever." Featherstone grew up to be a famous killer for the Westies gang.

When I walk around New York, I see the ghosts of my older relatives. There's the horse market outside the Flatiron Building where a white stallion broke free and ran down Twenty-Third Street. There's the wooden stand at Thirty-Fourth and Broadway, where a cop held up colored lanterns before there were traffic lights. Out in Rockaway and Gerritson Beach, there are the bungalows they built when you could rent a stretch of sand from the city for two dollars.

I still hear their songs and their expressions. They'd say our ancestor, John Hennessey, a cabinetmaker on Thames Street "came home in tatters" from the Civil War. They recalled neighborhood characters who'd purposely get arrested for vagrancy come wintertime, so they could get "three hots and a cot" in jail. Girls were warned, "Whenever a girl whistles, the Virgin Mary cries." Brides were given my great-great grandmother's mystifying birth-control advice: "Make tea in the kitchen, but spit in the parlor." In the era of spittoons, that must have been her way of explaining the rhythm method.

It didn't work too well, since her daughter, Auntie Lala, had eight kids. One summer, one of her twins, Irene, was swimming in a lake and drowned. Lala was heartbroken, but then she became pregnant again—with another pair of twins. She was overjoyed to deliver Josephine and Juliette. She was pushing them in a pram near Madison Square Park one day when there was some kind of explosion in the street. Juliette died in the pram. Lala's sister, Juliette, after whom the baby had been named, asked if the family could pretend that it was Josephine who'd died. That way, Juliette would still have a living namesake. Lala, beset with grief, agreed to rename Josephine "Juliette." The pathos of this story compelled my family to keep telling it nearly one hundred years later. And that's where I got the sense that telling true stories was an important thing to do.

My parents and their four children lived for a time in the Bronx, on Blackrock Avenue, near Castle Hill Avenue, about eight blocks from the projects where Supreme Court Justice Sonia Sotomayor grew up. Singer Jennifer Lopez later lived two blocks down Blackrock and went to our school, Holy Family. My father bought all the papers. He made sure I followed columnist Pete Hamill, who helped wrestle the gun away from Sirhan Sirhan when he shot Bobby Kennedy. But I would also read the "Suzy Says" society column in the *Daily News*. "Suzy," the pen name of Aileen Mehle, allowed me to escape from the Bronx into a fantasy world. She wrote about the ladies who lunched and the film stars I'd see on the three TV channels that all showed classic movies every day at 4 o'clock—the same ones Meryl Streep has said inspired her to become an actress. Don't get me wrong; our street games were fun. But it was a tonic to dream about Mrs. Muffie McFancyton dancing at galas with her silk Yves St. Laurent evening gowns and her jewels. Little did I know that the designers and party planners and hotels and florists all had press agents who pushed Suzy to plug their clients. No matter. I pictured the Astors and the Vanderbilts and the Whitneys swirling around chandeliered rooms with movie stars. It was dreamy. Knowing the players in Suzy's column also came in handy years later, when some of them got into trouble.

I became more politically conscious after my cousin Eugene O'Connell, an acting class buddy of Danny DeVito, was killed in Vietnam. I got my first job at thirteen. I lived in the South, the Midwest, and the West, working in factories, hospitals, and kitchens. I even sold Fuller brush products door-to-door. I bought a 1957 pink Ford Fairlane in Tennessee for $175. I ended up finishing college at UC Berkeley, where I became friends with Mark Dowie, the investigative journalist who exposed the exploding Ford Pinto, environmental activist David Helvarg, and *Mother Jones* cofounder Dave Talbot, who went on to create Salon.com.

I finally made my way back to New York and started looking for a job in the media. I worked for the *Downtown Express*. It was a scrappy neighborhood paper with only one other reporter, Jere Hester, and a great editor, John Cotter. It was in a building where the elevator doors regularly opened onto the brick between floors. Fluorescent bulbs hung higgledy piggeldy from the ceiling. A girl once came up to me as I sipped coffee. "Are you almost finished?" she asked in an annoyed tone. "You're using the Office Cup!"

At night, I worked as a typesetter for *New York*. The magazine's editor, Ed Kosner, presided over an amazing stable that included critics John Simon, David Denby, and Gael Greene and writers Nick Pileggi, Joe Klein, Michael Daly, Stephen Dubner, Chris Smith, Anthony Haden-Guest, Eric Pooley, Richard David Story, Michael Gross, Peter Blauner, and Peg Tyre. After contributing short pieces for two years, Jeannette Walls hired me as her assistant on the "Intelligencer" column. Jeanette was funny, statuesque, and had red hair that fell over one eye like Jessica Rabbit. It wasn't an accident that Jeannette gave this struggling Bronx girl a chance. Jeannette had gone to Barnard and lived on Park Avenue. But, when she knew me better, she confided that she'd grown up poor, tramping around the country with her family. I kept her secret. She later turned the whole story into her beautiful bestseller, *The Glass Castle*. Jeannette had reinvented herself and she encouraged me to do the same. She suggested I needed a makeover. That night, I went to an AIDS benefit where fashion designers donated clothes you could buy. I found a yellow Christian Lacroix suit that looked like it could hang in Jeannette's closet. It was a little expensive, but I remember Fran Drescher telling me, "If I have to pay retail to benefit humanity, so be it!" I bought that suit.

While the young Joanna rebelled and ricocheted around America, I stuck to the straight and narrow.

I was born in Chicago and grew up on the North Shore in Highland Park. The town has some magnificent lakeside mansions and landmark houses by Frank Lloyd Wright and other Prairie School architects. Orson Welles and Michael Jordon lived there (quite a few years apart). Director John Hughes used Highland Park as a location for *Ferris Bueller's Day Off* and many of his suburban comedies. We did not live in one of the mansions. My father, George Sr., had been a mechanic on bombing runs over North Africa during World War II. Later, he became an architectural engineer with the Department of Housing and Urban Development. He managed to afford a sweet cottage built in 1926 on a ravine surrounded by old oaks. It was just big enough for our little family of three. We were middle-class Catholics in a neighborhood where most of my friends were wealthier and Jewish. We were kind of a minority group within a minority group. I went to a lot of fun bar mitzvahs.

We lived a few blocks from America's oldest outdoor music festival, Ravinia. All the legends performed there—Ella Fitzgerald, Aretha Franklin, Joan Baez, Bob Dylan. We'd get cheap tickets on the lawn. Ravinia gave me my first glimpse of fame. My parents were by no means star worshippers. But I would say my mother, Peg, was a born gossip. She guarded the most trivial details of our family like they were Kremlin files—although she didn't mind prying into *other* people's business. On more days than I could bear, I was locked in a car with Mom and her women's club friends as they chattered about who'd had too much Scotch or why some teacher had had to resign. The year I graduated from Highland Park High School, two of my classmates, Gary Sinise and Jeff Perry, started the Steppenwolf Theatre. My mom and her friends clicked their tongues over the "experimental" plays Gary and Jeff were producing in the basement of the Immaculate Conception Church. "You wouldn't believe the language they're using!" my mother would say.

My church activities were confined to serving Mass as an altar boy and attending Boy Scout meetings as an Eagle Scout. As coeditor of the high school paper, I'd already set my sights on journalism. We didn't know anyone in the media, but Chicago had a proud newspaper tradition going back to Ben Hecht and Ring Lardner. Everybody followed Pulitzer Prize–winning columnist Mike Royko as he jumped from the *Daily News* to the *Sun-Times* to the *Tribune*. He took on Mayor Daley repeatedly and blew the whistle when Chicago cops were guarding Frank Sinatra on the taxpayers' dime. Irv Kupcinet, the *Sun-Times* columnist who was king of Chicago's nightlife, must have also been an influence. I didn't read "Kup's Column" daily, but even as a kid I'd try to stay up for his talk show, where the cigar-smoking Kup would have everybody from Muhammad Ali to Jimmy Hoffa to Linda Lovelace yakking around a coffee table. At Brown University, I majored in semiotics—the study of signs and symbols. It was a completely impractical concentration. But Roland Barthes's essays opened my eyes to the political and societal messages embedded in everything from fashion to wrestling. And my professors let me try my hand at what was then called "the New Journalism"—novelistic nonfiction a la Tom Wolfe and Hunters Thompson. I was able to slip some of my "impressionistic reporting" into *Fresh Fruit*, an alternative weekly I helped edit. I then managed to get into Columbia's Journalism School, which gives out the Pulitzer Prizes. My professors there, most of whom had worked at the *Times* or CBS News, taught by holding up the city's tabloids as examples of ethical failing—particularly Rupert Murdoch's *Post*, which the *Columbia Journalism Review* called "a force of evil."

After Columbia, I spent my days writing a book about the secret world of New York's rooftops—a sort of John McPheeish portrait of the beauty and horror that lurks above our heads. At night, I drove a taxi, and later, wrote and produced for Channel 5 News. The roof book was never published but it got me an agent and some magazine work.

In 1983, I landed an assignment with *Esquire* to interview Anthony Perkins, who was about to return to the screen as Norman Bates in *Psycho II*. I'd never done a celebrity profile before. Having flown out to L.A., I rang the bell on Perkins's Hollywood Hills house as nervously as Vera Miles checking into the Bates Motel. But Tony couldn't have been more welcoming. For years, he'd refused to talk about Norman. But he opened up to me about his struggle to escape his most famous role. He made dinner. Afterwards we were hanging out in the kitchen when he reached into his freezer and pulled out a big bag of pot. He loaded up a little pipe, took a toke, then offered me some. I figured one hit couldn't hurt—it'd help establish intimacy with my subject. I quickly found myself in the straitjacket of some phantasmagoric weed. Tony, who was kind of high-strung, kept jabbering on about working with Hitchcock. Meanwhile, I was trying to keep my melting brain from leaking out of my ears and nose. I fumbled through my notes, trying to remember what I'd come to ask him. Finally, I blurted out the obvious question: "Uh, what was it like shooting the shower scene with Janet Leigh?"

"Everybody finds that scene so terrifying," said Tony. "I find it quite funny. The blood was actually chocolate syrup. Also, for all the stabbing, you never see the knife touch Janet's body."

To demonstrate, Tony grabbed a carving knife from his cutlery set and began walking toward me. Norman Bates was suddenly looming above me with a gleaming blade.

"Tony," I said, trying to remain calm. "Please put that down."

Tony plunged the knife into the air a few times before returning it to a drawer.

"It was really quite funny," he repeated.

I complimented myself on defusing the situation. Later, I realized that Tony, who was an old pro at interviews, had given me my opening scene. Leaving out the pot, of course. Good thing my tape recorder was running or I wouldn't have remembered a word he said. I thought the interview had gone pretty well, but when I returned to New York, an editor asked me if I'd asked Tony about his gay past. Gay past? I'd met his vivacious wife, Berry Berenson, and their tween sons, Elvis and Osgood. Even if I'd known he'd had a gay past, how could I bring up such a personal question with a movie star?

My editor pressed me to call back Tony, who was nice enough take a few more questions. I asked him about his early shyness and anguished youth. Finally, I got around to asking whether he stayed in touch with Grover Dale, the choreographer I'd been told had been his partner for six years. Perkins chuckled. He seemed to sense I'd been put up to this. He said that he and Dale had been "roommates" and that Dale too had gotten married (to *Nine* star Anita Morris) and that they often vacationed with Tony and Berry. It was obvious Tony wasn't ready to come out—yet. But shortly after I handed in my piece, he admitted to *People* that he'd had "homosexual encounters [that felt] unsatisfying." (Tab Hunter, Rudolf Nureyev, and Stephen Sondheim were among those Tony "encountered," it was later reported.) My profile, which now looked behind the curve, got killed. It was a bummer after all the work I'd put into it. But I'd learned the coin that lay in a star's private life.

I was trying to make ends meet as a freelancer when, in 1985, I met Richard Johnson. Tall, blonde, and model-handsome, Richard had just started editing the *New York Post*'s Page Six column. We had mutual friends and Richard had recently written about an investigative story I'd done for *Manhattan, Inc.* about white-collar prisons—"Club Fed." He asked if I'd be interested in working with him two days a week. I never read Page Six. I didn't consider myself a "gossip." But it would be a regular check, with health insurance! I'd still have time to pursue my real work. And it'd just be two days a week, wouldn't it?

3

"Tart it up a bit."

Richard gave me the address of the *Post*—210 South Street. I wasn't sure where the hell that was. I got off the subway at Fulton Street and started walking many bleak blocks—under the Brooklyn Bridge, past some housing projects, past the stinking sidewalks of the Fulton Fish Market, which brought to mind Chicago columnist Mike Royko's crack that "no self-respecting fish would want to be wrapped in a Murdoch paper." Finally, I reached a gray, block-long, five-story building on the East River. Its backwater location made me wonder about the gang of renegades I was joining. Why did they need to be isolated from the general populace? That first day, the temperature was arctic. Homeless guys were warming themselves around fiery oil drums under the iron girders of FDR Drive across the street. Pig-knuckled *Post* drivers were having coffee and grilled blueberry muffins at the South Street Diner while their trucks were loaded with bales of crime, sports . . . and gossip!

I rode upstairs on a freight elevator with ink-smudged pressmen whose hearing, I later learned, had been pretty much devoured by the machines they tended. The pressmen wore square hats they made from newsprint—tabloid origami. When I got to the fourth floor, the grimy newsroom looked like it hadn't been cleaned since William Randolph

Hearst built the place in 1927 for the *New York Journal*. Old papers were strewn everywhere. Police and fire radios squawked. Editors barked orders from the "rim"—a horseshoe of desks. A few editors wore bow ties and green eyeshades. Photographer Louie Liotta still kept his press badge stuck in his hatband, just as he did in the 1940s when he worked for Weegee, the legendary lensman, who'd hand Louie rolls of film to "air mail" back to the newsroom via carrier pigeon.

A few touches of modernity had crept in. Miraculous "facsimile machines" now spat out press releases. Some reporters now wore "beepers." Computers had sidelined the typesetters. (The union saw to it that they held on to their jobs, even if that meant doing nothing but playing cards in what they called "the rubber room," because the boredom drove them nuts.) But reporters still did research by calling the paper's library for "the clips"—old, yellowed articles snipped and filed in folders. Editors sometimes pecked on typewriters. Photos came out of the darkroom. They were black and white, since the paper had no color presses. New Yorkers didn't seem to mind. Most of them still got their news from the *Post*, the *Daily News*, or the *Times*. They never missed their favorite columns. Yes, there was TV, but twenty-two minutes of news, weather, and sports didn't satisfy news junkies and sports fanatics. CNN was just five years old—*if* you had cable.

When he bought the *Post* from liberal publisher Dorothy Schiff in 1976, one of Rupert Murdoch's first reforms was to dedicate an entire page in the front of the paper to gossip. Gossip columns had traditionally been the epistle of one man or woman, like Earl Wilson or Hedda Hopper. Murdoch's newly hatched Page Six was team reported, though it carried one byline—that of its editor.

That was fine with me. I preferred to stay under the radar. I wasn't eager to advertise to my Brown and Columbia classmates that I'd wound up working at the *Post*, on a gossip column much less.

Safe to say, the newsroom at the *Post* was a bit different than at the *Times*. Murdoch had dragooned a gang of Brits and Aussies to teach the locals how he liked it done. A Murdoch "hack" would do anything to get his exclusive. One who covered a murder trial famously ran out of the courtroom ahead of the press pack, called in the verdict from a public phone bank, taking care to cut the cords on all the other phones so the competition couldn't use them.

The emotional temperature of the *Post*'s newsroom would rise as the day wore on, reaching the boiling point around six p.m., when the greatest minds—that is, the most deranged—would gather around the city desk to hatch the screaming front page, known as "the wood" because in the old days the letters were so big they had to carve them out of wood. A mushroom cloud of cigarette smoke would form as headline ideas flew back and forth, producing louder and louder laughter. The rapid-fire spitballing created flash-bang headlines guaranteed to ambush anyone walking past a newsstand. Among the eternal woods were GRANNY EXECUTED IN HER PINK PAJAMAS . . . BOY GULPS GAS, EXPLODES (a teenage suicide) . . . EATEN ALIVE! (a pretty Bronx zookeeper mauled by tigers) . . . I SLEPT WITH A TRUMPET (heiress Roxanne Pulitzer's musical sex aid) . . . KHADAFY GOES DAFFY (about the Libyan dictator's rumored cross-dressing) . . . PINEAPPLE IN A CAN (acne-scarred dictator Manuel Noriega goes to prison). A story about Father Bruce Ritter's "mentoring" of teenage boys prompted someone to suggest: OUR FATHER WHO ART IN KEVIN. But that one was ruled beyond the pale, even by *Post* standards. Anyone was welcome to lob a suggestion. Some priceless "heds" sprang from the heads of Dick McWilliams, Jimmy Lynch, Al Ellenberg, Dick Belsky, and even fishing columnist Kenny Moran, who dubbed some whacked wise guys as DEADFELLAS! The most famous headline—HEADLESS BODY IN TOPLESS BAR—was often attributed to Vinnie Musetto. It was most likely a team effort. But Vinnie, a copyboy-turned-managing-editor-turned-film-critic, was a character. Sometimes he zoomed around the newsroom with his arms stretched out like a seagull. Other times, he'd climb on a desk to blow reveille on a bugle.

Of the many odd ducks in the *Post*'s aviary, the most majestic mallard was the metropolitan editor, Steve Dunleavy. Born in Sydney in 1938, Dunleavy was a dashing rake with a graying pompadour, an aquiline nose, and a tooth that fell out at inopportune moments. His reporting methods were ingenious and sometimes unscrupulous. He'd charmed the pants off one of Ted Kennedy's "boiler room" girls to get to the bottom of Mary Jo Kopechne's drowning at Chappaquiddick. He'd slipped into a white hospital coat and pretended to be a bereavement counselor to get quotes out of the parents of one victim of "Son of Sam" killer David Berkowitz. When he was trying to win the confidence of a Jewish person over the phone, he'd introduce himself as "Don Levy."

The "Street Dog," as Dunleavy was known, never seemed to eat, except for the occasional grilled cheese sandwich. Tobacco and alcohol were his main food groups. He'd sometimes sip on a Budweiser tall boy in the newsroom, but he tended to do his daytime drinking in the second-floor tavern above the South Street Diner or around the corner in a mob social club where he might check out a tip with some wise guys over a hand of poker. His nighttime imbibing often took him at Elaine's at Eighty-Eighth and Second Avenue. One night, he got into a donnybrook with manic record producer Phil Spector, who pulled a pearl-handled gun on Dunleavy. Steve apparently disarmed him with a kangaroo punch to Spector's schnoz. On another night, the story goes, Steve was slipping some wood to a Norwegian heiress on a snowbank when a snowplow invaded their lovemaking, leaving Dunleavy with a broken foot. Steve kept his wife and family out on Long Island so, if an evening ran late, he'd sometimes return to the *Post* to crash. He might curl up under a desk. One time, a secretary was sent to fetch him in the executive sauna. She found him looking even more pallid than usual. "Mr. Dunleavy's dead!" she screamed as she ran back to the newsroom. But Steve seemed indestructible. He once showed me a burn mark on his hand where he'd stubbed out a cigarette to win a bar bet in Hong Kong.

Nothing sobered Steve up like the smelling salts of a good story. One day, I'd gotten a tip about Bernhard Goetz, the geeky electronics technician who had recently shot four teenagers he believed were muggers on the subway. The tip wasn't earth-shattering, just that Goetz had been seen in upstate Rhinebeck, shopping for milk bottles from his father's old dairy farm. My source said Goetz was "very sentimental" about the dairy. Someone suggested, "Dunleavy might know how to reach Goetz." When I relayed the story to Steve, he snapped to attention. From memory, he dialed a number and left a message: "Bernie, it's Dunleavy. Call me! Urgent!"

Goetz confirmed that, in addition to rescuing injured squirrels in Union Square, he collected milk bottles. The mental picture of the ruthless vigilante puttering around yard sales made for a decent paragraph. Gradually, I got better items. Murdoch's mandate was that Page

Six cover the "corridors of power." The Page should have gossip about people who mattered—or who mattered to Murdoch, for whom the column was an agency for punishing his enemies and rewarding his friends. This being the "Go-Go '80s" on Wall Street, Page Six tracked the traders and the raiders, the arbitrageurs and the greenmailers— from the boardroom to the bedroom. I landed an interview with Texas billionaire Ross Perot, who told me about his private commando rescue of hostages held in Iran. I also got wind of a howler about labor kingpin Victor Gotbaum's dog knocking an undertaker into an open grave at a family funeral in Greenwich, Connecticut.

The main criteria for a good Page Six item was that it tell some-thing that someone—somewhere—didn't want repeated. In 1986, I got myself onto a July Fourth cruise into New York Harbor for the centen-nial celebration of the Statue of Liberty. President Reagan and First Lady Nancy were aboard. So were French President François Mitter-rand, General William Westmoreland, and Governor Hugh Carey. At one point, emcee Bob Hope asked the black-tie crowd, "Hey, have you heard? The Statue of Liberty has AIDS! Nobody knows if she got it from the mouth of the Hudson or the Staten Island Fairy." There were enough groans that Hope instantly blamed his writers for the callous gag. But I saw the Reagans laughing. The next day, I wrote a long item about Hope's astonishing "joke" and the First Couple's delight in it. The story set off more fireworks than I'd seen that night. AIDS activists slammed the Reagans and Hope for their insensitivity. Hope's defense initially was that I'd taken the joke out of context and that there weren't supposed to be any reporters on board. But when the outrage didn't die down, Hope apologized. Elizabeth Taylor later got him to do several AIDS charity benefits as a penance.

The *Post* was hardly at the forefront of AIDS awareness, certainly not when the closeted former Joe McCarthy henchman Roy Cohn was a regular visitor to the newsroom and an invaluable source to Page Six. And the paper was not in the habit of running anything that caused bother to the Reagans. But even Republicans found it offensive that Hope had dared to suggest that Lady Liberty had that queer disease. Dunleavy had posted a sign in our cubicle to remind us that every item should have "CONFLICT!" And the Hope item had that.

I had been working at Page Six for a few months when Dunleavy took me aside.

"You've been turning in some nice items, mate," he said. "But if I may make a suggestion, tart it up a bit. I am *not* saying sensationalize the stories. But make them cheekier. And make the sentences shorter, like people talk."

Obediently, I began to have people "romping" and "canoodling" on "sexcapades." One politician didn't criticize another; he "blasted" him. Claudia Schiffer was "the Teutonic Temptress." Nightclub regulars were "party barnacles." And pretty much everything was "shocking."

I found out how much fear the column could cause. Merely saying, "Hi, I'm calling from Page Six," prompted a moment of stunned silence on the other end of the line. I usually tried to wade in with a couple of innocuous questions, but experienced media handlers knew better. Rex Reed, the film critic, brought me up short: "Listen, kid, what are you after? I know Page Six doesn't call unless they're trying to dig up some dirt."

A common reaction to a call from Page Six was to tell the reporter, "This is not a story." That's when you *knew* you had a story. Once, we got a call from a deli owner who said that Carl Bernstein, the Watergate sleuth, was weeks late in paying his take-out tab. Had Bernstein burned through all the money he'd made off *All the President's Men*? At that time, he'd become better known as the schnook who cheated on his wife, Nora Ephron, who'd turned her woe into the hilarious *Heartburn*. All the same, Bernstein didn't hesitate to lecture me on journalism.

"This is a not a story," he said, on cue. "I am more than happy to answer your questions but I can't right now. . . . I promise I will call you back."

A few minutes later, the deli owner called Page Six back to say, "Mr. Bernstein just came in! He paid his bill. There's no problem anymore."

So was there *no* story? No, just a different one, which began, "Page Six gets action!"

My friend-turned-editor, Richard Johnson, was the most easygoing of men. But God help the cur who besmirched his reputation, or the reputation of Page Six. One time, when the *Village Voice*'s Joe Conason dared to call him "undependable," Richard paid a visit to the offices of the leftist weekly and asked Conason to step outside. When Conason refused, Richard's fist delivered its message to Joe's jaw. When *Daily News* gossip columnist Betty Liu Eberon took a shot at Page Six, Richard wrote her a letter, warning, "Betty Liu, I'll be waiting in the tall grasses." Despite Richard's dedication to accuracy, the fact-checking at Page Six was a bit more relaxed than what I'd been taught Columbia's J-School. Each day, the Page Six team raced the clock to nail down twelve items for publication that could each be a libel land mine. A star's lawyers might accuse us of showing "reckless disregard," but, as Dunleavy would say, "The beast must be fed!" When a tip was really good, we'd joke, "It's too good to check!" Items that would definitely get us sued—accusing someone of adultery or drug use, for instance— might be run "blind," without naming names. The description of the adulterer or drug user had to be broad enough to apply to something like sixteen or seventeen people, according to our lawyer at the time. If it wasn't a potentially "actionable" item, one source was usually enough, at least for a one-sentence sighting of somebody at a bar or restaurant. But even one sentence could cause a lot of trouble if we found out the next day that the actress who supposedly had a glass of wine had been sober for twenty years, or the Knicks forward who was supposedly break dancing was actually on the team's injured list. But good luck getting a correction. The paper's legal fallback position was that it was only a gossip column. Gossip, the *Post's* lawyers argued, was a kind of protected speech, like satire or opinion. No doubt they would have gotten an argument from the *Post's* founder, Alexander Hamilton, who was tarred by the pamphleteers of his day for his affair with married mistress Maria Reynolds.

The imperturbable Richard usually calmed the offended party by saying, "I owe you one." Good sources were entitled to better treatment, however. The *Post*, for instance, didn't report that Roy Cohn had been disbarred. But it was sometimes hard to keep track of who was on the protected-species list. I'd just gotten to Page Six when Richard flipped me a tip about some kind of embarrassing production delay on the set of *Sweet Liberty*, a comedy Alan Alda was directing in the Hamptons. I found out some details Alda apparently didn't want out. The morning the item ran, Richard got an angry call from the movie's publicist,

Bobby Zarem, one of the column's most valued tipsters. The movie's producer, Marty Bregman, had just reamed Bobby and now Bobby was reaming Richard. Richard hung up the phone. His ear was practically glowing red. "Man," he said in his spare baritone. "I don't know how that one got through."

Marching orders as to who should and shouldn't be written about often came down from the executive suite upstairs, where Mr. Murdoch had an office. You'd see his fist-like face only occasionally. But even when he wasn't on the premises, his influence was felt. His will was usually channeled through the Post's editor in chief, Roger Wood, an Oxford grad who'd run London's *Daily Express* and the Sydney Morning Herald Group. Wood was on the short side, but he had a towering authority. When he wished to give instructions to the much taller Dunleavy, he rested his hands on Steve's shoulders and pressed downward, until they were eye to eye. One day Wood approached Richard.

"Dear boy," said Wood. "Are you familiar with a Richard Mineards?"

Mineards was another British transplant who made a nice living as a "royals correspondent" while moonlighting as a publicist for posh shops and restaurants.

"Yeah, he gives us items," said Richard.

Wood said Mineards had told one of his swank PR clients not to advertise in the *Post* because it was too down-market.

"I'd like you to call this Richard Mineards and casually ask him who his clients are," Wood went on. "Make a list. Then make sure you never write about any of them again."

Of course there were much bigger names on the enemies list. Leading the motorcade of despised "limousine liberals" was Paul Newman. The Oscar winner had been maligned by the paper since the early '80s, and, in 1983, told *Rolling Stone*: "I could sue the *Post*, but it's awfully hard to sue a garbage can." After that, Newman wasn't mentioned, even in the TV listings. But in 1986, when I joined Page Six, the column decided to do battle with him on the monumental issue of his height. Maureen Dowd had written a profile of the actor in the *New York Times Magazine* in which she called him a "lean" five-foot-eleven. A sportswriter at the *Post* had told Richard Johnson that he'd recently stood next to Newman at the theater and he couldn't have been taller than five-eight. Page Six did a forensic analysis of photos of Newman and offered to give $1,000 to charity for every inch he was over five-eight. Newman raised the bet—challenging the *Post* to make it $100,000.

The *Post* finally backed down on Newman. But there was plenty of other ax-grinding, so much so the newsroom sounded like a lumber camp. Mickey Rourke was among the celebs that, Richard thought, needed to be cut down to size. In 1988, the *Post* ran a photo of Rourke holding hands with model Terri Farrell. The caption noted that the actor was married to actress Debra Feuer. Other items followed. Unfailingly, they depicted Rourke in an unflattering light, usually with a photo of him from *Barfly*, looking like a punch-drunk hobo.

One day, I answered the phone at Page Six. Mickey Rourke was on the other end.

He said, "Yo, is Richard Johnson there?"

I said, "No, he's on vacation right now."

He said, "You tell him that I'm going to kick his ass when he gets back." In the background, I heard some guys yelling, "You tell him, Mickey, you tell him!"

Mickey went on, "I'm tired of those lies he's writing about me, and we're going to settle this man to man."

The feud went on for years. Richard finally challenged Rourke to a boxing match. The bout never came off but did yield a classic *Post* headline that claimed the only thing Mickey Rourke can box is pizza.

The usual human motivations drove people to call Page Six: envy, revenge, personal glory. Manning the switchboard made you feel like a priest in his confessional—or a phone sex worker. Though the tipster was often a stranger, the two of you quickly developed an intimate relationship. It had the air of a cheap affair. Your confidante could grow cross with you if were too skeptical or took too long to run the item. And there was a tender trust: you could ruin your confidante by exposing her, but then she'd never call you back with another item.

Sometimes the relationship became too intimate. I once fielded a call from a woman who said she was Robert Redford's girlfriend. She said they'd had a fight, that she was angry with him. She said she was tired of living in the shadows and was ready to go public. She certainly knew a lot about Redford and his schedule. She was quite intelligent.

She had a really sexy voice. I called Redford's publicist to ask about her. I got a call back from Gavin de Becker, one of the country's top personal security specialists. He said the woman I'd been talking with was mentally unhinged and that she'd been stalking Redford for some time. Redford had had some close calls with past "admirers," one of whom had a pistol in her purse when she was arrested. De Becker said he wanted to get this woman "help." He asked if I'd assist him by arranging to meet her and that his team would provide me with backup. "At no time will you be in danger," he assured me, which told me this could get dangerous. But the next time the woman called, I suggested we meet. She suggested we meet in a cemetery. She started to seem more disturbed and less sexy. I was having second thoughts about our graveyard rendezvous. Maybe she was, too. She stopped calling, or maybe de Becker's people found her on their own.

Then there was David Hampton. In 1983, when he was nineteen, David conned some well-known New Yorkers—including my high school classmate, Gary Sinise, and my former journalism school dean Osborn Elliot—into believing that he was the son of Sidney Poitier. David served some time, then disappeared from New York. In 1990, I heard that John Guare had written a play about the escapade called *Six Degrees of Separation*. Somehow I tracked David down. I asked him if he'd like to see the play with me. He was only too eager. David had a regal demeanor, which grew queenlier when a few audience members recognized him, apparently from his mug shot. Afterward, over dinner, David griped that James McDaniel, the actor who played him, looked too black. I don't know what he thought of Will Smith in the movie version. In any case, David proceeded to file a $100 million suit against Guare for stealing his life story. Guare tried to get a restraining order against David, saying that David had threatened his life. David did admit to me that he went to the play's opening looking for Guare. "I wanted Guare to think I had a gun in my pocket," he said. "It was really a jar of Vaseline." Once, I was in the shower at home when the phone rang. David said, "I hear water running. Are you washing the dishes or," he paused seductively, "yourself?" I almost got my own restraining order.

Broadway was just one of my beats. In the evening, the Page Six team would fan out to movie premieres, rock concerts, art shows, club openings, private tastings, black-tie recitals, Yankees games, cruise ship launches, sarcophagus unveilings, and many, many parties. All without charge. Such was the power of seeing your name in boldface. Just opening the invitations took much of an hour in the morning.

More and more, I found myself in places I'd only dreamed of. Or never dreamed of. My first trip out of the United States came courtesy of Peter Gatien, the eye patch–wearing club impresario who flew a bunch of us to the opening of Limelight in London. Vic Damone invited me to his dinner show at the Café Carlyle. He shot me a wink when he changed the lyric of "The Lady is a Tramp" to "she loves Page Six and reads every line." I spent hours on the phone with writers Harold Brodkey and James Toback, two procrastinating geniuses who found talking with me a good way to avoid work. I found myself at a dinner for four at Mr. Chow's with Andy Warhol. I discovered the white-wigged sphinx secretly had a lot to say. And no one had better gossip!

There were some strange nights. I tagged along with Richard and some friends to the Olympic Tower aerie of Saudi arms dealer Adnan Khashoggi. After checking out his Matisses and Picassos, indoor glass-walled pool, and mink-covered, double king-size bed, we departed in the wee hours. In the cab, one of our group confessed that she'd stolen an antique clock from the billionaire. At first, she said, "Ah, he won't miss it." Then the kleptomaniac realized that Khashoggi certainly had video cameras in every room. She was determined to return the clock before he found it missing. Since everyone else in the group was too afraid (or high) to walk into the lobby, I ended up being the one who left a bag with the clock with Khashoggi's concierge.

The lifestyle became intoxicating. I was still writing for magazines, but more and more, my two days at Page Six dominated my week. I enjoyed the instant gratification of seeing my stories on the newsstand by midnight. I spent weeks crafting a profile of ambient music maestro Brian Eno for *Esquire*. I never met a person who'd read it. But a paragraph on Page Six would create instant tremors. The rest of the media would repeat it. I'd been afraid that my career would be ruined if anyone found out I was writing for Page Six. But I discovered that magazine editors actually returned my phone calls now that they could benefit from me.

I was at the *Post* one day interviewing Joseph E. Levine, the venerable producer of *The Graduate*, *The Lion in Winter*, and *Carnal Knowledge*. I was trying to get him to admit something. I was coming at him from every direction, but he wouldn't budge.

"I am *not* telling you," insisted Levine, who died later that year. "But I will say you're obviously good at what you do."

It was evasive flattery from an old huckster. But I began to feel that maybe I could live with the shame of writing gossip.

4

Post Script

I t was an exciting time. The tabloid war was raging. And yet I still wasn't ready to settle down at Page Six.

I'd met a rogue Secret Service agent named Marty Venker. Marty had protected Presidents Nixon, Ford, and Carter, as well as some gamey dictators. He'd become disenchanted with the Service and started leading a double life—guarding the president by day, going out to punk and sex clubs at night. He eventually had a nervous breakdown, quit the agency, and became a hot nightclub DJ. I wrote a *Rolling Stone* story about him and, later, a book, *Confessions of an Ex-Secret Service Agent*, the first unvarnished history of the Secret Service. Warner Bros. hired me and my friend, Russell Levine, to write an action adventure based on Marty's story. I went out to L.A. to work on the screenplay. After about six months, we ended up in the usual screenwriter purgatory, where some producer wanted us to make the female lead more like a girl he was dating. The project went into turnaround and I turned around and came back to New York. As cool as it was living in Laurel Canyon and writing around a swimming pool, I found the life kind of boring. It sure wasn't the *New York Post*, where every day brought another crazy tale to share.

I wasn't sure they'd want me back at the *Post*—Bay Rigby, the mad genius artist whose cartoon was the centerpiece of Page Six every day, had taken a year off to surf the world and paint. One morning Bay showed up in the *Post* newsroom to reclaim his job. He was a handsome, strapping Aussie in his thirties, but he looked like hell. His shirt was wide open. He was obviously at the end of an all-night bender. He staggered off to find the editor in charge, Lou Colasuonno, who was in the men's room. Bay told Lou he wanted his job back. Lou said he was sorry but the paper was happy with Sean Delonas, the buddy Bay had lined up to fill in for him. Bay responded with typical panache. He didn't just say, "Fuck you"—he spelled it out in urine at Lou's feet.

Fortunately, they let me back at the *Post*. I arrived as both tabloids were struggling for air. All the shots that the *Post* had taken at liberal Senator Edward Kennedy had come back to haunt Murdoch. Kennedy had managed to get a bill passed forcing Murdoch to sell the *Post* if he wanted to hold onto WNYW-TV, the foundation of his new Fox Broadcasting Company. In 1988, Murdoch sold the money-hemorrhaging paper to real estate magnate Peter Kalikow. Two years later, the *Daily News* was at death's door. Management at the Tribune Company had refused to negotiate with the pressmen, who went on strike.

Joanna recalls:

Well before the strike, I was talking with the *Daily News* about coming over from *New York Magazine*. There was an opening at Apple Sauce, the gossip column the *News* had launched to do battle with Page Six. I came in for an interview. The paper's editor, the great Jim Willse, asked me what I thought of Apple Sauce.

I said, "Well, for starters, I'd change the name. It connotes mush." I'd prepared a list of 47 alternative names, but Willse interjected, "I thought of that name." Oops.

Willse hired me anyway. My familiarity with the "Suzy" set came in handy again. One day, an editor yelled out, "Any of you ever heard of John Gutfreund?" I raised my hand. The CEO of Salomon Brothers and his wife, Susan, were the king and queen of "nouvelle society" thanks to their conspicuous consumption. They'd spent twenty million redecorating their Fifth Avenue duplex. The editor said, "Well, that numb nuts thought it was a good idea to hoist a twenty-two-foot-high

Christmas tree into his apartment by crane. A worker just got hurt. Get up there!" I was delighted. It was the kind of hard news story I loved. I was a correspondent on the front lines of the class war.

Then, about six weeks after I started at the *News*, the pressmen struck. So did the other unions, including the reporters and editors in the Newspaper Guild. Well, most of the reporters. The ones who believed in the common cause picketed outside the Daily News Building, twenty-four hours a day in the middle of winter. I remember Larry Hackett, the future editor of *People* magazine, always took the lobster shift when the temperature and the time were both in the single digits. I'd barely started to work but I was ready to walk out. The leaders at the Newspaper Guild told me not to. They said since I was a "probationary reporter" and not a member of the Guild, I should continue working under protest. The Guild liked having eyes and ears inside the newsroom. But then the Tribune Company hired scabs to replace the striking reporters. One day, folks in madras shirts and white pants showed up from other Tribune papers. One woman was supposed to work on Apple Sauce with me.

I walked into Willse's office and said, "I can't work with her." It had been my dream to work for the paper my family had been reading since I was a kid. But I walked out of the building—in tears.

Brilliant editor Amy Virshup let me write a cover piece on the strike for the *Village Voice*. In retrospect, I regret criticizing some great *News* photographers and reporters for crossing the picket line. I'd been shocked to see progressive columnist Jack Newfield, champion of the working man, walk into the newsroom. But, ultimately, it was none of my business. Maybe Jack was right: the months-long strike nearly killed the *Daily News*.

Serendipitously, Richard Johnson had just left the *Post* to work on a TV show. So the *Post*'s new metro editor, John Cotter, my boss at the *Downtown Express*, hired me to coedit Page Six with Frank DiGiacomo, a deft writer who'd been working under Richard.

The newsroom of the *Post* was also much more freewheeling than I was used to. No tip was too crazy to check. I got a call one day from a source who said she was at a party in L.A. where Kirstie Alley had shown up with her pet baby possum. My source said, "The possum starts to go *squeak, squeak, squeak*. Like it was hungry. And Kirstie said, 'Oooh, ooh, baby, baby, Mommy's here.' And she turned to a publicist and said, 'Say, aren't you nursing a baby right now?' She wanted the publicist to give the possum some of her milk! They were talking about having the publicist breast-feed the possum. But because the possum already had teeth, the publicist was apparently afraid of doing that. So she expressed her breast milk into a bottle. Kirstie Alley then fed it to this baby possum." I could barely believe the story myself. But I called the publicist. Not only did she admit it, she crowed, "I did it, and you know what? I'm proud of it!"

Not everybody was so forthcoming. For a while we'd been hearing that Kevin Costner had not been faithful to his wife, Cindy. But accusing someone of adultery is libelous. Then, while Costner was over in England shooting *Robin Hood: Prince of Thieves*, the British tabs got wind of a strip club receptionist he was supposedly shagging or snogging or whatever they say over there. Now it was out there. We decided to take a run at it, adding what we knew. Costner was then at the height of his career as a leading man. His agent was Michael Ovitz, who at the time was known as "the most powerful man in Hollywood." If it came out that Costner was cheating on his wife of twelve years, it could hurt his family man image—and his bankability. So Ovitz called me. He didn't flat out deny that his client had been with another woman. He just said things like "Kevin loves his children" and "Kevin and Cindy have not separated." Of course there was the mandatory denunciation of those "British rags." Then came the insult—how could I, as a journalist, sink to their level? Then came the clincher. He said, "I would be personally grateful if you would drop this story."

Whoa! The mighty Ovitz said he'd *owe me one*. I said, "I'm sorry. We're going to have to go ahead with it." People used to say that when Michael Ovitz got mad, he didn't scream—he got very, very quiet. Sure enough, he lowered his voice and repeated, "I said that I would be *personally* grateful." Now, most people wanted to stay on Ovitz's good side. I guess I was too naïve to be scared. I repeated what *I'd* just said: "I'm sorry, we have to do this story." The story ran and there were no repercussions. Maybe Ovitz knew it was true. Maybe even *he* didn't want to get into a war with Page Six.

Celebrities usually let their agents or publicists do the talking. But sometimes the star takes matters into their own hands. One day, I was talking to a friend who had been to a small party at Sean Penn's house while Penn's beautiful wife, Robin Wright, was away. During Penn's house party, the friend went wandering through the house to find a bathroom—and popped open a door to find Penn horizontal with one of the female guests. The friend quietly closed the door and tiptoed away—but, like many of our sources, felt compelled to file it with central. I called Penn's reps, but Penn called back himself. He said, through gritted teeth, "I have a family. I have a family." (At that time, he had a one-year-old daughter who, safe to say, couldn't read.) To Penn, the problem was not that he may have been cheating on his wife. It was that she was going to find out. Talk about shooting the messenger. Sean actually had shot at the media helicopters covering his wedding to Madonna. I think he would've happily organized a firing squad for me. This second-generation-Hollywood brat also allegedly hit Madonna with a baseball bat, did time for slugging a photographer, and, once, before my eyes, smashed his cocktail glass on a small sculpture that an artist had offered him with outstretched hands. Of course, this was before he reincarnated himself as Saint Sean of Haiti.

Joanna had been at the *Post* for a few months when there was more tabloid upheaval. Liz Smith, who'd been the star gossip at the *Daily News*, since 1976, had jumped to *New York Newsday*. (She was said to have landed the richest columnist contract in newspaper history.) The *Daily News* hired Richard Johnson to replace Liz. His new bosses wasted no time making use of his skill as an assassin. Using the pen he'd sharpened at Page Six, he poked at the *Post*'s new publisher, Peter Kalikow, for building an enormous dock for his yacht. Richard recommended that Kalikow, who also had one of the world's biggest Ferrari collections, could make better use of his money by rehiring the reporters he'd laid off. Kalikow quickly sent word that he wanted someone to dig up something on Richard. A copygirl said she'd seen Richard getting his hair cut at Frederic Fekkai's posh salon at Bergdorf Goodman—and that he didn't get a bill. Joanna ran the tidbit with the snarky line: "Watch for Fekkai's name in boldface in the *News* soon." The next day, Richard faxed a credit card receipt from Fekkai. Joanna felt a little bad taking a shot at an ex–Page Sixer. Especially since Richard's item about Kalikow's dock said exactly what *Post* reporters were thinking. But even Richard probably understood that it was just business. as they say in the mob. He whacked our boss. He had to get whacked.

Says Joanna:

Another story I initially approached with dread concerned Woody Allen. Early in 1992, a source told me he'd seen Woody kissing one of Mia Farrow's adopted daughters in a dark corridor outside Madison Square Garden's VIP suite. I loved Woody Allen's movies. I once walked through a blizzard to see one on opening day. But I had to check out the tip.

I called Elaine Kaufman. Woody ate at her restaurant all the time. I ran the story past her. "That's bullshit!" she roared. I called other folks who knew Woody. They knew nothing. My original source kept nosing around. One person who'd been on Woody's set told him, "I did see Woody leaving his trailer hand-in-hand with one of the adopted daughters." I called Woody's publicist Leslee Dart. She said the story was "absurd." I honestly think she didn't know the truth.

I didn't have enough to go on then. But, a few months later, as I was leaving work, our assistant who protected us from crazoid callers said, "Wow, I had a doozy today. Somebody says Woody Allen is sleeping with his stepdaughter." I whirled around and said, "What? Did you get a name and number?" She said she threw it away. I dove into her wastebasket and dug under the Diet Coke cans until I found the scrap of paper. I called the number. The person said Woody was in a romantic relationship with Mia's adopted daughter, Soon-Yi Previn. The person said Mia and Woody's relationship had deteriorated during the past two years. Mia felt betrayed by the affair. She'd lifted Soon-Yi out of poverty in Korea and sent her to the best private schools. Mia had demanded that Woody end the affair. She wouldn't let him see their two adopted children, Dylan and Moses, or his biological son, Satchel. That explained why Woody had just sought custody of the three children.

I called Leslee Dart again. Woody apparently knew the jig was up. Leslee confirmed what was going on. Woody had fallen in love with Soon-Yi and, as he said himself later, "The heart wants what it wants."

My editor, John Cotter, put the story on the front page with the headline WOODY LOVES MIA'S DAUGHTER. But Cotter wanted more. He yelled, "Bring me red meat!"

I called my source, who said, "Do you care that Mia found Polaroids of Soon-Yi naked on a bed that she recognized as Woody's?" Um, that would be a yes. The next day the *Post's* front page screamed, MIA'S GOT NUDE PIX. I was working with Marianne Goldstein, a great reporter. We found photos of Woody and Soon-Yi together at Knicks games a few months earlier. The affair had been playing out in front of everyone. In another photo, I noticed Soon-Yi had a book bag with a college crest, the words "New Jersey," and a name that began with "R." Could Soon-Yi be a student at Rutgers? Ramapo? We pulled out a dictionary with a list of American colleges. Could it be Rider University? The photo desk dispatched dauntless lensman Paul Adao to the campus. He came back with a picture of Soon-Yi giggling with her classmates.

The photos ran with Woody's claim that Mia had tried to blackmail him for $7 million in exchange for keeping the affair quiet. Cotter did cut the name of Soon-Yi's college out of our story. He growled, "Why don't you just give the *Daily News* directions?" The front page blared: "Woody: Mia tried to SHAKE ME DOWN."

The day the story ran, another one of Mia's adopted daughters, Lark Previn, called me. She said her mother wanted to know where Soon-Yi was. I told Lark that I'd heard that Mia had broken a chair over Soon-Yi's head when she found out about the nude pictures. I said I was concerned that Mia would hurt Soon-Yi. Could I come over to discuss this with Mia? I heard some muffled conversation in the background. Mia was obviously there coaching Lark, who said that wouldn't be possible.

Mia did let Lark come to talk to us at the *Post* the next day. Marianne and I sat down with her in the editor in chief's office. Lark pressed us about Soon-Yi's whereabouts. I wasn't about to give up her location, but I wanted to try to talk to Mia. I said I was going to have to get Mia's word of honor that she wouldn't harm Soon-Yi. Lark used the editor's phone to call Mia, who got on the line. In her little-girl voice, Mia swore that she and Soon-Yi's siblings only wanted to tell Soon-Yi that she was welcome to come home. I told Mia I'd try to get a message to Soon-Yi. As soon as Lark left, Marianne had the brilliant idea of hitting redial on the phone. That's how we got Mia's private number. A few days later, we called it. Mia told us, "I will always love Soon-Yi. I don't blame her for this." Headline: MIA TALKS.

We had eight Woody front pages in a row. I don't think I've ever had a job that was so much fun. Most nights, we'd hit the media hangouts—like Maguire's on Second Avenue, owned by Steve McFadden aka "Pally." Or the Lion's Head on Sheridan Square. Cotter used to say he needed his dose of "Vitamin V," by which he meant vodka. I've never been much of a drinker but I loved trading stories. The bars were the great equalizers for reporters and photographers from all the papers and TV stations. There were future Pulitzer Prize winners Jim Dwyer and Mike McAlary, and John Miller from WNBC, who went on to become one of the foremost authorities on terrorism and an assistant director of the FBI. And a young, dedicated advocate for the homeless who never seemed to drink but liked the company. His name was Andrew Cuomo. He told me how he used to work in an auto shop where he took apart muscle cars and put them back together. Andrew said that's where he learned how to approach social issues: if you could just spread out all the parts, you could solve the problem. Like his father, he became the governor of New York.

We'd often end up at Elaine's where you didn't know what would happen. I'll never forget the night. It was the bad side of 3 a.m. McAlary, Cotter, and I were hanging out with Gianni Uzielli, who used to be married to Henry Ford II's daughter Anne. Gianni was wondering what had happened to his girlfriend of the moment. He was worried that she might have passed out in the ladies' room, so he opened the door. He found her in a compromising position with Keith Hernandez, the dashing first baseman who'd helped lead the Mets to a World Series victory in 1986. Gianni returned mournfully to his barstool. Slinking out of the restaurant, Keith put his hand on Uzielli's shoulder and said, "Sorry, Gianni." And the party went on.

I was having a blast with these guys, but as time went on, I ended up spending more evenings with someone else.

5

"Have You Two Met?"

I'd been out of the office when Joanna first showed up at the *Post*. I think I'd been off in Guatemala, exploring the ruins at Tikal. Someone introduced us. Joanna said she been reading my stories. I said I liked hers.

One thing we had in common was that we both enjoyed seeing Sean Penn explode. Before Joanna had gotten to Page Six, I'd done a story about Penn's behavior on the set of *At Close Range.* I had a source who'd been on the shoot. He told me that Penn had gotten mad at the prop master for not using real champagne in a scene. I'd been told that, shortly thereafter, the prop master found feces in his box of candy. People on the set suspected that Penn had left the stool sample. I had some fun interviewing a psychoanalyst who discussed Freud's theories about the anal expulsive personality versus the anal retentive—Penn being the former. I also called Robin Wright, who'd just started dating Penn. I knew Robin and her family. I must have been crazy, but I asked her what she made of Sean's alleged prank. I wanted to give her a head's up about this guy. She was horrified that I'd even called her about it. We didn't speak too much after that. Hey, she can't say I didn't warn her!

Joanna later found out that Penn was in good company. Once, the *New York Times's* venerable dance critic Anna Kisselgoff received a package. A source in the newsroom told Joanna that Kisselgoff was excited when she saw that it was from the great Rudolf Nureyev. But when she opened it, Kisselgoff found a stinking load of merde. Apparently, that was Nureyev's critique of something she'd written.

As I got to know Joanna, I became amazed by her energy. During the day, she barely sat down and she barely ate. She'd just pick like a sparrow at what I called "the all-day scone." She was also remarkably generous with the strange people who called Page Six as though it was a city agency help line. She was always taking time she didn't have to try to solve their problems—giving them suggestions on whom to call and sometimes calling on their behalf. She seemed like she didn't belong in gossip.

I didn't really come along on her pub crawls with Cotter and McAlary. As she says, "I'd be in saloons. He'd be doing readings at salons." But we got along. We ended up covering a lot of the same events and talking about things that had nothing to do with celebrities. We shared interests in some untabloidy things, like Yeats, the music of Central Africa's pygmies, and old French movies like *Les Enfants du Paradis*. We'd both ended up on Page Six in roundabout ways and were still wondering, "How did we get here?"

I'd been seeing a younger filmmaker and things weren't going so great. I turned to Joanna as my guidance counselor, telling her about our problems. Gradually, I realized that I was comparing my girlfriend with Joanna. My girlfriend and I broke up. I didn't know whether I stood a chance with Joanna, but I had to find out. I decided to test the waters by giving her a mixtape, the '90s equivalent of a sonnet. It began with the soundtrack from the famous scene in *To Have and Have Not* where Lauren Bacall tells Humphrey Bogart, "You just put your lips together and blow." One of Bogie's lines is "I know a lot about you, Slim."

Finally, I decided I had to speak my heart—no matter what the outcome. I suggested to Joanna that we cover the Gotham Independent Film Awards. Afterward, I asked her if she wanted to have a nightcap across the street at Sofia's, this little Italian restaurant on West Forty-Sixth Street. I nervously danced around different subjects before blurting out, "May I blaspheme?"

She thought I wanted to gossip about Frank DiGiacomo, who worked on the column with us. She said, "Okay."

I said, "Would you be willing to call one of these nights a date?" I had my whole spiel worked out. I said, "I know it's not always a good idea to go out with someone you work with. But look at all the couples who produced great work together—Louis and Marie Pasteur, Margaret Mead and Gregory Bateson, . . ." I went on and on. I didn't let her get a word in edgewise.

Finally, she smiled mischievously and said, "Why not?"

It was such a relief. We had a great conversation, as usual. When we stepped outside, I retroactively reclassified all our previous nights out as "dates." So figured I had grounds to move in on her.

We started this undercover office romance—nuzzling in doorways, staggering our arrival times at work. It had an air of espionage. Joanna claimed she actually thought I was a spy. I'd written a few stories about foreign dictators and the CIA. I was always disappearing to third-world countries. She read that Langley recruited a lot of people from Brown. One morning, around 5 a.m., we were in bed at my apartment and the phone rang. It was James A. Baker III, calling from Sakhalin Island in Russia. I jumped out of bed and started frantically taking notes. It was the first secretary of state I'd interviewed in my underwear. Joanna said she finally had proof that I was a spook. I said, "He was returning my call for a story!"

We tried to keep the fact that we were an item from becoming an item. But we weren't fooling anybody. One day, I got a call from Richard Johnson. He said, "George, I've heard the most delicious rumor about you and Joanna." I couldn't believe any *Daily News* reader really cared about us. But I thought that the *Post*'s editors might look askance at me sleeping with my "boss." I said, "Richard, I could get fired." Mercifully, he gave us a pass.

After a while, we started to relax. We'd walk into the *Post* in the morning together. Once, we were both invited to an eco-summit in Brazil. After visiting the Amazon, we went to Salvador, Bahia, home to Caetano Veloso, Joao Gilberto, Gilberto Gil, Gal Costa, and so many other singers Joanna and I loved. We'd samba down the cobblestone streets with or without music. We were strolling in our love haze past the crumbling colonial mansions. Old ladies kept making this hand gesture that we thought was a greeting. It turned out to be a signal that we were walking into a dangerous neighborhood. Which I guess marriage is. But I didn't heed their warning. I thought, there will never be a more romantic place than this to propose. We kept wandering up-hill until we reached the square of Santo Antonio, the patron saint of lonely hearts. There, at sunset, on the belvedere overlooking the bay, I presented Joanna with an antique gold ring I'd bought earlier that day.

Joanna says, "I had a feeling this might be coming. Jan Hooks, from *Saturday Night Live*, was with us on the trip. She told me she'd spotted George in the antique store 'shelling out mucho *cruzeiros.*' So, anyway, I said yes."

We floated hand in hand across the square to a cathedral where a wedding was going on. A little boy outside adopted us. He guided us to a sixteenth-century fortress where we hung out with a group of *bloco afro* percussionists who were rehearsing. It was like a dream, like we'd walked into the movie *Black Orpheus.*

After a while, we noticed it was dark. I looked at my watch and realized we were supposed to be back at the hotel, meeting up with some other reporters for dinner. The ladies present immediately picked up on the ring. One of the male journos, Jesse Nash, phoned in news of our betrothal to one of the columns in New York. It must have been a slow news day. But the *New York Observer* dubbed it the "Brazilian Engagement Shocker."

On December 12, 1992, we were married. Father Peter Colapietro, beloved by both his rich flock at Elaine's and his poor parishioners in Hell's Kitchen, did the honors at the Church of the Holy Cross. The worst nor'easter since 1950 lashed the nuptials, but December 12 being the feast day of Francis Albert Sinatra, the party was blessed by a superb orchestra of gray-haired Ellington and Basie vets who still swung hard.

Our Fred-and-Ginger-*Flying Down to Rio* romance had played out as one catastrophe after another befell the *Post* and the *Daily News.* In 1991, *Post* publisher Peter Kalikow filed for personal bankruptcy, putting the 191-year-old paper on the verge of extinction. Eccentric parking lot mogul Abe Hirschfeld and shadowy investor Steven Hoffenberg offered to save it. For about five minutes, when Pete Hamill was persuaded to be editor, it seemed they might. But Hirscheld turned out to be crazier than anyone expected (firing, re-hiring, and kissing Hamill for the cameras), and Hoffenberg later pled guilty to bilking investors out of $475 million. With the *Post* teetering on the brink of oblivion, even Democrats were forced to consider a previously unthinkable-savior—Rupert Murdoch. Governor Mario Cuomo lobbied the Federal Communications Commission to undo Ted Kennedy's handiwork and let Murdoch buy back his paper.

Before Murdoch's return, some Posties had started heading to the *Daily News,* which British press lord Robert Maxwell had acquired from the Tribune Company. John Cotter was among the first to flee to the *News.* But a few days before he was due to start, Cotter died of a heart attack. A few weeks after Cotter's death, Maxwell fell, jumped, or was pushed from the deck of his yacht, *Lady Ghislaine,* off the Canary Islands. It emerged post-mortem that Maxwell had "bought" the paper with millions stolen from his companies' pension funds. Editor-turned-publisher Jim Willse held the *News* together during bankruptcy proceedings until 1993, when real-estate billionaire Mortimer B. Zuckerman bought the paper. Zuckerman, who published *U.S. News and World Report* and *The Atlantic,* began to move the editorial chess pieces around the board. Among those he poached from the *Post* were star columnist Mike McAlary and editor in chief Lou Colasuonno and . . . Joanna.

"I left the *Post* mostly because I wanted to get out of gossip," Joanna recalls. "People thought I was crazy to go from editing Page Six to a general assignment reporter.

"As dedicated as I was to hard news, my editors kept asking me to do celebrity stories. They said it was a waste not to use my sources. And I wanted to help the paper. So, when Woody Allen and Mia Farrow started fighting for their son, Satchel, I was the one charged with finding out what was going on behind the scenes."

This made for some awkward conversations at home. I was still working for the *Post.* Joanna couldn't tell me what they were working on at the *News.* And I didn't want to know. But it could get tense in a restaurant when someone would tell both of us something juicy. How do you split that kind of tip?

For instance, we both talked with Donald Trump. Donald once invited Joanna to lunch at Trump Tower. They'd just sat down when she picked up her fork. Donald said, "Is that fork clean? Let me see it." Donald was a famous germaphobe. He squinted at the fork and told his waiter to bring Joanna a new fork. She picked it up. Donald grabbed it. He told the waiter, "No, I want a *clean* fork! Bring her another fork!" She thought she was never going to eat.

One of our marriage's early issues was who'd get custody of The Donald. One night, the phone rang in our apartment. We'd been hearing rumors that Donald was ready to marry his former mistress, Marla Maples. Joanna and I both jumped to get the phone; I grabbed it first and took the call out of earshot. I refused to tell Joanna that the Donald-Marla nuptials were on. The scoop was in the *Post*, not the *News*, the next day. Married or not, there would be no mercy!

6

Meet You On Forty-Second Street

Thankfully, another job opened up at the *Daily News*. Perhaps because of some past item that stuck in his craw, Mort Zuckerman didn't renew Richard Johnson's contract when he bought the paper. That freed Richard to return to Page Six. To patch the gossip flat, new editor Lou Colasuonno hired *Newsday*'s Linda Stasi, the *Washington Times*'s Charlotte Hays, and . . .

Me. Lou offered me my own column three days a week. I'd failed upward! The money was much better and it put Joanna and me on the same paper again. It was a thrill walking into 220 East Forty-Second Street, the landmark thirty-seven-story skyscraper built in 1930 when the *Daily News*'s two million readers made it America's largest newspaper. Above the door, the Art Deco stone relief was festooned with flappers and construction workers and men in top hats. The lobby had that giant revolving globe that they used in the *Superman* movies. Up on the seventh floor the newsroom stretched for a block. Anchored to the ceiling was a four-faced wooden clock that had glowered at sluggish reporters for decades. Nearby was a wooden copyboys' bench where Walter Winchell, who'd launched his career at the *News*, sat when he came begging for a job at the end of his life. The *News*'s lobby was lined with portraits of Cary Grant, Katherine Hepburn, Grace Kelly, and other stars who'd happily stopped by to pose for "New York's Picture Newspaper." Joe DiMaggio—the Yankee Clipper!—still dropped in to have lunch with revered sports cartoonist Bill Gallo, who'd fought on Iwo Jima. This was where Jimmy Breslin and Pete Hamill had hammered out masterpieces in less than an hour. I felt as though I was carrying the torch of *News* "saloon columnists" like Mark Hellinger, Danton Walker, and Ed Sullivan. I loved going to the library and looking through the yellow clips about debutantes who'd eloped and tycoons who'd made killings. The newsprint crumbled in my hands. Like fame. From dust to dust.

The *Daily News*, which billed itself as "the Honest Voice of New York," had its own share of characters. There was the guy who hurled a typewriter out a window. There was the codger in the library who sported a gray walrus moustache—and a lacy ladies' camisole under his shirt. There was the three-hundred-pound editor who'd sent summer copygirl Caroline Kennedy out for a breakfast six-pack. There was Victor Acosta, a sweet, roly-poly mailroom clerk who'd won millions in the lottery but didn't seem to understand that he didn't have to work anymore. There was the desk assistant with the mullet who, we found out later, was living in the basement. And there was the sports editor who was sleeping with two women at the paper, an editor and her secretary. When girlfriend number one found out, she asked her secretary to get a large cup of coffee—and promptly dumped it into their mutual boyfriend's lap. Bill Gallo, for one, could never fathom how this nebbishy sports editor had two women fighting over him. Gallo said, "I just don't see it."

When I got to the newsroom, they sat me at a desk directly opposite Charlotte Hays, who wrote her column on alternating days. Charlotte was a Memphis belle who seemed to have walked out of a Flannery O'Connor story—in her bare feet. Her desk had a southern gothic feel to it. Dead flowers sat in a dusty vase. A miasma of panic hung over her on the days she had to write. She talked to herself as much as to her sources. It was awkward for her and for me to be sitting within earshot of each other when we were dueling for stories. I was told that I could get help from the assistant she'd hired—Michael Riedel, a witty Columbia grad who went on to become Broadway's most-feared theater columnist. But after a few weeks, Michael, who was a gent at heart, sent me a message saying, "Charlotte doesn't want me to help you anymore. Ridiculous, I know, but I have to cover myself. So in the future, just message me for phone numbers. I don't mind helping you—the competition is between you and her, not you and me."

Fortunately, it wasn't long before I heard from some people who were excited by my new column: publicists looking for a fresh plot of newsprint to plant their items. Reporters still called them "flacks"—a bit of slang *Variety* is said to have coined in the 1930s in tribute to press agent Gene Flack. A barrage of publicity calls was known as a "flack attack." Flacks could be bothersome, but I had a soft spot for the old guys, the ones who'd fed items to Earl Wilson and Dorothy Kilgallen and the other legends: Eddie Jaffe, Harvey Mann, Bernie Bennett, Jack Tirman. A day never went by without at least two Smith Corona–typed pages from the indefatigable Sy Presten, who used to handle the Stork Club and signed his missives "Thanxy!" Mike Hall showed me a tattered thank-you note from "W. W."—Walter Winchell, whose thirty million readers once made him the most powerful columnist in America—thanking him for an item. Mike carried the note in his wallet like a holy relic. But he made no bones about how vindictive Winchell could be—like when he found out that several publicists had dared to attend a screening of *Sweet Smell of Success*, the savage send-up of Winchell starring Burt Lancaster and Tony Curtis. Mike remembered, "When we walked out of the theater, Walter stepped out of the shadows. He said, 'Hello, boys and girls. Howdya like the picture?' We knew what to say: 'It was a stinker, Walter!'"

The transaction between flack and columnist hadn't changed much since Winchell. The real-life versions of Tony Curtis's Sidney Falco character still swapped scoops for plugs. Plugs often came in the form of the flack's less-than-famous client being "sighted" at a restaurant, which was also a client of the flack. Or the plug might have "friends of" a real celebrity talking about his next project at the same restaurant, even though that celebrity might never have set foot in that restaurant. In spite of their casual acquaintance with the truth, the flacks still honored a code. It forbade them from "double planting" an item in two columns. They knew that "bum steers" could get them banned from the column. And if they screwed up, they knew that, like shamed samurai, they should "get buried."

The best of the flacks were like reporters: they had their own sources and did their own legwork.

No one was more dogged than R. Couri Hay, a well-born society gadabout who'd been a star columnist for the *National Enquirer* before opening his own PR company. One night, Couri spotted *Batman Forever* director Joel Schumacher with a handsome, younger man at the Gaiety Theater, an august male burlesque house in Times Square. Couri called me on his cell and gave me blow-by-blow commentary as he tailed Schumacher and his friend out of the Gaiety, down Broadway, and into the lobby of the Edison Hotel. Couri said, "They're getting on the elevator! Do you want me to go upstairs with them?" I said, "No, no, Couri, that'll be enough."

Bobby Zarem was also indispensable. By now, he'd forgiven me for writing that Page Six item about the production problems on *Sweet Liberty*. As a peace offering, he'd sent me a fluffy bathrobe with a note to "my new best friend." Of course the robe was emblazoned with the name of his latest client, Planet Hollywood. Bobby grew up in Savannah before going to Yale, where he became a great friend of Jane Fonda. He'd helped build the careers of John Travolta, Dustin Hoffman, and Arnold Schwarzenegger, among many others. Bobby was a large gentleman whose sweat-soaked shirt frequently hung out of his drooping pants. Some people thought he was separated at birth from Larry of the Three Stooges, though Al Pacino ended up playing a character inspired by him in the movie *People I Know*. Bobby's southern solicitousness was combined with a straight-talking, expletive-filled New Yorkese in a way that made him a pal to many stars. Michael Caine, Kirk Douglas, and Jack Nicholson never hit town without calling Bobby. He was out every night, always finishing at Elaine's. He was a good guy for a columnist to know.

I also heard from the paparazzi. The smart snappers figured out that they stood a better chance of getting their photos in the paper if they had a story to go with it. So they were soon regaling me with their tales of the hunt. "I don't do red carpet," young lensman Fernando Salas once told me. "There's no challenge there. Late at night, after the afterparty, that's when the stars get drunk and hook up." There'd be madcap car chases to and from the airport. More often, the confrontations between the paps and their prey took place on the sidewalk. David Duchovny, emerging from the Lowell Hotel with new bride Tea Leoni, threw a cup of scalding coffee on tiny Diane Cohen. David Copperfield did the same to another photographer who merely dared to snap him with Claudia Schiffer on a public street. The smart stars would make deals with their pursuers. Gwyneth Paltrow would promise Steve Sands her firstborn—that is, exclusive pictures of the baby—if he wouldn't haunt the door of the West Village townhouse she shared with her husband, Coldplay frontman Chris Martin. Jack Nicholson would find the paps camped outside his hotel and, rather than fleeing, put on a little show— striking poses and making his Jack faces. "Did everybody get enough pictures?" he'd ask them. "Good, good. Have a nice day." And off he'd stroll, free to pursue whatever mischief he had planned.

One of our favorite paparazzi was Arnaldo Magnani. Fellini himself couldn't have created a more classic specimen of the species. Arnaldo, who was in his sixties, owned a restaurant in the town of Cesenatico, on the Adriatic. In the summer, the tourist season, he'd drive around in his red Ferrari, living la dolce vita. Sometimes, he'd go on a stakeout in Italy. He once snuck onto the estate of Luciano Pavarotti and spent days waiting in the bushes for the great tenor to take a dip in his pool. Pavarotti had put on a lot of weight and nobody had gotten a picture of him with his clothes off. Arnaldo told me, "His gardener almost caught me. But finally, Pavarotti came out and dropped his bathrobe. His rolls of fat were beautiful—because I made a fortune off those pictures." Each fall, Arnaldo would come to New York to shoot celebrities. He was such a charming rogue that some stars actually looked forward to seeing him. I once saw him in the lobby of the Carlyle Hotel—coaching Eartha Kitt on her best angle. He'd hand a jack-o-lantern to Dustin Hoffman as he came out of Le Cirque. Dustin put it on his shoulder like a second head. Not every celeb was so obliging. Barbra Streisand, famously fastidious about her good angles, covered her head with a paper bag. But Arnaldo wouldn't be deterred. He ran down the block, climbed a tree, and snapped her when she took the bag off. Unfortunately, he fell out of the tree and broke a finger. But Arnaldo crowed, "I'm alright. I got the picture!"

Aside from Arnaldo, nobody had better info about which celebs were in town than Craig Castaldo. I didn't know that was his name till years later. Most people called him Radio Man, because he hung a small boom box around his neck so he could listen to ball games. Radio Man had been homeless at one point. Even after he had a place to crash, his wild gray beard and well-worn clothes made him the model of dishevelment. He had an ornate way of speaking, like he was a dethroned king. He loved the movies. Rain or shine, he'd ride his rusty old Schwinn from one movie set to another, scavenging food from the production's craft service people. Radio Man could tell me where any film was shooting. He got chummy with Robin Williams when Robin was playing a homeless man—who looked like Radio—in *The Fisher King*. George Clooney, Johnny Depp, and quite a few other stars took a shine to Radio Man. They helped him out by signing fan photos that Radio sold to autograph dealers. Arnold Schwarzenegger bought him a new Schwinn. When that was stolen, Whoopi Goldberg bought him another. When Whoopi hosted the Oscars, she flew Radio Man out to Hollywood, gave him the money to rent a tux, and handed him backstage passes. He brought his own radio.

Information could come from all sorts of people: cops, doormen, bodyguards, chauffeurs, strip club owners, party promoters, talent agents, producers, and every variety of lawyer—anyone who lived at the intersection where fame and mayhem collided. Private investigators were especially useful. I made it my business to know as many as possible. The private dicks were a jealous lot. When I ran an item about one PI, I promptly received a fax from another PI with some shocking allegations about the first one's "secret family." For a profession supposedly sheathed in stealth, some of its practitioners wanted a little too much attention. Frank Monte was an Australian investigator who claimed to have worked for designer Gianni Versace. He told me that Gianni had not been killed by serial killer Andrew Cunanan but rather by the Calabrian mob, for whom Versace was allegedly laundering money. The Versace family sued Monte and won a defamation case in which a judge concluded that Monte had "never had any relationship" whatsoever with Versace.

One of the private eyes you could always bank on was Joe Mullen. Joe had actually worked for Johnny Carson, Walter Cronkite, George Steinbrenner, Donald Trump—and those were just the people who gave him permission to talk. One night Joe invited me to dinner at Elaine's with a few of his buddies. They included G. Gordon Liddy, the mastermind behind the Watergate burglaries; Bob Burton, the bounty hunter who coached De Niro in *Midnight Run*; and Robert K. Brown, former Green Beret and publisher of *Soldier of Fortune* magazine. They were a lively group. When they weren't reliving a firefight in the Rhodesian Bush War, they were smashing pieces of strudel with their fists. Their collective testosterone level was soaring by the time dinner was over. We were all chatting on the sidewalk outside when I noticed that a squirrelly guy who reminded me of John David Hinckley had insinuated himself into our conversation.

Bob Brown said, "Can I help you, son?"

The kid had a sinister smile. He started reaching into a bag slung over his shoulder.

Bob Burton said, "What have you got in that bag?"

The kid said, "You want to see what I have in this bag?"

Liddy said, "Whatever you got in there, you better pull it out nice and slow."

The kid said again, "You want to see what I got?"

Burton, Liddy, Mullen, and Brown began reaching for their ankle and shoulder holsters.

Finally, the kid whipped out his secret weapon—an eight-by-ten photo of David Bowie.

"Bowie, man!" the kid proclaimed. "Bowie!"

He was just some groupie hoping to get an autograph from the Thin White Duke. The macho men looked so let down. Little did the kid know how close he'd come to annihilation.

Having built up my network of sources, I attempted to do a column that was a little different.

I had about a quarter of the space of Page Six. I couldn't fit in a lot of items, so I'd try to devote most of the column to one strong story. Some of the stories ended up in the main part of the paper. I wrote a three-part investigation about incest charges against Richard Nixon's "honorary father," pharmaceutical kingpin Elmer Holmes Bobst, whose name graced New York University's main library. The story was kind of a real-life *Chinatown*. I did another series on allegations that Fendi and Bulgari charged Oprah Winfrey, Sly Stallone, and other celebrities more than what average customers paid. Oprah's eyes bugged out when I told her at a party that, while many celebs were getting free jewelry, she'd allegedly been paying more than retail.

I also did the sort of items most people wanted in their gossip column. I landed scoops on paternity actions against Jack Nicholson and Don Johnson. One good story was a love child scoop in reverse. I'd heard Harvey Keitel had been dating the coat-check girl at his pal Robert De Niro's Tribeca Grill. The girl got pregnant and told Keitel he was the father. Keitel was ready to cop to it, but De Niro told him to run a DNA test when the baby was born. Sure enough, it turned out that somebody else was the father. I was at a premiere party for *A Bronx Tale*—fittingly, at the Tribeca Grill—when I saw Keitel. He had a reputation for not suffering reporters gladly, but I had to take my shot.

I walked over to him and said, "Hey, Harvey, I heard you got some good news."

His brow furrowed. "What's that?" he said.

"I heard you're not the father of your ex-girlfriend's baby."

Suddenly, I was looking at the Bad Lieutenant.

"*That's* a story?" he snarled, "You're going to *write* that?"

"Yeah, unless it's not true."

He stormed off. I took that as a confirmation.

Within a few months of arriving at the *News*, I learned that Charlotte Hays was being let go and that I'd be taking her space, writing five days a week. About a year in, *New York Magazine* ranked me third out of thirteen gossips, just behind Page Six and Liz Smith. "Rush has a reputation for being a decent guy—he's pro-feminist, pro-gay, and polite," the magazine ruled. I guess that explained why my "bitchiness" score was a shameful "1 out of 10," compared with Page Six's "8."

New York acknowledged that I had a challenge in working for the "socially ambitious Mort Zuckerman," who "is reported to expect only two things from his columnists: (1) that they write about his friends and (2) that they don't write about his friends." Mort had been the frequent victim of other columnists. His breakup with feminist icon Gloria Steinem had been the subject of endless items. His free-range dating continued to provide grist for Candace Bushnell's *Sex and the City* column. Though one of her characters dubbed Mort a "toxic bachelor," another proclaimed that "every guy in New York wants to be Mort Zuckerman."

I hadn't run afoul of Mort—yet. My scoop about anchor Peter Jennings leaving his wife, Kati Marton, for ABC News producer Kayce Freed had had Mort's media friends purring. But I knew I was pushing my luck when I sought to clarify the sexual identity of Liz Smith.

It was an open secret that Liz, who was still the most famous gossip columnist in America, was a lesbian. For many years, she'd lived with archaeologist Iris Love. But I'd heard that, lately, they were living apart, that Liz had turned her attention to a younger anchorwoman. Then, one day, Liz did a column on the champion dachshund that she and Love co-owned. She wrote quite affectionately about Love. Gay activists had been after Liz for years to come out—to use her platform to promote pride. So I called Liz and gingerly asked if she and Love were "back together." She was pleasant enough. In her husky Texan drawl, Liz said, "Iris and I have been friends and we continue to be friends." It was pretty clear to me that she wasn't ready to make any announcements in my column. So I was going to drop it. But Liz wasn't taking any chances. Within the hour, my editor, Betsy Pochoda, called me into her office. She said, "Mort just called me. He just got a call from his friend, Liz Smith." Betsy asked me what had happened. I told her. She smiled. She said Mort would be grateful if I left this subject alone, especially since Liz had written for the *News* for seventeen years. I was fine with that, since I'd never intended to out her. It took Liz another seven years before she wrote about her relationships with Love and other women in her memoir, *Natural Blonde*. But I'd earned my keep that day: Liz now owed Mort one. And that was half the reason rich guys bought newspapers.

I kept stirring up trouble. I'd heard about a woman who supposedly had had an affair with the male half of a prominent media couple. I called the woman and, to my surprise, she freely admitted that it was true. She said she'd met the flirtatious husband on the job and that their fling had lasted about six months. She went into some detail about their lunchtime liaisons. She said that, for an older man, he was quite an athletic lover. Even though she'd corroborated the rumor, I knew it would be impossible to use the married couple's names, especially since they were longtime friends of Mort. So I quoted the woman in a long blind item. The story set off epidemic speculation in media circles. Everybody was sure they knew who the married couple was—based on whoever they wanted them to be. I was relieved that so many power couples were considered suspects. Shortly after the story ran, I was invited to a big party thrown by the wife in question. People couldn't believe I'd dared to enter the lioness's den. She was not a lady who liked being seen as a victim. After keeping my distance from her, we found ourselves face-to-face. She gave me an Antarctic hello. She'd obviously seen the item. I asked a question about her new project. She gave me a clipped answer. Then my mind went blank. I stood there dumbly as her eyes hacked off my limbs, leaving my mumbling head and torso. Finally, she said, "Anything else?" I said, "Uh, no." She turned on her high heel. Fortunately, her husband took things better. One of his staff told me, "We were debating whether to show him your story, but we decided he better know that people were talking about him. He read it and said, 'Athletic? Good stamina? Sounds okay to me!'"

The story died down. But, a few months later, I got a call out of the blue from the husband. He said, "I saw your blind item. It didn't ring a bell for me. I know you have to follow up on these things. But, believe me, [my wife] and I love each other very much. We are very devoted to each other. We can't go to everything together. We each have to attend four or five things a night. People are envious of her. It's mean-spirited. Mark your card—it's not true." I had the feeling that he'd gotten frisky again and that his wife had lowered the boom. I didn't know what prompted the belated damage control, but I thanked him for calling. By the way, they're still together.

I jumped into hotter oil when I obtained a proposal for a biography of Motown founder Berry Gordy by Tony Turner, a former road manager for the Supremes and the Temptations. Turner, forty-two, promised his Gordy book would be even more personal than his two earlier works. Among other charges, Turner alleged that, in 1966, Gordy had showed him some "wrestling moves" at his Warwick Hotel suite in New York and that he'd then invited Turner to join him in the shower. "At the uncertain age of fourteen," Turner wrote, "Berry Gordy Jr. gave me my very first taste of sexual intimacy, followed by my first full sexual experience."

It was obviously a scalding allegation. No one had ever said anything like this about Gordy, who was famous as a ladies' man. He'd fathered five children—one with Diana Ross. I had Michael Riedel, who'd laid his mitts on the pitch, call Gordy's spokesman several times. He wouldn't give us any comment. It *usually* makes a reporter's life easier when someone doesn't deny a charge. But refusing to "dignify the charge" can sometimes work to the flack's advantage. It's a gamble, but editors sometimes won't sign off on a potentially actionable story if its subject doesn't say something. We made other calls to try to check out Turner's claim, but it came down to his word against Gordy's. And Gordy wasn't talking. We gave him a week to respond. Finally, the paper's lawyers felt we'd given Gordy every opportunity; we had Turner on the record in writing, and so we pulled the trigger.

Now Gordy deigned to speak. Within two days, he announced that he was suing the *Daily News*, me, and Turner for $250 million. In a statement, Gordy called the article "irresponsibly published, highly offensive, obscene, and completely false. I have no recollection of ever seeing this man except maybe on television. The fact that anyone can walk into a major newspaper and get something this damaging published without corroboration is downright frightening."

Gordy filed suit in Los Angeles Superior Court, where the libel laws were more favorable to public figures than in New York. The *News*'s lawyers argued that, for starters, the case shouldn't be heard in a California state court because the *Daily News* had a total of thirteen subscribers in California—most of whom were in prison. The paper succeeded in having the case moved to federal district court, which dismissed the action for lack of personal jurisdiction over the defendants. The US Court of Appeals reversed that decision, noting that it was not "unreasonable" for Gordy to feel most injured in California. First Amendment authorities around the country watched as the case dragged on for three years. Meanwhile, Tony Turner, whose testimony was critical to the case, was facing some serious health problems. The

News's lawyers began to worry that he might not be able to make it to a trial. So a confidential settlement was reached. Gordy and Mort supposedly closed the deal with a handshake over a round of golf. The *News* did not retract the story or admit error but apologized "for any distress or concern that its action may have caused Mr. Gordy."

They talk about lawsuits having a "chilling effect" on a free press. This one definitely left my teeth chattering. It was a huge distraction. The depositions went on forever. After my Gordy experience, even when I believed a story to be true, even if the lawyers green-lighted it, I made the calculation whether I cared enough about the scoop to risk being tied up in court for three years.

7

Our New Mattress

We had a new boss. A few months after hiring Lou Colasuonno as editor in chief, Mort had replaced him with Martin Dunn, a thirty-eight-year-old Brit who'd been running Murdoch's *Boston Herald*. Martin was a funny bloke who could turn himself into a dozen different Monty Pythonesque characters. But he was also a hard-charging Fleet Street gladiator who'd won glory taking Murdoch's *Today* tabloid up-market, boosting its circulation 20 percent in one year. The day he arrived at the *News*, Martin dispatched Joanna to L.A.

Over to Joanna:

Twenty-seven-year-old Heidi Fleiss had been just been charged with running a prostitution ring that allegedly serviced big stars and producers. She was instantly dubbed the "Hollywood Madam." I didn't mind flying to L.A. But somewhere over Nevada, I remembered I really didn't know how to drive. I had no choice but to rent a car, which I drove at about twenty-five miles per hour down the Santa Monica Freeway. I began inquiring about Heidi and her clients. She'd gotten her start working for Alex Adams, who was known as "Madam 90210." I went over to Madam Alex's mansion. She was a large lady who received guests in her giant powder blue canopy bed. I asked her questions while her Filipino maids served us tea and her Persian cat, George, licked her. Alex gave me some leads, but I really hit pay dirt when I met Heidi's estranged boyfriend, Ivan Nagy. Ivan was a TV director from Budapest. I invited him to my suite at the Chateau Marmont, greeting him with the only Hungarian I knew: "You're a little block of gold." Which he was. Luckily for me, he was mad at Heidi. It was somehow related to his ceiling being shot up the night before. Ivan gave me a copy of Heidi's big black scheduling book. It had the first names of her call girls and their clients. On one page, the name "Barry" was scribbled next to a phone number. I called the number. It turned out to belong to Barry Josephson, vice president of production at Columbia. The *Daily News* had one front page after another. Ivan also gave me a ton of photos from Heidi in her bikini on holiday. The paper made a bundle reselling the photos. The money almost covered my traffic and parking tickets.

Back in New York, I had to start chasing Mickey Rourke. His on-and-off girlfriend, Carré Otis, was modeling in the Fashion Week runway shows. Mickey was tailing her, having run-ins with security along the way. I was tailing Mickey. I followed him to an afterparty, where I talked to him and his buddy Tupac Shakur. They were laughing so hard they didn't realize their nostrils looked like powdered donuts.

Then there was the Saturday I went to a small lunch at Le Cirque, Sirio Maccioni's power boîte, to celebrate the twentieth anniversary of the place. I'm not a foodie, but I couldn't say no. For several hours, some of France's greatest trotted out their daring dishes, one more exquisite than the last. The room filled with suspense as waiters rolled in silver carts filled with porcelain bowls.

"And now, ladies and gentlemen," said Chef Alain Ducasse, "we present you with the greatest gastronomic delicacy on the face of the earth. These are the legendary ortolans, the songbird that one must eat whole, bones and all."

The waiters distributed the tiny birds, which had been force-fed millet in dark boxes, killed, soaked in Armagnac, and roasted. We were also presented with embroidered white linen cloths.

"According to tradition, you must put one of these cloths over your head," Ducasse explained. "That way, God will not see you experience such ecstasy outside of heaven."

The assembled socialites dutifully covered themselves with the schmattes. Le Cirque looked like a cafeteria for ghosts. They all began crunching away and groaning.

Our hosts asked us not to breathe a word of our ortolan orgy. They admitted that the ortolan was a protected species in France. But since we were in the United States, they claimed they weren't doing anything illegal. All the same, I asked my tablemate, photographer Aubrey Reuben, to discreetly snap a picture of veiled Food Network host Nina Griscom.

Back in the newsroom, our metro editor Richard Gooding asked, "Where've you been, Molloy?"

"Oh, just watching a bunch of rich people eat an endangered species," I said. Gooding grabbed me by my blouse. "Excuse me?" he said.

He told me to call animal rights activists. US Fish and Wildlife officers were soon descending on Le Cirque. They hit Maccioni with a big fine. Martin put the gastronomic outrage on the front page—complete with a picture of Nina Griscom chomping on Tweety Bird. The story went around the world.

Martin knew how to play a story. He had a lot of original ideas. But neither of us was prepared for the one he sprang on us in 1995. He proposed that Joanna and I write a gossip column together.

Of course we'd worked together on Page Six. We'd also collaborated on stories for the *Daily News*. But Joanna still harbored the hope of doing hard news. And we'd been trying to put a *little* breathing space between us. Some companies forbid married couples from working together—for the sake of the other workers. Everyone questions the judgment and objectivity of a husband and wife working together. I think they also question their sanity. Maybe because we arrived at the *News* pre-assembled, people just rolled with it. But cohabiting on one page could be risky—for everybody. It was like sharing a mattress in a window at Macy's.

And then there was the question of what to call the column. Joanna and I tossed around different names. Should we steal the name of the

African National Congress's gossip column—"Pssst"? Just kidding. Finally, Martin suggested just calling it "Rush & Molloy."

It sounded like an accounting firm, which I suppose it was. We audited celebrities. Once we agreed on the name, we knew what our mission was. Older columnists seemed to be carrying on the Louella Parsons/Hedda Hopper tradition of wanting to be friends with celebs. We didn't think that was possible. Our page was going to be a sticky glue trap for those two Hollywood cockroaches—hype and hypocrisy.

We wanted to be skeptical, but not cruel. We didn't want to be bitchy queens who tore down people just because they were famous. But it still had to be fun. Cranking out items was like comedy writing—except that comics don't get sued if the guy in the audience gets mad. And billionaires did get mad. Even with all their money, most of them couldn't afford a sense of humor. So we still had to obey the journalistic traffic lights. No item was too small, or too good, to check.

We wanted the column to be like a party where movie stars, senators, supermodels, financiers, quarterbacks, and rock stars were all drinking and dancing and getting into brawls. Getting the right mix of stories could be tricky. We covered celebs that minority readers and immigrant readers cared about. We wanted to make sure we didn't have a page full of white people. But items about the rich and powerful att-racted the A-list, who liked to read about themselves. We also believed that people in the outer boroughs should know what the robber barons were up to. We were infiltrating an elite that often abused its privileges. You can say that we had no business invading peoples' private lives. But that's where you saw their true characters. You had senators who wanted the support of voters and CEOs who wanted the money of stockholders. But their own wives couldn't trust them.

"Rush & Molloy" debuted as a full page on February 20, 1995. The first column included the news that pinup Pamela Anderson and Mötley Crüe drummer Tommy Lee, who'd met only four days before, had gotten married on a beach in Mexico. It was what the British tabs liked to call a "world exclusive" (as if most of the world cared). The column also included original items about John Kennedy Jr. and girlfriend Daryl Hannah's dogs, Paul McCartney and Yoko Ono's rapprochement, and actress Sharon Stone's nipple. More scoops followed: Andre Agassi hooking up with Steffi Graf . . . Madonna's jettisoning of Carlos Leon seven months after the birth of their daughter, Lourdes . . . a commodities trader buying the chicken-nugget-sized piece of Evander Holyfield's ear that Mike Tyson had bit off. Among other stories.

There was a rough science to what made a good item. Picture four quadrants labeled *Sex, Conflict, Fame,* and *Power.* Ideally, a story would straddle two. A billionaire didn't have to be a household name—we delighted in noisily exposing "quiet wealth." But an unknown billionaire would need to do some *schtupping,* feuding, or law-breaking to make the column. If a billionaire had a famous name (Newhouse, Lauder, Icahn, Koch, Kravis), the acquisition of more power could be enough. We were happy to get first word of a big deal. A really amazing story would overlap all four quadrants—say, a mogul cheating with an actress while the SEC investigated his IPO.

A satisfying item also involved an inverse ratio between the subject's fame and the subject's activity. A C-list celeb would need to rob a strip club for us to care about him. An A-list celeb just had to eat scungilli at a restaurant where you couldn't get a table. The president of the United States had to do practically nothing. Minutia about the truly powerful was irresistible to almost everyone. Even if you couldn't understand his economic policy, you sounded like an insider repeating the president's golf score.

Knowledge of these formulas didn't lessen the challenge of taking on the *Post*'s seasoned pros. Besides Richard Johnson, Murdoch's gossip posse now included Cindy Adams, who'd been writing her own column since 1979; Liz Smith, who'd just jumped from *Newsday*; and Neal Travis, the wily Kiwi who'd launched Page Six in 1977.

Items didn't come flying over the transom as they did when we were at Page Six. We had to work for them. One night, Universal was having a premiere of Rob Reiner's comedy *The American President.* No press was allowed—supposedly because it was a benefit. But I snuck in with a friend who had a ticket. I got ejected, so I snuck in again. The following day, Page Six had an item griping about the press ban. Rush & Molloy had a conversation with the movie's star, Annette Bening, and her husband, Warren Beatty.

By no means did this happen every day. But, most days, we held our own. While Page Six was then locked into the graphic prison of a cartoon and two fixed headshots, we had paparazzi pictures and, usually, a huge silhouetted photo of a starlet we called "the fifty-foot woman."

Another battleground was the red carpet. At a big movie premiere at the Ziegfeld Theater, you'd be wedged cheek-by-jowl along a rope line with thirty reporters and their camera crews. Like most assembly lines, the red carpet produced a shabby product.

Stars were usually racing into the theater. So they didn't have much time to talk. If you had a controversial question, their publicists were there at their side to tell them not to answer it. If you did get an interesting quote, the eavesdropping reporter next to you was likely to steal it or to ask the same question you just asked, so they could claim it was *their* quote. That's why I usually preferred to try to catch the actors at the after-party—after they'd had a few drinks.

If there was no after-party, or if we couldn't crack it, the red carpet was unavoidable. The best strategy was to think of a concept or theme. For instance, at the premiere of Tim Burton's musical *Sweeney Todd*, we asked one and all to donate a few thoughts on blood, since Burton splashed around a lot of it in the film. "I like to keep my blood inside me, thank you," said Johnny Depp, who played the Demon Barber of Fleet Street. Had he ever lost a lot of blood? "Yes," he deadpanned. "But I found it!" Depp's pal, Keith Richards, said he was only creeped out by "other people's blood." Had he seen the Broadway version of Stephen Sondheim's ghoulish musical? "Nah," said the cadaverous-looking Rolling Stone. "But I knew the original Sweeney Todd. He gave a hell of a shave!" And so on. Sutured together, the quotes made for an amusing read.

The crimson conveyor belt sometimes delivered people you didn't care to speak with. Typically, it was an eight-year-old who played the son of the lead actor. But the kid's publicist might be the gatekeeper for the actor you needed to talk to. And so, the publicist might whisper that, if you talked with the kid, you'd get five minutes with the star. Deal!

Sometimes nothing could make you talk to a proven bore. One night at a fashion event, I was standing next to Jeannie Williams, who wrote for *USA Today*. Calvin Klein was coming down the carpet. He turned to take a question from Jeannie, but she lowered her recorder and said to me, "You can have him. He never says anything interesting." I was taken aback because Jeannie was a sweetheart who'd suffered through years of vacuous starlets. But, after thinking about my own brushes with Calvin, I said, "You're right. I can't recall a usable quote I've ever gotten out of him." Meanwhile, Calvin was standing there, kind of glassy-eyed, listening to us discuss him. I finally said, "Thanks, Mr. Klein. No questions."

Though we tried to avoid the pack, we couldn't help but join certain mass migrations. Like a couple of wildebeests, we headed in March to L.A. for the Oscars. We usually stayed at one of the hotels our friend, André Balazs, owned on Sunset Boulevard—the Chateau Marmont or the Standard. André had done a brilliant job converting The Standard from an ugly 1960s retirement home; instead of wrinkly seniors, it was now filled with toned hipsters who never seemed to stop dancing, even at breakfast. There were DJs everywhere at The Standard. We half-expected to open our shower and find a DJ in there. The Chateau Marmont, built in 1927, was a more elegant place, where dark Spanish décor conjured the feeling of old Hollywood. But things could get lively. One day, around noon, a bomb scare caused the LAPD to evict us from our room. Like other guests, we tried to dampen the panic by heading to the pool. There we found Irish director Jim Sheridan, who suspected the phoned-in threat might be related to his IRA sympathies. Most of us were in our swimsuits. That is, except for *Reservoir Dogs* star Michael Madsen, who groggily emerged from the cottages where John Belushi had overdosed in 1982—dressed in black leather jacket, pants, and motorcycle boots. Just the outfit for a dip!

Our Oscar *haj* always included certain pilgrimage sites. On Saturday, around noon, we'd go to the Independent Spirit Awards. The Spirits were created to salute makers of low-budget films. The first Spirit Awards we went to was like an Elks Club lunch, if John Waters were an Elk. Then, as "fringe" films started winning Oscars, the Spirit Awards attracted major stars, which attracted media from around the world. The televised circus now needed a big top tent on Santa Monica beach. But it still had a boozy, irreverent vibe. It was easy to grab a word with

Woody Harrelson as he took a hit at the oxygen bar or Jodie Foster as she availed herself to free Frye boots and a Chantelle thong (still a potent mental image) in the swag suite.

After the Spirits, we'd hit the Miramax cocktail party at the Beverly Wilshire. Guests like Mick Jagger, Barbra Streisand, and Madonna were just hors d'oeuvres. The centerpiece was the "Maxy" awards—chocolate statuettes that Miramax founders Harvey and Bob Weinstein presented to their Oscar nominees (who could number twenty in a good year). In return, Harvey and Bob would put their stars to work—dragooning them to play each other's characters in sketches written by the likes of Tom Stoppard and John Irving. Ben Affleck would ape Harvey by donning a prosthetic gut. Gwyneth Paltrow would wear a plastic nose and glasses, *a la* Roberto Benigni. Kevin Spacey would slip into a dress to channel Charlize Theron. And, anointing himself a rabbi, Robin Williams would bless everyone in fake Hebrew, thanking them "for coming to the Weinstein family's bar mitzvah."

Of course, Sunday was the big day—the Academy Awards.

The first year I covered the Oscars, I figured I'd better try to go to the ceremony. So I threw on my tux and drove downtown to the Dorothy Chandler Pavilion. I was directed to the press pool backstage. After someone won an Oscar, the Academy people would trot the winner from one room to another—from the photographers to the TV crews to the print reporters. It was a like a sheep dip. You'd be watching the ceremony on a TV monitor. The presenters would be opening the envelope. You'd hear, "And the winner is . . ." Suddenly, the sound be cut and someone from the Academy would bellow, "We have Anna Paquin!" You couldn't hear the live acceptance speech in the auditorium, but you could hear some stringer from Slovenia asking eleven-year-old Anna Paquin if she was happy. It was frustrating. Then Paul Newman appeared. He'd just received his first Oscar—the Jean Hersholt Humanitarian Award. He took some questions. Then I saw him heading into the hallway. Back when I worked for the *Post*, Newman never would have talked to me. But I figured I stood a chance now that I wasn't working for Murdoch. The one way a reporter could get out of the media stockade was to go to the bathroom. So I told the security guards that nature was calling me. I tailed Newman and discovered that he actually was heading to the men's room. So we did the interview at the urinals. On the way out, I was apprehended by a publicist who demanded to know how I'd gotten out of my pen. They were about to throw me out when I told them I was leaving.

From then on, we watched the Oscars on TV at a party. Once the Best Picture Oscar was handed out, it was off to the parties where the real stars showed up. The winners always stopped by the Governor's Ball, the Academy's official Academy party. A lot of celebs would hit Elton John's annual AIDS fundraiser, where you could always depend on Elton (A) dissing the Oscar show as *boring* and (B) making up for it with some surprise musical guest like Prince.

But the main event was the party thrown by *Vanity Fair* editor Graydon Carter. Graydon first hosted the bash in 1994, after the death of agent Swifty Lazar, who used to rule the night with his dinner at Spago. At some point in the evening, pretty much every Oscar winner—past, present, and future—stopped by. The limos would be lined up around the block as one star after another was deposited at Morton's restaurant, which had been completely transformed. There were topiary sculptures painted in colored light. The crowd of fans screamed with each arrival. Photographers splashed the winners with flash as they hoisted their Oscars like golden barbells. Inside, there was a Himalayan range of cleavage—adorned with borrowed diamonds, sapphires, and emeralds. You couldn't turn around without bumping into Bono or Cher or Iman or some other one-named icon. Even stars were starstruck.

For a gossip columnist, it was like shooting fish in a barrel. Only, we were *never* supposed to overtly interview anyone. God forbid that Graydon's press empress, Beth Kseniak, saw you writing something down. We'd have to duck behind a bush or in a bathroom stall to scribble a quote.

I would try keeping a small recorder wrapped up in a cocktail napkin or tucked in my breast pocket behind my handkerchief. Trouble was, it was hard to be sure when the damn thing was switched off and on. Only two people ever spotted that little red recording light—Ryan Gosling and Diddy. Don't try to pull anything over on those two!

You often got more by not letting on you were a reporter. You witnessed a lot of emotional moments just standing there. Like when Oprah saw her idol, Sidney Poitier, walk in with his lifetime achievement award. She clasped his face with her palms and kept repeating, "My God, my God!" You just had to listen and watch. You could see people hooking up—Ellen DeGeneres and Anne Heche, Ellen Barkin and Ron Perelman. There was always some awkward intersection of ex-lovers. Madonna would hold onto Guy Ritchie when Sean Penn walked by. Matt Damon would dodge Winona Ryder. Tom Cruise would come in with Katie Holmes and immediately run into Penelope Cruz and Nicole Kidman.

As the champagne flowed, you could count on someone getting sloppy. One time I sat down in a wicker chair near the bar. Anna Nicole Smith was sitting next to me. She was obviously feeling no pain. She hiked up her blue spaghetti-strap dress to show off her legs, opening and closing them in the air, like a nutcracker. Her date, an actor named Branscombe Richmond, was kind enough to stand in front of her crotch. He said, "I'm blocking the view." I asked her how the party had been so far and she started griping about Oliver Stone. She slurred, "He can kiss my white ass!" Apparently, Oliver had been seated between Anna and Candice Bergen and he had chosen to talk with Candice. Anna ended up dashing into the ladies' room, where Dolly Parton watched her lose her cookies.

Some of the best scenes happened around 3 a.m. when you'd see Hilary Swank and Kevin Spacey and Julianne Moore and Russell Crowe dancing and drinking and eating In-and-Out burgers. One night, the party was almost over when Paul McCartney showed up with Heather Mills. The DJ was playing "I Will Survive." Paul started acting the song out and spinning Heather around the empty dance floor. They were oblivious to onlookers, including that one old Beatles groupie staring at them from the corner—Rupert Murdoch.

8

Westward Ho!

Back in New York, we returned to work in the *Daily News*'s new newsroom. Looking for more (and cheaper) space, Mort had moved the paper out of the Forty-Second Street building that had been its flagship for sixty-five years. It caused a bit of heartache—not only for us, but for many New Yorkers who thought the *Daily News* should be in the Daily News Building. The paper's memorabilia—vintage Speed Graphic cameras, models of two airplanes it once owned, and its famous framed front pages (FORD TO CITY: DROP DEAD)—was shipped to 450 West Thirty-Third Street, near a windswept stretch of Tenth Avenue favored by valet hookers who drove around topless in cars without license plates.

On our first day in the new office, we were all unpacking our stuff. I was going through the mail when I noticed an odd-looking box wrapped in brown paper. I didn't recognize the return address and my name was scribbled in weird handwriting. We often received bizarre hate mail from crazy readers. The security director at the *News* had just sent around a memo telling everybody about a new mailroom scanner. We were supposed to let security X-ray any suspicious packages. So I handed this package to a security guard. Then I went to a movie premiere for a couple of hours. When I came out of the premiere, I got an urgent page from Joanna.

Instead of scanning the package, the security guard had called the NYPD Bomb Squad. The police came over in the big armored truck they use for detonating explosives. Our editor, Martin Dunn, happened to be having dinner at a nearby restaurant and saw the truck and squad cars tearing past with their lights flashing. He thought, "Hmm, where are *they* going? Could be a story." He phoned in the tip, only to find out every editor and reporter was standing outside the building. The cops in their Kevlar suits had evacuated the newsroom. And this was on our first night there, when everybody was battling the new system to put out a paper!

The mysterious box turned out to contain my new business cards. Some incendiary device! I burned the edge of one card with a match and handed it to Martin. He was not amused.

Even on a day without imaginary bomb threats, the newsroom was a tense place. Everyone felt the pressure to find original stories, make them accurate, and get them in on time. The pressure felt amplified when one was working with one's spouse.

We'd each write our own stories, which we'd send to our Features editor, Larry Hackett. Joanna's a much faster writer. Sometimes, she'd finish her items and have to run out to an event. So I'd go over the column with Larry. Sometimes I'd tinker with her Joanna-isms. She liked to end items with these moxie Bronx interjections like "Natch!" and "Yikes!" I'd cut those out.

"He wouldn't tell me," says Joanna. "He had no right to do that. God help anyone who touched his deathless prose! We'd also end up with too many items at the end of the day. He'd put his items in first!"

Sometimes I'd write something that offended a source of hers. Or vice versa. One of us would have to apologize to our source. We actually figured out that the old good cop/bad cop interrogation routine could help us get more information out of people. I could say to someone who didn't want to talk: "I'd like to help you. If it were up to me, I'd skip the whole item. But Molloy is dead set on it." Or we'd reverse roles. Joanna would say, "I can't control George. He's so stubborn! You know what he's like. Maybe if you talk to me, I can talk to him."

When we had arguments, we usually worked them out. Shared passions brought us back together. The more seventeen-year-old "superstars" we'd have shoved in our faces, the more we appreciated the old stars.

I had the pleasure of talking with Peter O'Toole a couple of times. He was such an old pro. He'd say, "You won't get any gossip from me!" But he was a corker. When I asked him how he stayed so thin, he said, "I eat like a horse. It's a family trait. We're frightfully good artists with the knife and fork, but we all look like we were just dug up."

We hit the jackpot when we saw Claire Trevor sitting with Douglas Fairbanks Jr. at an Oscar party in New York. Trevor had won the Academy Award for Best Supporting Actress in 1948 for her incandescent portrayal of a broken-down moll in *Key Largo*. Joanna asked her about the famous scene where she sobs the song "Moanin' Low" so her gangster boyfriend (Edward G. Robinson) will give her a drink.

"'Those were real tears," Trevor recalled. "I was terrified. All through rehearsals, I kept reminding [director] Mr. [John] Huston that I couldn't sing a note, and that he had promised me singing lessons. After we started shooting, I kept asking him, 'Mr. Huston, when is my singing coach coming?' He would say to me, 'Very soon, Claire, very soon.' And then one afternoon an assistant came and told me that Mr. Huston was bumping up the shooting schedule and that we would do the song right then. I pleaded, 'Mr. Huston, I can't do this!' He said, 'You'll be fine, Claire, just fine.' So I had no choice once they called 'Action!' but to sing and cry!"

We both got on the phone with Joan Fontaine, the only Hitchcock star to win a Best Actress Oscar (for *Suspicion*, 1941). She told us how Joseph Kennedy wanted to shack up with her. "His son, President Kennedy, said to me years later, 'Let's see, he would have been sixty-five then. I hope I'm the same when I'm his age.'" I asked her about the rumors that Rita Hayworth's playboy husband, Prince Aly Khan, had had an affair with her in Paris. She'd only say, "Oh, but the Aly Khan was a *daaarling!*" From then on, whenever Joanna and I wanted a laugh, we'd say to each other, "Oh, but the Aly Khan was a *daaarling!*"

Maureen O'Hara, the star of *The Quiet Man*, agreed to a sit down in an Irish bar when she was named Grand Marshal of the St. Patrick's Day Parade in 1999. But she refused to be drawn into controversy when I asked what she thought of organizers banning gays from marching.

"Don't!" she commanded. "I don't wish to be involved in it."

Off the record, she assured us that some of her closest friends were, or had been, gay. Among them, she said, was her longtime collaborator John Ford.

Our jaws dropped.

"I saw him kissing another man," she said.

John Ford—the married, macho director of Westerns like *Stagecoach* and *The Searchers*?

"I know what I saw!" she insisted. "But that's off the record!"

We kept the deal. Five years later, she shared the story in her memoir *'Tis Herself*, adding that she saw the kiss on the set of *The Long Gray Line* and that the other man was a major Hollywood actor.

We were big on Lauren Bacall ever since I gave Joanna my *To Have and Have Not* mixtape. I saw Bacall at a party and told her agent, Johnny Planco, that I'd read Warren Beatty wanted Bacall or Katharine Hepburn to play his aunt in *Love Affair*. Johnny said, "I wouldn't ask her [about] that." I asked her anyway.

"What!?" she said. "How old do you think I am?!"

She was almost seventy at the time, but she didn't like to be reminded of it. Johnny said, "I warned you."

Our column began to attract loyal followers, some of whom were rather strange. There was the mysterious society lady who whispered into the phone like Norma Desmond in *Sunset Boulevard*: "Do you know who [New York philanthropist] Mrs. Milton Petrie was before she became Mrs. Petrie? Ask around!" There was the man ready to tell all about his former law partner, one of America's most prominent attorneys— who apparently had a weak bladder. "I have more information about his incompetence . . ." the tipster said, "and his incontinence!" There was the reader who never forgave us for reporting that cops at Aqueduct Racetrack had busted a stable hand for having intercourse with a horse named Saratoga Capers: "How dare you reveal the name of a rape victim!" And there were assorted delusional women who called faithfully to give status reports on their "relationships" with Steven Seagal, Prince, and, curiously, former secretary of commerce Robert Mosbacher. They usually left long, expletive-filled, 2 a.m. voice mails—transferring their anger at their neglectful fantasy boyfriend to us.

One time, security at the front desk called and said, "I have Mrs. Jon Bon Jovi here to see you." When I went out to the lobby, I didn't find the rock star's longtime wife, Dorothea. I found an attractive, young Japanese woman who'd been calling night and day trying to find out where Bon Jovi lived in New Jersey. She said she had to get there because "we have to go on our honeymoon." I told her I didn't know his address, but I knew he had a lot of security and vicious dogs and that she would definitely be arrested if she trespassed. She thanked me for the information and left. She ended up on a thirty-day hold in Bellevue that night.

We began to see that we could use some help in dealing with these odd customers—not to mention in covering the night's events. We were told we could hire an assistant reporter. We thought we knew just the guy. Baird Jones had gone to Buckley, Groton, and Columbia and claimed to have a law degree and three master's degrees. He was friendly with Andy Warhol, Keith Haring, Mark Kostabi, and a lot of artists. He had a huge collection of paintings by celebrities, as well as infamous public figures like Jack ("Dr. Death") Kevorkian and serial killer John Wayne Gacy. Mostly, Baird promoted parties that starred a freaky cast of characters. "Danny the Wonder Pony" was a masochistic stockbroker who wore a mask, leather shorts, a saddle on his back, and a bridle in his mouth. He gave women "pony rides." Baird's parties also featured "dwarf-bowling"—where guests sent a little helmeted man on a skateboard hurtling toward some pins. Governor Mario Cuomo called for the "sport" to be outlawed. Baird himself had gone on TV talk shows proclaiming himself a virgin and claiming he represented the National Chastity Association.

He was in his forties and he lived with his mother in a rambling apartment on Fifth Avenue. He had some quirks. He wore his pajamas under his seersucker suit because, he said, "It saves time getting dressed in the morning." He also never took his baseball cap off. On the other hand, he was a walking encyclopedia of celeb trivia. Baird would interview stars at parties and get some pretty good quotes. He'd give the quotes to us on the condition that we sourced them to "Webster Hall curator Baird Jones." Webster Hall was a rock club that paid him for the plug.

Baird had never had a real job before. But we decided to give him a try. He *was* eager. Sometimes too eager. He had a gift for alienating celebrities. He'd pelt them with questions till they screamed. Quincy Jones called him "the nerd with bad breath." Which made Baird obsessively spritz himself with Binaca. The worst encounter was with Arthur Miller at the playwright's eightieth birthday party at Sardi's. Everyone knew you *never* asked Arthur Miller about Marilyn Monroe, to whom he was once married. So what was Baird's first question? "Do you ever dream about Marilyn Monroe?" Amazingly, Miller apparently said he did. Baird asked, "What kinds of dreams are they?" Like he was going to give Arthur Miller Jungian analysis. Miller went crazy. He said, "I'm going to knock your block off." The octogenarian chased Baird around Sardi's. When he caught him, Miller punched Baird so hard he flew against a buffet table.

Later hires went better. We found a surprising number of well-adjusted, Ivy-educated young people who actually wanted to write gossip. Though they may have lacked Baird's dwarf-bowling skills, our subsequent legmen showed ingenuity at sneaking into no-press parties by posing as waiters and publicists. Two days after Heath Ledger's tragic overdose, our reporter Sean Evans used some kind of starlet sonar to find Ledger's last girlfriend, Mary Kate Olsen, kissing another guy in a basement club on the Lower East Side. The attractiveness of our female reporters proved useful in getting face time with male stars. James Franco, Diddy, Ethan Hawke, and George Clooney were among those who hit on or made out with our captivating interviewers.

The *Daily News* didn't make a big deal of the fact that Rush and Molloy were married, but we became a curiosity to others in the media. *New York, W, Gotham, Details,* the E! Channel, and *Entertainment Tonight* did profiles of us. In its annual ranking of New York's "most-gossiped-about" people, the *New York Observer* judged Rush & Molloy "the most fair of the gossips, or at least diffuse in their attention. . . . The husband-and-wife *Daily News* duo doesn't seem to have a boldface agenda. Or maybe they just have to step lightly around Boss Zuckerman's star-studded social life." In another article, the *Observer* observed, "George

Rush is unusually mild in a field crowded with neurotics, while Joanna Molloy likes to give the average celebrity a good kick in the ass."

"George Rush and Joanna Molloy are cheerful and intelligent, a nice married couple," Kurt Andersen wrote in the *New York Times Magazine*. "They are also hard-wired cynics. . . . They are a kind of living screwball comedy: sassy Irish-American working-class girl from the Bronx (Jean Arthur?) competes against wry Ivy Leaguer from suburban Chicago (Jimmy Stewart?), fall in love, marry, form a tabloid gossip tag team, and disagree amusingly."

In his *Times's* column, "On Language," William Safire tipped his hat to Joanna for coining the term "stalkerazzi" to describe predatory photographers. Tribune Media Services replaced Marilyn Beck's long-running syndicated column with Rush & Molloy, promising subscribers "the best celebrity journalism from New York to Hollywood and points in between." Among the two dozen papers that signed up were the *Denver Post*, the *Cincinnati Enquirer*, the *Cleveland Plain Dealer*, the *San Diego Union-Tribune*, the *Kansas City Star*, the *Sacramento Bee*, the *Toronto Star*, and a little paper in New Zealand—perhaps seduced by the obscene-sounding come-on that the column was perfect for "your tight news hole."

We began appearing regularly on the new tabloid-style TV shows—*Inside Edition*, *Hard Copy*, *Extra*, and *A Current Affair*. Iris Dugow, a director on *Designing Woman*, *Growing Pains*, and *Ellen*, called us to ask if she could pitch our lives as a sitcom. (Studio execs "loved the idea," she said, but worried about the legalities of using the names of real celebs in the script.)

While shooting his comedy, *The Paper*, Ron Howard and his cast camped out for weeks in the *Daily News* newsroom. Howard asked Joanna if she'd give Marisa Tomei tips on playing a gossip columnist. He also offered her a cameo in a scene as a reporter. They sent Molloy to a hairstylist on the set. Kidding around, Joanna said, "Make me look like Madonna." The stylist made her curly hair pin-straight. As soon as Howard saw her, he said, "What have you done?! You don't look like that!" Joanna argued, "I could!" Howard shook his head. That was the end of her movie career.

We experienced the other side of stardom when the publisher of *Hamptons Magazine*, Randy Schindler, didn't like something we'd written about him. So he fabricated a scurrilous item in his magazine about us. I must say it isn't pleasant when people make up shit about you. The *Daily News's* lawyer, Anne Carroll, sent him a libel letter, demanding a retraction—just like the ones we usually got. Our brush with fame was complete!

Well, not quite.

Frienemies

Next up was the experience of celebrity friendship, or what passed for it. Now that we occupied a sizeable chunk of real estate in the paper, more of our subjects were willing to speak to us directly. Sometimes, they'd been injured by another column and hoped we'd give them a fairer hearing. Sometimes, they were hoping to enlist us in their battles—charitable, political, and personal. We were still determined to keep our distance from our subjects. But we often found ourselves drawn into their dramas.

It would usually start with jokey interactions. Oscar winner Geoffrey Rush would call me "cousin," even though we knew of no genealogical lineage. At a party, Alec Baldwin gave me winking advice on strengthening our marriage. He was telling me I needed to take Joanna on a getaway when she tried to interrupt. "Dummy up!" Alec told her, "I'm getting you a vacation!" Joanna challenged Kevin Bacon to a game of "Six Degrees of Kevin Bacon." She thought she'd stump him by saying, "Bruce Springsteen." He said, "That's easy. I costarred with Tom Hanks in *Apollo 13*. Tom Hanks starred in *Philadelphia*. Bruce Springsteen wrote the song for *Philadelphia*. Next."

We started getting notes from our subjects. Once I did an item about Calvin and Kelly Klein arriving together at some event "defying rumors of a breakup." I'd never met or talked with Kelly Klein, but the next day, she sent me white tulips with a note that simply said, "Thank you." Years later, after their divorce, I thought about those tulips when I heard about Calvin inviting a younger guy up to his apartment. The guy told our source that as he was leaving Calvin told him, "Take some underwear!" Apparently, Calvin kept packages of CK briefs on hand as lovely parting gifts.

Sometimes we'd stumble into family feuds. Once, we heard that Danny Aiello Sr. was telling his neighbors that his actor son never visited him. I got on the phone with Danny Sr. He admitted he hadn't been much of a father, that he hadn't been around for his kids. But he said he was sorry and hoped that he could have Thanksgiving dinner with his family. I called Danny Aiello and relayed his father's appeal. He told me how the old man had abandoned his six children and his wife, who was blind. Danny said he didn't think he could ever forgive the codger for the hell he'd put his mother through. I said that I understood but that his father sounded sincerely regretful. Danny called his dad. They talked. Danny agreed to give the old guy another chance. I told our editors we had this heartwarming story for Thanksgiving. They loved it. Then, the day before the holiday, I heard from Danny. He and his father had had an argument. Danny said, "He hasn't changed at all! He's still a selfish bastard! He's no longer invited to our dinner!" Meanwhile, the story of their touching reconciliation was all laid out! So I called Danny Sr. and begged him to apologize—for *my* sake. I went back and forth between father and son, trying to broker peace. Finally, Danny agreed to let his dad come to dinner. We'd achieved a rapprochement—if only for a few editions of the paper.

Our acquaintance with Roberto Benigni also took a few hairpin turns. Joanna and I were big fans of *Life Is Beautiful*. He'd managed to write, direct, and star in a movie about a Nazi death camp that was both funny and tender. We did an interview with him in the café at The Mercer Hotel. Almost every answer was a performance. The waiters were all listening in. He told us how, after World War II, he and his family lived in a stable. "We didn't have money to go to the movies," he recalled. "So me and my sisters, during the summertime, we would go behind the drive-in and watch the movie from this sunflower field. Every night we went to watch the movie backward." Even though they couldn't hear the words. When he finally could afford a ticket, he discovered that cinema had "a power greater than Stalin or Hitler ever had."

Our admiration of Benigni didn't keep us from running a story that threatened to hurt his movie's Oscar chances. We'd heard that Steven Spielberg didn't like *Life Is Beautiful*—that he was about to walk out of a screening until his wife, Kate Capshaw, told him to sit down. The folks at Miramax, who released Benigni's movie, were worried. If Academy voters heard that the director of *Schindler's List* thought *Life Is Beautiful* made a mockery of the Holocaust, they might not vote for it. The Miramax people lobbied us hard to drop the item. They suspected Spielberg's camp of trying to sway Oscar voters toward his movie, *Saving Private Ryan*. But we ran the item. It was balanced—we quoted a Shoah official who pointed out that concentration camp prisoners had used humor "as a weapon." Right before the Oscars, I ran into Benigni in L.A. He said, "Mamma mia! What you wrote was very good, but the way [the Italian papers] used it—they took some pieces and said, 'Spielberg: "I hate the movie! The movie is revolting!"'" Benigni said he and Spielberg had just had lunch and Spielberg told him he "loved" *Life*.

After Benigni won his Oscar, Joanna sent him a little gift. He'd told us that, when he was young, his family had one book, Dante's *Divine Comedy*. His mother made him read it, again and again, until he memorized it. He still performs it all over the world. Joanna happened to have a nineteenth-century edition illustrated by Gustave Dore, so she left it off at his hotel. Hours later, she was in the midst of our deadline, when our tenacious reporter K. C. Baker fended off what seemed to her like another crazy caller. "Listen pal," K. C. snapped, "I told you, Joanna can't talk!" Only when we got home did we find a divinely comic message on our voice mail from Benigni, thanking Joanna for the book. We'll save that tape forever.

Tom Cruise was another professional charmer. Back when he and Nicole Kidman were making *Eyes Wide Shut*, everybody was trying to find out the plot of Stanley Kubrick's psychosexual drama. Kubrick had sworn Cruise and Kidman, who played married psychiatrists, to secrecy. But when I saw Cruise at the *Vanity Fair* Oscar party, he was surprisingly willing to talk about the months-long shoot. He brushed off talk that Kubrick had made him dress in women's clothing. But he admitted the director was demanding. We spoke for close to a half hour in the middle of a roaring party. I was struck by his focus—how, while he was speaking to you, everyone else in the room vanished. I don't know if that was his training in acting or in Scientology, but he was one of the more intense people I've met. Maybe he was just intent on dispelling rumors that his real-life marriage was coming apart. "Nic and I are very good to each other when we're [filming]," he said, adding that they found their characters' kinky mind games "exciting." Just in case anybody had any doubts, Cruise made quite a display of kissing Kidman that night.

But, by 2001, Cruise had filed for divorce. Shortly after he filed, his reps denied to us that he'd hired thuggish, wire-tapping private eye Anthony Pellicano. But after Pellicano was arrested, investigators found a recording in the detective's so-called "war room" of a phone call between Tom and Nicole.

We knew some people in Nicole's camp. She'd always been friendly. But now that she was out from under Tom's thumb, she was much saucier. No actress was more skilled at bantering with male reporters. I'd ask her what was happening with her and Lenny Kravitz or Q-Tip or Jude Law or whoever she'd been linked with recently. She'd laugh and say, "Oh, George, you're so baaad!" She might not tell you much, but we'd always have a pleasant chat. You didn't want to hurt her.

Even more forthcoming was Courtney Love, who'd usually call us one minute before our 5 p.m. deadline, about the time she was waking up. Joanna would say, "Courtney, why do you always have to call now?" She would talk for an hour, but it was fascinating to see how her mind darted around, sometimes brilliantly. Courtney is what you might call a fourth-generation motherless child. Her great-grandmother, sugar-cane heiress Elsie Fox, was too busy partying with Scott and Zelda Fitzgerald to take care of her daughter, Paula Fox, and tossed her into a foundling home. Paula became an award-winning writer but put her daughter, Linda Carroll, up for adoption. Linda and one-time Grateful Dead manager Hank Harrison had Courtney. But, after they divorced, Linda was off to New Zealand, leaving Courtney to grow up with friends and in foster homes. When we learned all this, we understood why she did drugs and why her own daughter, Frances Bean, was taken away from her at various times. It was clear Courtney deeply loved Frances. But Courtney just couldn't get out of her own way. It didn't help that the other love of her life, Nirvana's Kurt Cobain, killed himself with a shotgun.

Even in her depths, when she'd call us from some precinct or clinic, she had a wicked sense of humor. When she was arrested in 2003 for narcotics use, she told me, "Cops and two ladies in white coats came to my house. I got jackbooted. My mouth was taped shut. They put a ping-pong ball in my mouth. And, honey, you don't get to say you're sorry for that, because it wasn't in bed." She was always brutally honest about her misadventures. Once, when she snuck out of Dr. Drew Pinsky's rehab program, she said, "I looked like a fucking bag lady. I had no shoes. I had to hide in a bush like four [blocks] away. Then I see a house with two fourteen-year-old girls in it. So I knock on the door and I say, 'Hi, I'm Courtney Love. I'm leaving the loony bin.'" But she swore to us that she wasn't a danger to herself. She'd say, "I'll be here after the cockroaches."

It was always fun to hear who was and wasn't on Courtney's shit list. She said Drew Barrymore and Pamela Anderson had been good to her. She wasn't a big fan of Madonna. "Every decade has its big star, and Madonna was it in the '80s," she told me. "But the '80s are over." She'd have something to say about the men in her life—Fred Durst, Billy Corgan, Trent Reznor, Russell Crowe, Ed Norton. She always brought up her beloved Kurt. There'd be some tears. Then she'd wipe the sniffles and launch into a rant about Kurt's former band mates, Dave Grohl and Krist Novoselic, whom she was suing. She claimed that people handling her money were ripping her off. We tried to help her. She said she had boxes of evidence in L.A. It was more than we could take on, but we introduced her to our investigative editor, Rich Pienciak. He went out there but even he was overwhelmed by Courtney.

More and more, we found ourselves becoming romantic advisers to our subjects.

We'd jumped the gun when we wrote an item linking Matt Dillon and Marisa Tomei. But it gave them ideas. "It wasn't true—then," Tomei later confided. "But after you wrote it, Matt and I said, 'Why not?'"

At the premiere party for *Carlito's Way*, Penelope Ann Miller confided to me that, yes, she'd had an affair with her costar, Al Pacino, during the making of the film. But now, as she stood in the ballroom of the Plaza Hotel, she felt nervous being in the same room as his girlfriend-of-record Lyndall Hobbs. Maybe Miller thought that, by going public with the romance, Pacino would be forced to choose. But Hobbs hung in there for another four years, until Pacino and actress Beverly D'Angelo became so flagrant that he brought her to a Yankees game. (He did disguise himself in a fake beard that kept falling off.) D'Angelo went on to have twins with Pacino. She also took custody of me as a confidante when she and the *Scarface* star got into a child support battle, letting me know whenever Pacino was late with his $50,000-a-month payment.

We'd also get whispered updates from Fréderique D'Arragon during her globe-girdling romance with Ted Turner. Fréderique, a French artist of noble birth and independent means, had known Captain Outrageous since 1969, when she used to crew (and bunk) with him on yacht races. In 1999, when his marriage to Jane Fonda went south, we heard he was back with Fréderique. She didn't want to talk—then. Within a year, though, she called to tell us she and Ted would be celebrating her birthday at the Rainbow Room. Just in case we wanted to send a photographer. The strong-willed adventuress became Turner's constant companion. When he said publicly that he felt "suicidal" after Gerald Levin pushed him out of AOL Time Warner, Fréderique acknowledged that the bipolar billionaire was taking the antidepressant Paxil but assured us, "He's enjoying life." She phoned in from one of his ranches to douse reports that Ted had been fooling around with Fonda again. (Fréderique did not appreciate the actress calling her "my favorite mistress of my ex-husband.") But by 2003, Fréderique and Ted had reached an impasse. He wanted her to join him on yet another fly-fishing trip. She wanted to go to Tibet. "He likes people to come when he calls," she told us. "He wanted his space; now he's got it."

Bill Maher told us at Michael's restaurant one day that he wasn't worried that his new girlfriend, "video vixen" Karrine Steffans, would turn on him, as his last girlfriend, centerfold model Coco Johnson, had done. "People say I'm into black women," said Maher. "I'm just into women who are real, and they happen to be black." Unlike Johnson, Steffans didn't file a $9 million palimony suit against the comic. But the lady known as "Superhead" did gab with us about their "explosive" love-making. Maher also "made me a better person," said Steffans, who'd written a bestseller about her romps with Usher, Diddy, and Shaq, to name a few. She and Maher eventually decided to take a break. "Bill is free to go out and date," she told us. "The difference between me and whoever he's fucking now is they're not getting what he gave me."

The Rush & Molloy counseling service also had male clients. During the epic Trump divorce, Ivana had done her talking to the *Daily News*—via Liz Smith. The Donald's transmitter had been the *Post*, which had been so kind as to run a front page attesting that he'd provided mistress Marla Maples the BEST SEX I EVER HAD. With the divorce over, Donald and Marla had invited us to their wedding at his Plaza Hotel—a modest affair, in the way the Ringling Brothers circus is modest.

I once received a photo that appeared to show Marla lying naked on a bed and lifting one of her legs into the air. Donald said the photo was doctored—that someone had put Marla's head on someone else's body and he accused her estranged publicist, Chuck Jones, of sending the photo.

"Chuck's a sick puppy, George," said Donald, adding that the *Post* had also received the photo. Whether because of Donald's power or, as Donald preferred to see it, the *Post*'s decency, "Nobody has written anything."

I wrote something—a story reporting the photo's existence and Donald's allegation that Jones was waging a smear campaign against Donald and Marla. Jones, who spoke with us regularly, later admitted showing nude photos, which he claimed were real, to "people who asked." He also admitted having sexually gratified himself with Marla's shoes.

In spite of my bringing the situation to light, Trump still returned my calls. At one point, the voluptuous Anna Nicole Smith, then married to elderly tycoon J. Howard Marshall, was claiming her bodyguard had beaten her. Fleeing her apartment, she sought refuge in Trump's Plaza Hotel.

I asked Donald why, of all places, she'd come to his hotel. He chuckled deeply. "Anna likes me *very* much," said Donald. "She likes me *a lot*."

I said, "Really? Donald, have you two ever hooked up?"

"Hey, hey, you don't mess around, George!"

"Well, have you?"

"Listen, you can just quote 'a friend of Donald' as saying, 'Anna likes Donald very, very much.'"

After the *National Enquirer* reported that a police officer had found Marla in a compromising position with her bodyguard, she and Donald divorced. Single again, Donald called us at home to talk about his latest conquests. In one conversation, I said, "I can't keep track of all your girlfriends, Donald. Remind me, there's Kylie, there's Kara, there's Celina . . ."

"And don't forget Kimberly Hefner," Donald interjected.

"I thought she said she never went out with you."

"Ask me if I've *had* her," he laughed. He jumped off the phone before I could.

Perhaps we did get too close to one of our regulars. Kirk Douglas's drug-addled son, Eric, would call to clarify his latest arrest or stint in rehab or eviction from an airplane. Much as we enjoyed talking to him, we sensed he was becoming a little too attached when he left a message.

"Boy, your voice sounds so sexy," rasped Douglas, who, sadly, overdosed at age forty-six. "It's getting to be a three way between you, Joanna, and me. That's a sweet wife you have. If ever you decide to do some swapping, give me a holler."

10

Pleas For Mercy

Our interactions with celebrities grew still more personal when they heard we were expecting a baby. Even if they hadn't so much as played a doctor on TV, they offered advice. Rosie O'Donnell commanded: "Get the Baby Bjorn snuggly! It's the only one that doesn't hurt your back." Warren Beatty often had trouble completing one sentence, but the cad-turned-dad told me in no uncertain terms: "This will change your life forever." He was right about that. On April 15, 1998, our page featured an item headlined "Rush Delivery!" Larry Sutton, who was filling in for us, wrote: "In case you were wondering why your favorite gossip columnists are missing from today's page, we have the answer: It's a boy!" Despite Joanna's having laid bare their affair, Woody and Soon-Yi sent a note and flowers. Barbara Walters sent a rocking horse. Crusty Lauren Bacall suddenly transformed into a mush-ball, always asking, "How is that baby?" Kathie Lee Gifford, still smarting from our item questioning whether the world needed her *Christmas with Kathie Lee* book, sent "Baby Rush" one of her other books with a note saying she hoped he enjoyed her work even though "your parents don't like me." (Not true.) And when we finally came up with a name—Eamon, after Eamon De Velera, the NYC-born leader of Ireland's revolution—Madonna pronounced it "strong . . . and sexy."

All this attention was nice but we had to ask ourselves again if we'd grown too chummy with our quarry. We'd vowed we wouldn't be toadies to the stars. Still, I recalled that even my tabloid tutor, Steve Dunleavy—as unblinking a crucifier of celebrities as you'd ever meet—had admitted that some celebs should be spared. Dunleavy had told me that the old stars—"the class acts"—showed respect for the working press. "Cliff Robertson," said Dunleavy, "now there's a real gentleman."

Who could argue that certain celebs had earned themselves a little leniency? Hadn't Danny Glover given a fifty to homeless guy on Fifty-Seventh Street? Wasn't George Clooney helping refugees in Darfur? You sometimes had to cut a celeb a break when it came to their children. Some star offspring were fair game because they chose to go into acting or they got themselves arrested. But many celeb kids, certainly the little ones, were innocent bystanders.

Once, a source reported seeing Ivanka Trump among a group of teens passing a joint in Central Park. We called Ivana's spokeswoman who called Ivana who called Donald who called us back. "We checked it out," Donald said. "It's not true. Somebody else was smoking." We gave her the benefit of the doubt.

Donald was less reluctant to see Ivanka's name in the column when she modeled in a Fashion Week show.

Donald said all the big designers were asking for Ivanka to model for them.

"She has an amazing look," Donald said with typical understatement. "She's very much in demand. She's already in the ranks of Naomi Campbell and Kate Moss."

I said, "I think she looks more like you than Ivana." Which wasn't necessarily a compliment.

He said, "A lot of people say that. I don't want to say that. But *you* could say that."

I laughed and said, "See, you could have been a supermodel."

"That's right," Donald said, "but then I wouldn't be talking to you."

Decency, not friendship, guided us when reporting on illness. We only reported potentially fatal illnesses with the subject's cooperation. In

1996, we put in a call to producer Dawn Steel, one of the first women to head a major studio, after hearing that she'd been diagnosed with a brain tumor. Her friend, producer Linda Obst, called back to remind us what an unforgiving town Hollywood can be.

"There's a kind of horror of disease in the movie industry that could be injurious to Dawn's progress," Obst said. "We'd like to keep it out of the news until we have a prognosis. There is a chance she will pull through. Right now, we want to create a safe place around her."

We backed off, as we did when we heard *Harper's Bazaar* editor Liz Tilberis had ovarian cancer. Both became models of valor and activism before they passed away. Sometimes, when we kept their treatment to ourselves, celebrity patients would circle back to us when they were ready to speak. That was often when the supermarket tabloids were nailing together a coffin for them. Appreciating our early discretion, singer Carly Simon called us to announce in 1998 that she'd been diagnosed with breast cancer and was undergoing chemotherapy. "The idea of people stopping me on the street to say, 'I'm so sorry' is kind of a downer," she said. "Then I have to comfort *them*. I'm doing fine." Carly pulled through. Jerry Orbach was not so fortunate. The beloved *Law and Order* star revealed his prostate cancer to us on December 1, 2004. Eleven days later, he was dead.

We became the tasteful transmitter for less dire news—like a couple's decision to separate.

When calling to confirm someone's heartbreak, you had to try to overcome the assumption that a gossip columnist had no heart.

I once asked our new assistant, Kasia Andersen, to call the wife of an NBA star to find out if they were still living together. Kasia is a very smart woman, but early on, she came off a little Nordic, a little cool. So she called the wife and in the most matter-of-fact way said, "Hi, I'm calling from the *Daily News* to confirm that your husband has left you." Before I could grab the phone, the wife had hung up on her. I said, "Kasia, put yourself in that woman's shoes. Imagine what you'd feel like if the man you loved had dumped you. You've given up your career to have his children and now he's out fucking some young bimbo. How would you feel?" Kasia started biting her lip. I said, "First you'd cry. And then you'd pull yourself together. You'd get mad! And you'd call a lawyer to get what you had coming to you. And you might even call a gossip column to blow Mr. All-Star's little secret sky high. Now, if only there was someone at a column who understood, someone who'd been through it herself, who you could trust. You could be that person." Kasia turned into a great reporter.

Even star handlers who wouldn't normally trade in gossip felt safe defending a client's good name by snitching on someone else's client. For instance, one of the supermarket tabs had reported that *Ally McBeal* star Calista Flockhart was secretly seeing her show's creator, David E. Kelley, the husband of Michelle Pfeiffer. But an impeccable source told us: "They got the wrong producer." In fact, Flockhart was sleeping with Jeffrey Kramer, the show's co-executive producer. Our source explained: "David is getting a little annoyed about the confusion. He thinks Jeffrey should clear it up. But Jeffrey—even though he's separated from his wife—doesn't want her to know about Calista." We were happy to clarify things.

Having a rapport with the stars was nice. But it came at a price. Barely a day passed without some plea for mercy. At the Four Seasons premiere party for *Wit*, director Mike Nichols's HBO movie about a woman battling cancer, I interviewed Nichols as he puffed on a ciga-rette (indoors, no less). I asked if the movie hadn't made him want to give up smoking. "George, could you possibly not mention that I was smoking?" asked Nichols. He said his wife, Diane Sawyer, would "kill" him. We left it out.

Sometimes the intrigue went deeper. At a small dinner one night, Mariah Carey poured her heart out to me about her cold war with estranged husband Tommy Mottola. Although they were separated, Tommy, as chairman of Sony Music, still controlled her career. Carey claimed that the man who had made her a star now wanted to destroy her. She contended that her jealous ex had gone round the bend since she'd started dating dreamy Yankees star Derek Jeter. She pointed to a string of Page Six negative items, which she believed were covered with Tommy's fingerprints. She hoped we'd be kinder to her.

Rush & Molloy had written a snarky item here and there about Carey—pointing out the number of late nights the then-Mrs. Mottola had spent partying with rapper friends. But we'd probably written more unflattering stories about Mottola—reporting his rejection by a coop board, his Hamptons neighbors' displeasure with his dock plans, and rumors of his possible ouster at Sony. Finally, one of his handlers called. "Tommy would like to meet you," the handler said. "He could be a good source for you." I agreed to a sit down in the dimly lit basement of Scalinatella on Third Avenue. There, Mottola lamented about what had become of Carey now that "daddy's not there to make everything better." He pitied Jeter, whose hitting had suffered, he contended, since he got mixed up with Carey. Mottola said that some of what we'd written about him hadn't been accurate, but that he'd like to make a fresh start. "From now on, call me directly," said Mottola. "And I'll keep an eye out for items for you."

In the coming months, Mottola kept his word, calling in some very timely information. He also invited us to some AAA-list gatherings where we glimpsed rare scenes, like the first meeting of Madonna and Bob Dylan. ("I've always been a fan of your music," the groveling Material Girl told the taciturn rock god.) Cleverly, Mottola was trying to make himself so valuable as a source that we wouldn't want to cross him. He actually didn't go out of his way to bury Mariah, perhaps because he'd found a new Galatea: the Mexican singer Thalia Sodi. His romance with Thalia brought us to a crossroads with Mottola. In September of 2000, we heard that the couple were planning to marry and that Mottola had visited St. Patrick's Cathedral to discuss having the wedding there. Mottola told us they hadn't set a wedding date and that he had just been paying a call on Edward Cardinal Egan, whom he said he'd known for a while. The following month we heard that Thalia and Mottola had picked the first week of December for their wedding. Again, Mottola denied any wedding but said we'd be the first know if they had one. A few weeks later, Page Six reported exclusively that the couple would have two weddings, on December 2 and 3 in New York and Mexico City. Page Six also had details of Mottola's bachelor night out with pals Danny DeVito, Russell Crowe, Tom Cruise, and Nicole Kidman. His decision to make the announcement there may have had something to do with our questioning how Mottola could marry in a Catholic church—much less New York's most famous Catholic church—when he was a divorcé who, according to our sources, had adopted the Jewish faith for his first wife, Lisa. A generous donation perhaps? Mottola insisted he'd never left the church. An Archdiocese spokesman wouldn't explain why an exception was made for this divorcé but insisted that Cardinal Egan "does not know Mottola and had nothing to do with Mottola's marriage at St. Patrick's." After that, we had less interaction with Mottola. Sony finally released Mariah from her contract, but the following summer she suffered a week-long, headline-making episode of "exhaustion." Private eye Jack Palladino told us Carey had hired him to investigate Mottola's "smear campaign," which friends believed had driven her over the edge. Mottola insisted, "I am deeply saddened by Mariah's illness, and I remain completely supportive of her, both personally and professionally. Any allegations that I have tried to hinder her career are completely untrue."

Our coverage of her ex made Carey even friendlier toward us. But we were beginning to see the rash you could catch by rubbing shoulders with the stars. We'd stumbled into the good graces of Julia Roberts by debunking a *Post* story in which a paparazzo claimed he'd seen her French-kissing a female bartender on top of the bar at Hogs & Heifers. The bartender told us that the photo of Roberts "kissing" her ear actually captured the actress yelling, "If he keeps taking pictures like that, I'm getting off the bar." The day our story ran another vase of white tulips and thank-you note arrived—this time from Roberts. A few flowers didn't stop us from covering Roberts's ups and downs as usual. Then, one day, someone told Joanna that she'd been nuzzling *Law and Order* actor Benjamin Bratt at the Soho restaurant Kinkao. After we called her publicist to check it out, my phone rang.

The caller said, "George? This is Julia Roberts. What are you writing now about my boring life? If you write about me every time I have dinner with someone, no one will ever ask me out. They'll say, 'Don't bring her, she just causes trouble.' I'm never going to get a date."

I said, "I'm pretty sure you'll never have trouble getting a date."

She said, "If you write about this, photographers will hang around me while I'm trying to shoot a movie. Look, Benjamin and I are just getting to know each other. If anything starts to brew, I'll call you. You'll be the first to know."

I said we'd hold off on the item. Julia thanked me profusely. Before she hung up, she said, "I think it's so great that you get to work with someone you love!"

As it turned out, my wife was none too pleased that I'd fallen for this movie star sweet talk—which was followed by more tulips. Joanna was even more annoyed when Page Six published the scoop on the Roberts/Bratt romance.

One day, Julia's publicist, Marcy Engelman, told us her client had just had dinner with Jennifer Lopez at Campagna, where they talked about *Chambermaid*, a new romantic comedy J. Lo would star in and Roberts would coproduce. Nice sighting, interesting project news, we ran the item. A few days later, Lopez's publicist, Alan Nierob told me his client had never been at that dinner. "You got snookered, my friend," said Nierob.

I called Marcy Engelman and said, "What the hell? Have you lost your mind?"

She admitted she'd lied about J. Lo being there but said, "You did a big favor for someone, and I'm sure they'll remember it."

I said, "Who?"

"I can't say," she said. "Look, don't make a big deal out of it. Aside from J. Lo's publicist, who's going to know?"

Ignoring her recommendation that we not attract attention to the fact that we'd been gulled, we ran an item asking, "Does Julia Roberts know that her own handlers planted a fabricated sighting of her having dinner with Jennifer Lopez? We're sure Julia isn't hurting for publicity."

Engelman had insisted that the item mention that Roberts and Lopez dined with Roberts's former agent, Elaine Goldsmith-Thomas, who now worked for Joe Roth at Revolution Films. Page Six later deduced that, with Roth leaving Revolution for Disney, "Thomas [was] looking for a new job. Insiders point the finger for the false item at Thomas. 'She wanted to make herself look like a big *macher*,' said one."

We became acutely aware that many people were trying to manipulate us.

Once, I got a tip that one of the big network news anchors had been having a long affair. His alleged mistress was a highly educated woman who traveled with him whenever he went "on assignment." He supposedly promised her that he was going to leave his wife. He and the mistress were making plans to start a family. The mistress had waited and waited. Then she found out he'd gotten himself a second mistress—a younger woman. Now the first mistress was threatening to file a palimony suit if he didn't fork over big bucks for the years she'd invested in him. I called the woman. She was cordial. She didn't deny an affair. But she wouldn't confirm it either. She said, "I might have something to say to you, but not right now." She referred me to her lawyer, whom I knew well. He acknowledged he was representing her but wouldn't say why.

I decided to try to get a reaction from the anchor. I got hold of his unlisted number. Every night, a few hours after he'd signed off his newscast, I called his home. His wife picked up a couple of times. I told her, "No message. I'll call back." I felt it wasn't my place to tell her what was going on. I also knew that, if I told her why I was calling, she'd scream at her husband, who then would never get on the phone. Finally, I did catch him at home. He handled the call perfectly. He showed no anger or nervousness. In his famously sonorous voice, he told me he respected our column. He thanked me for giving him the opportunity to comment. "Unfortunately," he said. "I can't speak right now." I had the feeling his wife was standing there. He said, "Would you please call me tomorrow at the office?"

I said, "Will you take my call?"

He said, "Yes, I will."

But he didn't—not the next day nor the day after that. Without anyone on the record, our lawyers wouldn't let us say one of the giants of journalism was an adulterer. I later found out the anchor reached a generous settlement with the woman, which shut her up for good. Little did I know the role I'd played in their negotiation. A friend of hers told me: "Every time you called [the anchor], he offered her another $100,000."

Were we being used? Probably. The cheating anchor story had stalled. But usually, if the columnist and the source hooked up their cables correctly, both engines ended up purring. Joanna once scored a one-on-one interview with a famous defendant who was on trial. The day it ran, our friend, TV correspondent John Miller, called to compliment us on her "get." John knew something about "gets," having landed a one-on-one with Osama Bin Laden in his cave in 1998. We thanked John for the compliment but admitted that what the famous defendant told Joanna had been "a little self-serving."

"Hey," John quipped, "when self-serving meets exclusive, everybody wins!"

11

Clashes With The Titans

Woody Allen, Bill Cosby, Mariska Hargitay, Debra Winger, and Maureen Dowd were among those who wrote or phoned to thank us for being even-handed. But celebrity fan letters became rare as the years went on. Stars who thought we would take dictation found that we made bad stenographers. It wasn't that we didn't try to be polite. But, sooner or later, we'd ask some prying, impertinent question.

I'd be interviewing Gwyneth Paltrow, things would be going along fine, and then I'd ask, "Are you and Ben [Affleck] back together?"

"Well, I'm not telling *you*," she'd say with a smile. (Hmm, that wasn't a no.)

Other stars exercised due caution. Harrison Ford was chatting with me as he moved down the buffet line at a premiere party at the Four Seasons restaurant. Then a heavy-lidded, bearded crony came up to the heavy-lidded Ford. They hugged.

Ford: "Who are you here with?"

Crony: "Some ladies."

Ford (nodding toward me): "Careful, we have a spy here."

Nobody was better at spotting the dorsal fin of a lurking reporter than Princess Diana. I'd been tailing her at the Metropolitan Museum of Art's black-tie Costume Institute Gala. Finally, I got into eavesdropping range by backing up toward the princess, who was speaking with some other guests.

I was feigning disinterest in her—pretending I was looking at some Roman statuary. Then, just when the conversation was getting interesting, I felt someone tap me on the shoulder. I turned around. It was Diana.

"Could you please move your *ear-ah* over *there-ah*?" she decreed. She was pointing to the other side of the atrium. Busted, I smiled and slunk off—for a while anyway. I'd been to three events she'd attended. Initially, she had New York society falling all over itself. I watched Henry Kissinger feasting his eyes on her cleavage as she passed him some cookies. But by the time she'd gotten to this Met benefit, her spell seemed to have worn off. "She's looking old," whispered a woman who wished she looked as hot as Di.

The Princess's former sister-in-law, Sarah Ferguson, was also hyper-vigilant. When the Duchess of York was beset with money woes, her new American publicist, Howard Rubenstein, introduced her to his client, Weight Watchers. Rubenstein invited me up to his office to meet her. Knowing it was her birthday, I brought her a little cake, despite her endorsement contract. Fergie's eyes lit up when she saw it, though Rubenstein wouldn't let her eat it in front of our photographer. The disgraced duchess never really took off her tiara. Joanna once asked her about reports that she was expecting. Fergie scolded her for even posing the question: "You know better than that!"

She wasn't the only ex-commoner puffed up by a title. An ex-girlfriend of Ben Kingsley had introduced me to the knighted actor, warning me to be sure to address him as "Sir Ben." I never failed to do that. But once, during a phone interview, I came in for a dressing-down, merely by saying, "I read in a newspaper that . . ."

"Don't!" commanded the man who'd played the selfless Mahatma Gandhi. "I don't read anything about me in print. It's not written for me. It's written for people who are curious about me."

"Well, I can *tell* you what it said."

"I'm being dead serious," he interjected. "I don't read them. So is this a good idea?"

"It wasn't a *bad* article," I said.

"I'm saying I don't read them, and you're holding a newspaper under my nose! I'm trying to be polite, but . . ."

"Okay, then let me say that I *heard* that people who live in your village in Oxfordshire say you've become nicer since you married [fourth wife] Daniela [Barbosa de Carneiro, a Brazilian actress thirty years his junior]. One taxi driver said you're even tipping better."

"Oh, well," said Kingsley, chuckling with delight. "I hope they're talking about the right person."

Many celebs were only too happy to talk—and loudly!—*after* we'd run an item.

Our conversations with Alec Baldwin were usually friendly, but he called in when we reported that eavesdroppers heard him telling friends that his estranged wife, Kim Basinger, was a "prima donna" who insisted on bringing her own towels, bed sheets, and applesauce whenever they traveled. Then in the thick of a custody battle, Baldwin told us he'd meant "prima donna" as a compliment: "I was kind of extolling the virtues of my wife and her caretaking of my kid."

Once we quoted an interview that disarming *Village Voice* columnist Michael Musto did with Melanie Griffith. The Hazelden detox graduate had told Musto that, if her children "ask me if they could experiment with pot," she would toke up with them—rather than have them "go out and buy some shit that has weird psychedelic chemicals in it and fucks them up." Two days after the story ran, Griffith called us in tears.

"I'm insane," she said in her girlish voice. "I've gotten so many phone calls about your article." She confirmed that she had offered to find her kids "safe pot," but said, "You hurt me very bad, and, more than that, you hurt my family! I'm sorry I'm crying, but I've just had it!

"I'm not advocating that my children do drugs," she went on. "Because of my history with drugs, my children don't want to try anything."

We asked how she would find some "safe" grass, assuming her kids ever wanted to experiment. And would she light up with them, or just watch?

"You know what?" said Griffith, who was sitting with her fifteen-year-old son, Alexander. "After this whole thing, I'm not going to do it at all! I'm not going to try it with them. So forget it! The whole thing is absolutely gone now."

The next day we clarified Griffith's drug policy.

Our good relations with Carly Simon did nothing to appease her ex, James Taylor, after we suggested their reunion may have hastened his split with second wife Kathryn Walker. "Kathryn really didn't deserve that," the mournful folk singer told us. Sounding like he was still carrying a torch for Walker, he went on: "Kathryn is an extremely worthy and admirable and valuable person . . . I love her dearly."

There were much firmer reprimands. A question alone could unleash a lashing. When we phoned John McEnroe at his Central Park West apartment, he commanded: "Don't ever call here again!" At Le Cirque one night, Sharon Stone shut down my questions by offering unsolicited medical counseling. "You don't look well," she said. "Are you feeling sick? Don't talk! I think you should go straight home."

Painter-turned-director Julian Schnabel had apparently been reading our items regarding his film about fellow art star Jean-Michel Basquiat, who OD'd at twenty-seven. Among other things, we'd written that Schnabel's new wife, Olatz, whom he'd cast in the film, had forced him to digitally remove the bags under her eyes. Schnabel, famous for his canvases covered with broken plates, looked like he wanted to smash some crockery over my head at the *Basquiat* premiere party at his studio.

"The press unconsciously pushes people off the edge," Schnabel said, asserting that vicious art critics drove Jean-Michel deeper into drugs. "Maybe if you could learn *anything* from his story, you could be a little more generous and kind with people! And not shoot from the hip! You wrote about this film before it was made and you presupposed a lot of things! Now you can set the record straight because you have a pen!" We did end up lauding the performances of Jeffrey Wright as Basquiat and David Bowie as Andy Warhol. (When we asked Bowie if, like Warhol, he had a lunatic fan gunning for him, the Thin White Duke gestured around a room packed with Iman, Lou Reed, Dennis Hopper, Gary Oldman, Christopher Walken, Harvey Keitel, Bianca Jagger, S. I. Newhouse, Donna Karan, Spike Lee, and Gianni Versace and dead-panned: "Actually, everybody you see around you—they're all my security.")

Donald Trump had a few choice words for us. Once we heard that Trump had cut ahead in the ski lift line at Aspen. Two sources said

Trump had repeatedly used the express lane reserved for instructors and their pupils. In fact, ticket taker Tanya Hess confirmed, "Donald Trump did cut in line."

"It didn't happen," said Trump. "This story is total bullshit. Who told you this? Whoever it was made it up. You tell him I said he's a mother-fucking liar. Tell him to call me. Whoever it is doesn't have the balls because he knows I'll beat the fucking shit out of him." The idea that he'd had to go to the end of the line was empirically false, he concluded, because, "come on, do you think anyone would say that to *me*?"

We set off another holiday sport storm when we attended a celebrity golf tournament hosted by Michael Jordan in the Bahamas. One evening at a gala dinner, the former Chicago Bulls star stepped up to the mic and confessed how miserable he was running the Washington Wizards, whose record was then 7–32.

"Don't tell anybody I was down here," dead-panned Jordan, who had already riled his players by calling them "scared" and by skipping games. "I've got a job that is truly a fucking job."

We asked Jordan later where the Wizards were headed. "Only one place they can go—up," he said.

Our column caused an uproar in DC. We'd given Jordan credit at the top of the story for raising almost $500,000 for cancer-stricken kids. But our hosts accused us of ingratitude. One organizer said he'd been on the phone all day with Jordan and the furious members of his camp.

"Michael said it in an open room," admitted the organizer. "But, on a scale of 1 to 10, this was a 10. It was nuclear."

Anytime we wrote about Howard Stern we risked being jolted awake by a call from the King of All Media, who wanted to critique each sentence on the air. Once he summoned us to his studio to complain about items linking him with different women. He said he wanted to disabuse us of the notion that he was a letch. His first comment? "Nice rack, Molloy!" He guessed her bra size exactly.

"You're always saying I'm with this blonde or that blonde," he said. "It's the same blonde!" Namely, his future wife, Beth Ostrosky. "I've been cheating on her, with her!"

We often got calls from whatever publicist was handling Naomi Campbell that day (she went through many). But whenever possible, the supermodel liked to rebuke us in person. Our first brush with Miss Campbell came at the Cannes Film Festival, at a benefit for AmFAR at Chef Roger Vergé's famed Moulin de Mougins. Joanna whispered to auctioneer Sharon Stone that she should get Naomi to put her emerald-and-sapphire-studded navel ring up for bidding. (A Saudi prince bought it for $22,000, then agreed to pay double if Naomi allowed him the pleasure of removing it.) We'd recently reported that, back when she was dating Robert De Niro, Campbell had flushed a female rival out of his Tribeca loft by dialing 911 and reporting a fire at Bob's place. "Nothing like a ladder-and-bucket brigade to extinguish a couple's ardor," we'd observed. The sourcing on this tale was airtight. But when we introduced ourselves to Campbell, she took exception. "I would never do any such thing!" said the cover girl, whose exquisite ebony cheekbones looked like they'd been sculpted by Paul Manship. Still, she didn't seem upset about our charge. Given her lifetime rap sheet of assaults against employees and police officers, pulling a fire alarm was a schoolyard prank. Even when she was scolding us, the Naomi Campbell we met was a far cry from the harpy we read about in the papers. Whether she was calling in from Rio or giving an interview backstage before a bikini runway show, she was always a perfect lady.

"I'm remorseful and regretful," she said once as she braced herself for court-ordered community service after attacking her maid with a cell phone. "I'm taking my punishment, and I accept that." Her efforts to be good were sometimes comical. Once, after we had a non-controversial conversation with Campbell about her "godfather," Nelson Mandela, at a Friday night party, her publicist called at 9 a.m. on Saturday (when Naomi may have been going to bed):

"Naomi is in a panic," said the publicist. "She said she spoke to you, but she can't remember what she said."

Some people took our invasions of their privacy surprisingly well.

One Saturday night, a friend called to say that paramedics had just removed the corpse of flamboyant restaurateur Warner LeRoy from his building on West Sixty-Sixth Street. LeRoy, the son of *Wizard of Oz* producer Mervyn LeRoy, had created Maxwell's Plum as well as Tavern on the Green and had revived the Russian Tea Room. He was a big deal in New York. We called the city desk and told them to start pulling LeRoy's clips for an obit. Trying to confirm his death, we left messages with his spokeswoman and friends. Finally, as an afterthought, we checked the phone book and saw LeRoy listed at 100 West Sixty-Sixth Street.

I called the number. A man answered. I said, "This is George Rush from the *Daily News*. I'm sorry to bother your family at this time but I'm trying to confirm that Mr. LeRoy has passed away today."

The man said, "This is Mr. LeRoy. And I'm very much alive."

I said, "Gosh, Warner. I'm glad to hear that."

He took the call in stride. He said, "I've gotten other calls. I'm fine."

Sadly, cancer claimed him within a year. But I like to think he got some satisfaction out of quoting Mark Twain's line: "The reports of my death have been greatly exaggerated."

Another time, I heard that David Letterman had given up his trademark cigars "for health reasons." His producer, Robert Morton, confirmed it. So we did an item. The next morning, we got a call at home: "This is David Letterman." He was obviously concerned. He admitted he had given up cigars, but he didn't like the "health reasons" part. Maybe because there could be big insurance implications. He said his doctor didn't tell him to; it was his decision because "I was lighting one off another." Rather than yelling, he diplomatically asked, "How can we resolve this?" We let him have his say in a second story. We thought about his delicacy in dealing with us years later, in 2009, when he announced on his show that he was the target of an extortion attempt. Here Dave was admitting to "creepy stuff"—having "sex with women who worked for me on this show." But he did it in a way that made him seem vulnerable, even heroic for standing up to a blackmailer. It was a brilliant piece of damage control. He had the audience applauding him by the end.

Brad Pitt also showed his aplomb when I met him at a book party.

I was introducing myself when he said, "I know you. You're the guy who made me move." I was baffled. He explained that when he was in town shooting *The Devil's Own*, he'd rented an apartment in the West Village. "You put my address in the paper. Z-100 read it on the radio. I had guys ringing my buzzer all night, saying, 'Yo, Brad, come down and party with us!'"

Amazingly, he was smiling as he told me all this. I said, "I have no recollection of that item. We have a policy, after John Lennon's death, not to print addresses. But, if we did, I'm sorry."

The next day, I checked Nexis and discovered that Page Six—not Rush & Molloy—had done an item that didn't give Pitt's exact address but gave enough clues so any idiot could figure it out. I called Brad's publicist, Cindy Guagenti, and told her, "Just for the record, we didn't print Brad's address."

Four months passed. I was at the bar at Morton's in L.A. at *Vanity Fair's* Oscar party when I heard someone calling, "George, George." I turned around and it was Brad Pitt. He said, "Hey, Cindy told me that you guys didn't print my address. I wanted to apologize for what I said." What? A celebrity was apologizing? I said, "No problem," and we had a nice conversation about how he'd gotten into architecture and was designing furniture. We shook hands and I thought, *that Brad has class.*

Gabriel Byrne was another actor you could joke around with, though one joke got a little out of hand.

The year that Linda Fiorentino picked up the Independent Spirit Award for Best Actress, she announced to the crowd that playing an evil vixen in *The Last Seduction* had been murder on her love life. She said she hadn't had sex in three months. She added that she'd gladly trade her award "for a date with Gabriel Byrne."

Fiorentino told me later that day, "I really do have a crush on him. I figured this is my only chance to meet him." I thought I'd play Cupid. So I asked Byrne, who was at the awards, if he was ready to give Fiorentino some relief from her celibacy. He played along. "I'm flattered," he said in his brogue. "Three months, and she picks me? I wouldn't be a gentleman if I didn't call her." Over the next day, I kept running into him and asking, "Have you called her yet?" He'd say, "I'm working up my nerve." Urging him on was his ex-wife, Ellen Barkin, who came with him to the Oscars. She said, "I told him to go for it!"

I don't know whether they ever hooked up, but there were always a few ladies after him. At one point, he was talking with Madonna about a project and there were reports of him visiting her house in L.A. a lot. Byrne and I were talking after the premiere of his movie, *Smilla's Sense of Snow,* and I asked him, tongue in cheek, what was the nature of his visits. All he would say was, "Madonna is a lovely woman." Then I asked him about an interview in which his *Smilla* costar, Julia Ormond, hinted that they were dating. Again, Byrne would only say, "Julia is a lovely woman." Pushing my luck, I asked if Julia and Madonna were "lovely" in the same way. That was too much. He gently wrapped his fingers around my throat. I took that as a "no comment" and said, "Okay, I withdraw the question." I mentioned our little interaction in the column. The next time I saw him he said, "You got me in trouble with me mum. She saw what you wrote and said, 'Now why did you go and strangle that poor man?'"

12

The Spin Doctor Is In

No one wanted to throttle us more than Robert De Niro. The Oscar winner fiercely guarded his privacy. Yet, week after week, we found out things he didn't want known: that he'd fathered in-vitro twins with ex-girlfriend Toukie Smith . . . that he'd accompanied an investigative journalist to an underworld Paris screening of a snuff movie . . . that he'd collaborated with prosecutors on a sting operation to catch a paparazzo who'd tried to blackmail him . . . that he regularly saw a therapist about "commitment issues." No star kept his life better fortified than De Niro. We viewed him as the celebrity godfather of New York. No doubt he would have been thrilled to know we lived four blocks away from his Tribeca stronghold. It was always a treat seeing the Raging Bull pushing a baby stroller.

In all honesty, we admired his work. We were pretty sure the feeling wasn't mutual. Once, someone seated us directly in front of him at the Broadway opening of *Rent*. Sitting next to De Niro was his producing partner, Jane Rosenthal. After we'd chatted with Jane for a few minutes, we heard De Niro ask her who we were. She informed him that the dreaded Rush and Molloy were sitting within earshot. "Damn it!" he snorted, slamming his fist on the arm of his seat.

Little did De Niro know how close he was to one of our informants. I happened to be at his desk one Sunday when his phone rang.

"Is this George Rush?" asked an imperious-sounding woman. "I read your story about Robert De Niro giving Anne Marie Fox a ring. You have it all wrong."

"Oh really?" I said, incredulously.

"Yes. That woman means nothing to him. She is *not* his real girlfriend."

"Is that right?"

"*I* am his real girlfriend."

"Oh yeah? What's your name?"

"Grace Hightower."

"How come I've never heard of you, Grace?"

"Mr. De Niro and I keep our relationship very discreet. I was just with him in Las Vegas when he was making *Casino*. . . . I have to get out of this cab. But, next time, check your facts."

She hung up. I was sure she must be a stalker, like the self-proclaimed "girlfriends" of Robert Redford and Jon Bon Jovi.

Yet two years later, we learned something else De Niro had been concealing: he and Hightower, a former flight attendant, had just gotten married. The wedding news surprised even some of his closest friends. The bride and groom kept us in items for years. Nine months after their wedding, Hightower gave birth to their son, Elliott. The following year they renewed their vows *and* commenced a divorce action. They briefly called off their lawyers, only to launch one of the most spectacular custody battles we'd ever seen. In one court filing, De Niro claimed that while visiting the yacht of singer Marc Anthony, a jealous Hightower mistakenly concluded that her husband was fooling around with the captain's wife and punched De Niro in the side, breaking a rib. Incredibly, the couple stuck together, re-renewed their vows, and had a second child.

De Niro continued to be irked that we were finding out all this stuff. After one story, we got a call from publicist Stan Rosenfield, whom De Niro, George Clooney, Danny DeVito, Morgan Freeman, Charlie Sheen, and others had long depended on.

"Bob is quite upset with your story," said Rosenfield. "We're trying to figure out where you're getting your information."

"You know I can't reveal my sources, Stan."

"I understand," said the always affable Rosenfield. "But could you tell me, do people call you?"

"We hear things in our travels."

"Listen, Bob is very private. I'm trying to build a relationship here. I could have gone wide with the story when you called me about Toukie and the twins. I didn't."

"Stan, we do appreciate that. And, believe me, we haven't reported some of things people have told us about Bob."

"Is it one person who calls?"

"We have multiple sources."

"What if I gave you a name? You could just say no if it's not the source."

"I'd rather not get into that game, Stan. Bob has played enough Sicilians to appreciate the creed of *omerta*."

"We understand *omerta*."

"Stan, I don't think I can help you."

Stan then tossed out a pair of initials—which I'll change here to "L. K."

"L. K.?"

"Do those initials mean anything to you?"

They really didn't. I wondered whether I should do this "L. K." the favor of absolving him, or her, of suspicion. Then again, leaving a shadow of doubt over "L. K." would protect our actual sources.

"I really can't say, Stan."

"I don't like asking you these questions. But we think we have a special relationship with you and Joanna. I'm not saying Bob is going to invite you over for Thanksgiving, any more than you'd invite him over to your house for Thanksgiving."

"Excuse me, Stan. Please tell Bob he has a standing invitation to come over to our house any Thanksgiving."

More and more, publicists were bartering access in return for obsequious coverage. A few public relations agencies had come to represent most of the big stars. That gave them the power to dictate terms to the ballooning number of publications and TV shows built around celebrities. If you wanted an interview with Superstar A, you had to promise to put him on your magazine's cover—*and* throw in a feature on Rising Star B. If you wrote something unflattering about Superstar A, you could forget about ever talking to Superstars B, C, D, and E, who were also in the publicist's stable. Thus, most of the nightly entertainment shows became slavishly servile to the flacks. A show's interviewer wouldn't dare step on an actress's toes—though the interviewer could "reveal exclusively" the color of her toe polish! Interviews with stars typically took place on "junkets," where dozens of TV interviewers waited for their five or ten minutes with the star, who sat in front of a giant poster of his movie. The publicist instructed the interviewers which topics were off-limits—such as the divorce, the arrest, the client's last "misstatement." Just to make sure a sneaky interviewer didn't try to slip in a curveball question, the movie studio would supply the videotape. Only if the publicist deemed the questions acceptable was the tape surrendered to the interviewer.

Gossip columnists generally don't do such junkets. But we sometimes found ourselves at parties where the stars were quarantined in a roped-off VIP area where we were allowed to ask a few questions, provided we had a PR chaperone. We called this the petting zoo. Some publicists deemed us too risky to let into the petting zoo, even briefly.

One night, Joanna was at a premiere party. She'd had a great conversation with Paul Schrader, who wrote *Taxi Driver* and directed *Patty Hearst*. But a publicist from L.A., Simon Halls, refused to let her talk with his client, Skeet Ulrich. She really didn't care. She turned to chat with a friend. But then Simon Halls came over and said, "What are you still doing here?" Joanna joked, "I'm reading your client's lips." Halls grabbed her by the arm, pulled her through the restaurant, and shoved her out into the rain. Peggy Siegal, the venerable and not-to-be-trifled-with publicist, ran after her and tried to get her to come back. Peggy said, "He can't do that! This is my party!" When Joanna came home and told me what had happened, I drove over to the restaurant. I was going to punch this flack out but by the time I got there, he'd left. We didn't write a word about the premiere and it was years before we mentioned Skeet Ulrich.

While the big West Coast studios looked upon the New York gossip columnists as poisonous reptiles, Harvey and Bob Weinstein, the Brooklyn-born founders of Miramax Films, recognized that the columns drove much of the mainstream media. Every morning, interns assembled a "gossip pack" of clips for magazine editors and producers of drive-time radio shows, breakfast TV shows, and afternoon entertainment shows. The Weinsteins knew that gossip could turn an actor into a star—that, from Olivier and Leigh to Taylor and Burton, audiences paid good money to see a screen couple who'd had a location lay. Rather than infantilizing the actors and treating us as predators, the Miramax publicists allowed talent and journalists to have adult conversations. As a result, they got a lot of publicity, and, much to the consternation of the big studios, a lot of Oscar nominations.

Other production companies started wising up. They too started to reach out more—not only to promote their own movies, but to try to badmouth competitors. One producer might take us aside and ask if we knew that the real Oskar Schindler was a much more flawed hero than the one we saw in Steven Spielberg's movie. Another might ask if we were aware that John Nash, the Nobel Prize–winning mathematician Russell Crowe played in *A Beautiful Mind*, was a racist, bisexual sadist and a deadbeat dad? There was evidence if we knew where to look.

One producer kept a larder stocked with items he could trade in case you heard something bad about him or his movies. And there were some bad things, such as the audio recording a foe had surreptitiously made of his bedroom performance. The producer even kept a former columnist on a $100,000 retainer to come up with trade-worthy items. Sometimes we couldn't resist giving the producer a little poke. His extramarital affair had become so flagrant that we ran a blind item about him nuzzling his mistress in a hotel pool. The producer saw the item and sent his staff to buy up every copy of the *Daily News* in the seaside town where his wife was on vacation. His panic soared when a paparazzo offered us smoking-gun photos of the producer cavorting with his bikini-clad girlfriend in the surf. The producer took the pictures off the market, spending a small fortune. He even hired his paparazzo tormentor to be an official photographer at his parties, insuring the pap's long-term loyalty. Little did the producer know that *Daily News* editor Ed Kosner had already passed on the snaps, explaining, "Who wants to look at an old Jew in his bathing suit?"

Often we'd find out something about a person of power that was so risky it would never get past our lawyers. But that was not to say it didn't still have value. We'd phone the person of power—let's call him Mr. Doink—and ask him about it. Just to let him know we knew. He might shit a brick and beg us not to run it. And so we'd do him the favor of not running the item that we couldn't run anyway. And Mr. Doink would say, "I owe you one."

The killing—or postponing—of an item involved a quick calculation of the immediate value of the story divided by the long-term value of the source. Some people, like Tommy Mottola, became sources so they wouldn't become items. When a famous author was caught making out with a woman who was not his wife, he offered a dozen items about other people. Some people expected clemency even though they hadn't earned it. People who got in trouble often promised some scoop "down the road." Experience taught us that scoop rarely arrived.

Someone with clout at the columns could ask for clemency on behalf of a client, trading on past and future favors. That was why people hired certain publicists and lawyers, known as "fixers." Once when we were investigating Vogue editor Anna Wintour's then-young affair with financier Shelby Bryan, we got an unsolicited call from Ed Hayes, the sartorially resplendent attorney who inspired Tom Wolfe's character Tommy Killian in *Bonfire of the Vanities*. Ed represented many in the media.

"I hear you're doing a story on Anna Wintour," said Ed.

"How did you hear that?"

"Because her lawyer is your lawyer—me."

Ed didn't ask us to kill the story; he just wanted to find out if we were running it, which we were. Sometimes you had to explain to the fixer that the story was too big to ignore, that it was already on the editorial schedule, that somebody was bound to report it, somebody meaner, so it was better to do it now, to lance the boil. The fixer would try to dictate the spin as best he could. One morning, Joanna got a call from a big PR guy who'd planted a story that he'd envisioned as a hit on one of his client's enemies.

He said, "Molloy, what is *that* in the paper today? I gave you the exclusive! What are you doing to me?"

She said, "Well, I think the story is pretty balanced."

He said, "Exactly!"

The columnist's negotiating skill lay in knowing how to get some version of the story into the paper. For instance, Viacom chairman Sumner Redstone went ballistic when we inquired about his fondness for women who could be his granddaughters. After his threats to sue didn't make us back off, one of Redstone's handlers asked, "Why do you want to make an enemy of Sumner Redstone? Do you know what he owns? We'll remember this if you make it go away." We ran a story anyway—comforting Redstone's mouthpiece (and our paper's lawyer) with the opening line: "Some eighty-five-year-old men might be flattered to be linked with a much-younger blonde, but Viacom billionaire Sumner Redstone is fed up with the 'false and vile gossip' about him and a former flight attendant." We framed the story as a public service announcement that cleared up those awful rumors. Redstone must have thought we were an effective PA system. He also got on the phone again to rebut reports that he was feuding with his "friends" Tom Cruise, Steven Spielberg, and Jeffrey Katzenberg, as well as his daughter, Shari. "I talk to my daughter directly . . . every day," he assured us. "I love my daughter."

We also relied heavily on euphemisms. Back in Cole Porter's day, the columnists would say that two people having an extramarital affair had become "fast friends and dancing partners." Britain's *Private Eye* had contributed several classics. A drunk politician was "tired and emotional." Copulating diplomats were having "Ugandan discussions." The trouble was that if every journalist started using it, the euphemism itself became defamatory. So you had to try to coin new ones. When a rocker was smoking a joint, we would say he was "wreathed in fragrant smoke." A closeted gay actor would be at a notorious bar "enjoying the company of like-minded friends." Following her separation from her husband, an actress would be "comforted" or "consoled" by her hunky costar. Or you would call the two lovers "platonic friends" to indicate they were not. Walter Winchell defined it best: "Gossip is the art of saying nothing in a way that leaves practically nothing unsaid."

Many scandal-prone stars hired Los Angeles attorneys Jay Lavely and Marty Singer because of their fearsome reputation as libel litigators. Their cease-and-desist letters were masterpieces of intimidation.

Each resembled an actual court complaint, complete with extensive citation of case precedents. After receiving a few of them, we gleaned that, aside from quoting a few sentences from the article in question, they were essentially form letters. Not that we didn't take them seriously. But considering how much the firm was charging its clients for these letters, we wondered if Rush & Molloy should be billing Lavely & Singer for generating business. Once, Lavely sent a letter accusing Joanna of defaming his client simply because she'd left the subject of her call with his secretary, thereby spreading the rumor.

Over the years, we became friendly adversaries. Singer would say, "I know you're a decent guy, George. So I'm going to try to talk my client out of suing you." We would try to negotiate the "demand for retraction" down to a "clarification." Whenever possible, we'd throw a star's lawyer a bone by calling him a "pit bull" or a "Rottweiler." Which was a compliment. He in turn might tell us of some looming litigation—for instance, that thieves had made off with Salma Hayek's laptop and Penelope Cruz's camera and that any media outlets that published images belonging to the actresses would be prosecuted to the fullest extent of the law.

We also developed working relationships with certain well-paid "crisis managers" who helped famous people ride out their scandals and repair their reputations afterward. At least once a day, it seemed, we spoke to Howard Rubenstein, the soft-spoken mouthpiece of such controversy generators as Rupert Murdoch, George Steinbrenner, Imelda Marcos, Ronald Perelman, and Mike Tyson. Rubenstein, an attorney, had advised at least six mayors and four or five governors. Former governor George Pataki had famously said that if Rubenstein had represented the rats during the bubonic plague, town criers would have proclaimed, "Rodents Unfairly Accused of Mild Rash." As wired as he was, Howard displayed little ego or temper. He might say, "You can quote 'a friend' as saying, 'This outrageous accusation is a devastating betrayal of our family!'" But Howard was so mild-mannered that even one of his "angry" comments sounded avuncular.

A crisis manager knew how to minimize the fallout from an embarrassing announcement. If you had to file for divorce or release a bad earnings report, it was best to do it on a Friday, so the story would wind up in the Saturday paper, which fewer people read. Then again, if you had a client going into rehab, it could be better to announce it late on a Monday, after the deadlines of the checkout counter mags. That way the client had a week to peddle his version of events to the mainstream daily media, making the story old by the time the supermarket tabs went to press again. Or so the client hoped. A "no comment" was like an admission of guilt. Master crisis manager Mike Sitrick would advise clients, "If you don't tell your story, someone else will." Sitrick would recommend that a star fess up, get treatment, and move on.

You had to get ahead of the story. Take Ken Sunshine, Mayor Dinkins's former chief of staff and a spokesman for everybody from Leonardo DiCaprio to the city's healthcare union. Sunshine called one day asking if we were working on a story about percolating rumors that his client, Barbra Streisand, had had a fling with Israeli Prime Minister Benjamin Netanyahu back when he was ambassador to the United Nations.

"Uh, no," I said. "I mean . . . not *yet*."

"Well, *if* you were working on such a story," Sunshine said, "you'd need a response from me, wouldn't you?"

"Yes, we would."

"Well, I just happen to have one."

And so we received the Funny Girl's ready-made exclusive denial that she had ever *schtupped* Bibi. "I met the prime minister once at a dinner with a group of people," stated Streisand, who wanted to underscore her support for Netanyahu's Labor Party foes. "The hypothesis that there is anything more to our relationship is ludicrous and absolutely untrue. I wish the man much good luck. He'll need it."

The crisis manager knew when to send his client into the talk show confessionals so that Father Conan, Father Dave, and Father Jimmy could perform the same sort of absolution Hugh Grant received from Father Jay when he was caught in a car with Divine Brown (a hooker who later made us buy one of her autographed, lipstick-smooched T-shirts before she would give us an interview).

If the crisis manager couldn't get the client to change his behavior, he could try to create a diversion with a new story. When rumors about Michael Jackson's play dates with young boys were getting out, Sony Music, who had just signed a multimillion-dollar deal with him, wanted to assure America that Jacko was really quite normal. PR maestro Dan

Klores flew to L.A. for a meeting with the Gloved One. Someone at the meeting suggested that MJ hold a children's concert. Klores recognized that surrounding an alleged pedophile with kids might be counterproductive. Instead, Klores turned to Jackson and asked, "Have you ever thought about getting married?" Klores even suggested the bride—Lisa Marie Presley, Elvis's daughter. Soon afterward, the *Daily News* obtained the Dominican marriage license of Michael and Lisa Marie.

Even while we chuckled at the marriage (which lasted twenty months), we couldn't deny the creativity of Klores, who went on to become an award-winning filmmaker and playwright. We lived in a casbah crawling with such artful dodgers, where everyone told his or her version of the truth. When one of these spin doctors offered his diagnosis, we always sought a second opinion. But there was an element of trust. The better manipulators knew they could only tell a reporter so many times that their coked-up client was suffering from "dehydration," "laryngitis," or "exhaustion." The stand-up flacks would rather give you a "no comment" than insult your intelligence. They knew they'd have to keep dealing with you long after their client had fired them or they'd fired their client.

A few celebs like Jack Nicholson and Bill Murray dispensed with publicists altogether. A celeb had to be brave to do that. With no one spinning on your behalf, it left the press pretty much free to report what they wanted—but then, Jack and Bill figured, the press would do that anyway.

The absurdity of a flack's alibi was sometimes breathtaking. We'd seen Anna Wintour arguing with her new beau, Shelby Bryan, at the Met benefit she hosted. We'd seen Bryan storm out of the party. We'd seen the mascara running down Wintour's cheeks. We asked her spokesman, Paul Wilmot, "Why is Anna crying?" With a straight face, Wilmot said, "Tears of joy! She's so happy about the success of the event!" (Whitney Houston, who had also witnessed the drama, had a different take. We heard her say, "She'll fuck that boyfriend up!")

We kept track of the lies. In one year-end roundup, we wrote:

"As the year draws to a close, you can almost hear Burl Ives's Big Daddy character from *Cat on a Hot Tin Roof* shouting at the top of his lungs: 'Mendacity!'" Like Big Daddy, we called out the "prevaricators, equivocators, and deceivers" for their crimes. There was so much chicanery, malarkey, and bunco to choose from. We still cherish the claptrap Jessica Sklar offered one summer when we called her to ask if it was true that she was working up a sweat with her new gym buddy, Jerry Seinfeld. At the time, she'd been married for all of two months to Broadway theater heir Eric Nederlander, who had insisted that his bride get on a three-way conference.

"Now, Jessica, would you please tell Mr. Rush what you've told me," said Nederlander.

Nervously, she said, "I'm *friends* with Jerry. There's no romantic interest whatsoever. He and I have, like, basically the same schedule right now. I'm looking for a job and we just, like, hang out and talk at the gym."

Her trusting husband added, "I know all about their friendship. . . . Our relationship, it couldn't be more solid. Jerry Seinfeld is not going out with my wife, and if he were going out with my wife, then we'd have some real problems."

As it turned out, Nederlander had some problems. Within two months, he'd filed for divorce. Seinfeld initially swore that nothing was going on with Sklar. But within the year, they were engaged.

Seinfeld argued that the Nederlanders' marriage was already broken when he met Jessica. Despite our stories, he was nice enough to keep talking with us. He'd get on the phone to stump for Al Gore or talk about the Mets. His new wife was less forgiving. At a comedy benefit for her laudable Baby Buggy charity (which distributes used strollers and children's clothes to poor families), Joanna was talking with Jerry when Jessica barged in to declare, "Jerry's not doing any interviews!" Seinfeld waited till she'd walked off, then picked up the conversation. He told Joanna, "I want everyone to know what a wonderful person my wife is. She has absolutely no interest in being in the limelight. I wanted to out her." We had our doubts about the limelight part. But then, he was besotted with his bossy princess, even when, as he told audiences, she said, "I don't like the tone of your voice." As Jerry told me on another occasion, "When you're a married guy, one thing you learn is that it's no big deal to apologize. You don't even have to mean it!"

At least Jessica had given Seinfeld some killer material.

Media Relations

Some of our most prickly subjects proved to be other members of the media. They were a cagey bunch, probably because they themselves were master rope-braiders when it came to fashioning a quote. "We're off the record, okay?" a famous columnist would say. "That includes my saying that we're off the record." The editor of a publication known for its celebrity exposés would deny that he and his wife were on the outs, even after we'd talked to the private eye she'd hired to tail him and his mistress. Most of the time, our clashes with other media gladiators were confined to print. But things could get physical.

The British writer Anthony Haden-Guest was a fixture on our scene. Anthony was a brilliant writer on everything from art to terrorism. But he drank—a lot. Maybe that was because his half-brother, *This is Spinal Tap* actor Christopher Guest, had edged him out for the title of Fifth Baron Haden-Guest. At least Anthony could take pride in being a model for pickled reporter Peter Fallow in Tom Wolfe's *Bonfire of the Vanities*. Like Fallow, Anthony had once Xeroxed his privates at a *New York Magazine* Christmas party. ("Yes," another guest had drily remarked to Joanna, "but was it letter or ledger size?")

Anthony's party antics earned him the nickname "Anthony Hated-Guest." One of his running gags when he saw a mate at a party was to pretend he was angry and lunge at your neck, as though he was going to strangle you. He did it with a lot of people. Usually, I was able to deflect him and we'd have a laugh. One night, though, I was at a book party at the Park Avenue home of Knopf editor in chief Sonny Mehta. I was talking with Candace Bushnell and didn't notice Anthony sneaking up on me. By the time I did see him, he had his thick fingers wrapped around my throat. This wasn't like Gabriel Byrne. He was really choking me hard. I kept waiting for him to let go. Candace exclaimed, "Anthony, he's turning blue!"

I finally broke his grip and pushed him away. I would have punched him, but it was a formal party. Candace said Anthony went on to a restaurant, where he passed out. The next day, I told my private eye friend Joe Mullen what happened. We decided to have some fun with the Park Avenue Strangler. Joe put me in touch with his son, Joe Jr., a top personal injury lawyer. Joe Jr. drafted a lawsuit demanding $1 million in damages. Then Joe Sr. had a rather large bodybuilder serve the papers on Anthony. Joe would never give me all the details, but he said the service was "quite forceful."

I doubt Anthony even remembered strangling me up till then. But suddenly, he was very remorseful. He sent me a letter begging for forgiveness and asking if we couldn't "settle this as friends." Richard Johnson did an item about the suit. I dropped the action shortly after that. Ever since then, Anthony couldn't be more solicitous. He's also lightened up on his drinking—though that may have more to do with his losing a $500,000 art collection when he forgot to pay his storage bill.

Our main combatants—journalistically speaking—were at the *Post*. Despite my past invasion of her love life, Liz Smith always gave us a big Texas howdy; she'd even drop us notes, complimenting us on stories. We also became red carpet buddies with the *Post*'s other grand dame, Cindy Adams. Cindy worked out of the Park Avenue penthouse, previously owned by billionaire Doris Duke. She shared her aerie with her husband, legendary joke man Joey Adams, and her Yorkshire terrier, Jazzy. Cindy had won many beauty contests in her youth—she was once crowned Miss Bagel by the Brooklyn Better Bakers Union—and had gone on to travel the world. But she never lost her appreciation for our surprising city, usually signing off her column with the tag line: "Only in New York, kids!" She had a big heart and a sassy, streetwise voice. But we learned early on not to cross her.

Once, when we were still at Page Six, we were working on a story about a fight that had broken out at an Aspen party between two socialites—Dewi Sukarno, the ex-wife of the late Indonesian president Sukarno, and Minnie Osmena, the granddaughter of former Philippines president Sergio Osmena. Minnie had made an unkind allusion to Dewi's past as a Ginza "hostess," provoking Dewi to cut her face open with a wine glass. Minnie needed thirty-seven stitches. We called Dewi. We got a call back from Cindy Adams. Cindy specialized in dictators and their wives, having scored exclusives with the Shah of Iran and Imelda Marcos. We'd forgotten that she'd co-written President Sukarno's autobiography and that he'd given her a three-paneled screen carved entirely of jade.

She said, "I understand you called Dewi Sukarno. Dewi is a dear friend of mine. If anyone writes about her, it will be me."

Our editor worked out a deal, wherein Cindy wrote about what Dewi wanted to talk about and we wrote about what she didn't. So everybody was happy.

Years later, after we jumped to the *News*, the publicist for director Roman Polanski asked us if we'd run his response to Cindy's claim that he considered Adrien Brody an ungrateful "punk" for not thanking him enough when Brody picked up his Best Actor Oscar for *The Pianist*. Even before Cindy's item, we'd quoted Polanski's pal, producer Robert Evans, as saying that "the kid should have gotten down on his knees." But now here was Polanski, insisting, "I feel enormous gratitude and love for Adrien... What more can I say to dispel these lies?" It would have been irresponsible not to run his quote.

The next time we saw Cindy she said, "They were trying to get someone to run that statement. You were the only ones who did." I said, "Well, we didn't mention you by name." She said, "You urinated on me," and she marched off, leaving me feeling like a fire hydrant just visited by Jazzy.

A paper's gossip column was often the catapult for hurling fireballs at another paper. Every other day, we or Page Six would chide the competition for some slipup. Errors were mercilessly noted. Off-hours, we'd often be clinking glasses—like the German and British soldiers celebrating Christmas together on the Western Front in 1914. Once, leaving a yacht party during the Democratic National Convention in Boston, I grabbed what I thought was my blazer. Later that night, I discovered I'd taken the party-scarred jacket of Page Six's jolly reporter Chris Wilson. It wasn't a big deal till I also realized Chris had my jacket—containing the lineup of Rush & Molloy stories for the week. I woke him up the next morning, apologized, and casually offered to deliver his blazer. I'm still not sure whether Chris checked the pockets but, sometimes, rival columnists actually *gave* each other story tips. When we couldn't get an item past our editors or lawyers, and we were pissed off enough about it, we'd slip the tip to the other team. We'd then have the pleasure of showing our minders that, because of their hesitancy, our opponents had now scooped us! Occasionally, when a British journo feared that a story about the royal family would incite official UK press watchdogs, he'd feed it to us, so he could more safely report on our report.

Cordial as he was when we met, Richard Johnson was a muscular point guard in the tabloid arena. He reamed sources he suspected of giving us items. We locked antlers with Richard most conspicuously when Joanna got a tip about a nineteen-year-old actress who was found naked and dead in the hotel room of an older television producer. Earlier in the evening, the actress and producer had met at Bowery Bar. It happened that, like so many businesses looking for plugs on Page Six, Bowery Bar employed Richard's wife, Nadine, as its publicist. Joanna had no choice but to call her for comment on whether Bowery bartenders had served the underage actress liquor. Molloy asked Nadine not to tell Richard about her story. What was in the *Post* the next day? A story about the dead actress. Shortly afterward, we ran into Mr. and Mrs. Johnson at the Metropolitan Museum of Art's Costume Institute gala. Joanna accused Nadine of tipping off Richard. He swore that the *Post* already had been working on the story. Joanna apologized to Nadine. But the next morning, I discovered something miraculous on my voice mail. There was a recording of Nadine Johnson, talking with someone in her office about our encounter the night before. "God, Richard is such a good liar," she chuckled in her husky Belgian accent. "Last night with Joanna Molloy at the Costume Institute . . ." Suddenly, Nadine realized she'd missed the beep. "Oh shit!" she said before hanging up. The *New York Observer* did a story about the "power couple" contretemps, labeling it "an impending gossip apocalypse."

In the end, we all laughed about it. For all our public dart-throwing, Richard thought it wise to stay away from private areas. "Nothing personal, okay?" he proposed one night at Elaine's. Remembering how he'd once overlooked our newsroom affair, we did our best to forget some lively stories about his extracurricular activities. Once, we couldn't help slip in a blind item: "Dear Mr. X: You're too famous now to go to Casa La Femme and lock yourself in the rest room with a woman. Our phone was ringing before you two surfaced."

We discovered we weren't the only ones with a non-aggression treaty. Rush & Molloy regularly made digs at "Citizen Murdoch." When the United Jewish Appeal-Federation honored the *Post*'s overlord, we mocked the unctuous speeches of Henry Kissinger and Sumner Redstone while quoting human rights picketers who branded the tribute to the "HuMONEYtarian" as a "festival of hypocrisy." But then came the day when we heard that the divorcing media mogul was staying at Soho's hip Mercer Hotel with a much-younger Asian woman. Hoping to catch him there, I called Murdoch's room at all hours and dispatched a photographer. When neither Murdoch nor his companion could be trapped or snapped, Rush fell back on calling Murdoch's mouthpiece, Howard Rubenstein.

I sent Howard questions about the divorce—what percentage his estranged wife Anna would get of the family holding company—and about this mysterious Asian woman. Howard called back and said he'd shown the questions to Murdoch. Howard told me, "I won't say what he said, but he was not happy. He told me, 'Call Zuckerman.'"

Howard also represented Mort Zuckerman's Boston Properties. Apparently, with Howard's intervention, Rupert had done Mort the favor of killing a couple of Page Six items about Mort's personal life. Howard said, "If you run this item, it's going to be World War III."

I called Mort. I could almost hear his blood vessels swelling as I recounted my exchange with Howard. Mort said, "Listen, I don't want to get into a pissing match with Rupert!"

Ultimately, both moguls agreed to a story reporting that Rupert and Anna had reached an "amicable" settlement, that Anna got their palatial New York spread, and that Rupert was living in a hotel. There was no mention of the younger woman who was sharing his suite.

A couple of weeks later, that rag, *The New York Times*, broke the news that Murdoch, sixty-one, "has been dating Wendi Deng, thirty-one, a vice president in Hong Kong of Star TV, Mr. Murdoch's Asian satellite-TV service." Within a year, Rupert and Wendi were married. Our Murdoch items always had to be reviewed, but no one stopped us from repeating withering stories from a memoir by his butler, Philip Townsend (who portrayed him as a homophobic philistine) and a biography by Michael Wolff (who claimed a domineering Deng had come between Rupert and his older children).

Joanna once saw Rupert and Wendi and their daughters at a service at Old St. Patrick's Cathedral on Mulberry Street. Frankly, she was shocked. She ran after him after Mass like she was chasing down a celebrity outside a club. Identifying herself, she asked, "Mr. Murdoch! What were you doing in there?"

He was incensed. "My wife teaches Sunday school here!" he snapped. "This is my parish church!"

"I'd love to talk with you about that," she said. "I've worked for you twice. How about an interview?"

"No, I don't think so," he said. "I'm shy."

Bashful as he claimed to be, Rupert turned to Mort for help in 2008 when Murdoch-watchers started to make much of the time Wendi was spending on projects with MySpace cofounder Chris DeWolfe. Looking to snuff out rumors that their marriage was in trouble, the Murdochs appeared together at a party at Michael's restaurant. The same night, a photo of the happy couple was delivered to the *Daily News*, where editors were told it *must* run the next day. The picture didn't cure the ulcer that was apparently growing in the marriage. Five years later, in June 2013, Rupert filed for divorce, stating that his relationship with Wendi had "broken down irretrievably."

Mort interfered with us less than his critics suspected. Early on, we heard from him a couple of times. Once, our spy saw Liz Rohatyn, wife of investment banker Felix, taking his firm's helicopter to the Hamptons without her husband. Felix called Mort, who then called us to say Felix, the former US ambassador to France, was, of course, reimbursing the company for her fare. Another time, we had the bright idea of calling DreamWorks billionaire David Geffen to see if he wanted to debunk a French magazine claim that he'd "married" actor Keanu Reeves. We heard back instead from Mort, who said Geffen had assured him it was a fiction.

But, after a while, Mort may have gotten tired of playing publicist for his friends. Once, we discovered some rather interesting court papers in the divorce of supermarket billionaire Ron Burkle, a major Democratic donor and a buddy of everybody from Michael Jackson to Bono. In the papers, Burkle said he didn't want his estranged wife, Janet, exposing their twelve-year-old son to a boyfriend Burkle said had pled guilty to attempted murder. Janet alleged that Ron had had private eyes tail her and had installed security cameras that captured her and said boyfriend having rough sex. The papers were in the public record. We had a right to report their contents. Rather than having a lawyer or spokesman deal with us, Burkle tried to have the story killed—using the good offices of his friend Bill Clinton, who sat on the board of Burkle's Yucaipa Co. We were told that either Clinton or his right-hand man, Doug Band, lobbied Mort to shelve the article.

Nothing makes a reporter lock his jaws on a story like being told he can't do it. But we never heard a word from Mort. So over the next few weeks, I proceeded to report the story. On the day before it was due to run, Doug Band called me to ask if I'd trade the Burkle story for tips down the road. I politely declined.

That night, Burkle himself called me. He said, "Do you have any kids?" We spoke dad-to-dad. He said that he wanted to keep his son out of the spotlight. I could understand where he was coming from. I said, "I wish we'd had this conversation when I first started working on this story. Right now, the paper is on the presses." I suggested that, in the future, he might consider talking with reporters, rather than trying to Bigfoot them. The next day, he said he thought we'd been fair—"but I still wish you hadn't run anything."

We knew a party was A-list if Mort was there. He'd be talking with his friends—Elie Wiesel, Nora Ephron, Charlie Rose, Barbara Walters, Diane von Furstenberg, and Barry Diller. Mort would always smile and make a little conversation, while keeping us at a bossly distance. Unfortunately, we had to read more than once in the *Post* about an elite gathering where there'd been some juicy confrontation—and where, among the glittering guests, was listed one Mort Zuckerman, who hadn't told us about it. We appreciated that Mort prized discretion, and that *we* were supposed to be working for *him*. But ever so delicately, I asked the real estate magnate (estimated worth: $2.4 billion) if he'd occasionally be our legman—share things he picked up in his travels . . . when he thought it appropriate. To his credit, he tried once or twice. When he did phone something in, he'd inevitably quip, "Do I get my usual tip fee?"

One afternoon, right on deadline, he called me out of the blue.

"Have you heard any good gossip?" Mort asked.

"Um, uh. Let's see . . ."

"I have some news," he interjected.

"Oh really?"

"Yes. I'm getting married."

I was gobsmacked. The man Candace Bushnell had called the "toxic bachelor" was finally hanging up his spurs?

"Wow! Congratulations! That *is* news."

"Liz Smith has been calling. But I don't think I should let the *Daily News* be scooped."

"I agree. Well, what can you tell me about your bride?"

"Her name is Marla Prather. She was just named curator of the department of twentieth-century art at the National Gallery of Art in Washington."

"How long have you known her?"

"We don't need to get into that."

"Okay."

"She just turned forty."

"Good, good. How old are you again?"

"We don't have to get into that either." (He was then fifty-nine.)

"Okay."

"I don't want to make a big deal out of this. Just low-key it—a couple of lines at the end of the column."

"I understand."

I wrote up a simple, four-sentence announcement and read it back to Mort.

I asked, "Is there anything else you want to say? Like—I don't know—how you found Marla after . . . after . . ."

". . . After much research? Thanks a lot, George."

We left it at that. After informing our editors of our publisher's engagement news and his wish that it run at the end of the column, we headed off on our nightly rounds.

The next morning at 8 a.m., the phone rang at our apartment. It was Mort and he was apoplectic.

"Would you please explain to me what I'm reading in your column today?" he sputtered. Spittle was practically flying out of my phone.

"Uh, jeez, Mort, I haven't seen the paper yet."

"Didn't I say to 'low-key' it? Didn't I? Do I have to put it in your contract?"

"Yes. I told that to everybody."

"Then why is it the lead story with a headline across the entire page that says, MORT THE MARRY-ER: PUBLISHER'S HAPPY NEWS?"

"I don't know. They must have changed it after we left."

"*Who* changed it? Whose idea was this?"

"I don't know. I guess everybody was happy for you and wanted to surprise you."

"Yeah, this is some surprise."

He hung up. I knew the witch hunt was about to begin. I returned to our bedroom.

"Sell the apartment," I told Joanna. "We're about to be fired."

Later that morning, our editor in chief, Martin Dunn, took responsibility and talked Mort down. At the end of the day, Mort called me. He was in a much better mood.

"Liz Smith is fuming," he said, mischievously. "But everybody else is calling to congratulate us."

That night, we saw him at Elaine's, where Carl Bernstein, Graydon Carter, Howard Stringer, and other pals were slapping him on the back and making jokes about the eternal player finally taking himself off the market. He looked giddy with joy. Maybe we'd keep our jobs a little longer.

One day we got a call from Terry McDonell, one of the country's most talented magazine editors. McDonell, who'd been managing editor of *Rolling Stone*, was working again with its founder, Jann Wenner, on relaunching Wenner's *US Weekly*. McDonell said Wenner would like to hire us. Wenner's admiration came as a surprise. Years ago, I had done a Page Six item about a boat party in St. Bart where he'd dressed up in drag. More recently, we'd written about him leaving his wife, Jane, for fashion designer Matt Nye, and Jann and Matt's ensuing dramas. Nevertheless, we had a number of stealth meetings with Wenner and McDonell. We told them we were flattered by the invitation, but we had reservations about *US Weekly*'s fluff content—its focus on mainstream pop gossip. McDonell admitted the mag's readers probably wouldn't know the politicians, financiers, and power players who were part of our mix. However, Wenner was offering us nearly double our current salary. If we were going to write gossip, we might as well get paid top dollar.

We decided to see if Mort would match Wenner's offer. Mort invited me up to his office in the fifty-nine-story Citigroup Center, which his company, Boston Properties, owned.

The office was like being in the cockpit of an airplane. You could see halfway across America. Around the room were awards and photos of Mort with assorted world leaders. After congratulating us on the birth of our son, he turned a desk photo around to show me his daughter, Abigail, who was just a year older than Eamon.

"She likes younger men," he said, with a wink.

I'd never seen Mort generate this much charm, at least in my direction. I felt a bit like George Bailey being offered a cigar by Mr. Potter in *It's A Wonderful Life*.

"Now what's this I hear about you and Joanna going to *US Weekly*?" he said, making a sour face when he mentioned the magazine. "You don't want to do that. You'd be squandering your talent."

Mort admitted that he was surprised by the success of our column, which now took up two pages of the paper.

"To be honest," he said, "I didn't think it would work."

It was nice to know we'd always had his complete confidence.

"Jann Wenner has promised us a lot of space and freedom," I said. "Oh, and money."

"Well, we've all heard that before," he said.

Mort didn't match Wenner's offer, but he did offer a significant raise. After several weeks of negotiations, we decided to stay at the *News*, figuring we'd be able to write stories with a little more gravitas. We sent our regrets to Terry McDonell and to Wenner. Not one to lose, Wenn struck back that afternoon. He offered our two sterling assistants, Marcus Baram and Marc Malkin, twice their salary to take the jobs he'd offered us. Understandably, they leapt at the chance. No hard feelings. Two more graduates of our school for scandal had made good.

That same week, we happened to be invited to a birthday party for our friend, André Balazs. His wife, Ford Models president Katie Ford, had told us it would be a '70s costume party, so we'd tracked down the tackiest clothes we could find. Joanna was in triple-belled disco pants. When we got to the party, we saw only two or three other people in costume. Katie said, "Oh, God! I forgot to tell you I ditched the theme idea. But, um, you look fabulous!" As if it weren't bad enough that Robert De Niro, The Band's Robbie Robertson, Microsoft cofounder Paul Allen, and assorted supermodels were staring at us, in walked Jann Wenner. Getting a load of my leisure suit and medallions, he looked relieved to have dodged a couple of losers. I told Wenner that I was sorry our talks hadn't worked out. As for stealing our reporters?

Wenner smiled slyly and said, "Can't help that."

14

Camelot on the Hudson

O f all the famous people we covered, few stirred such mixed emotions in us as the Kennedys. Like many raised in Irish Catholic families, we grew up revering the family. But, at the *Post*, the only good news about Ted Kennedy was bad news. The point was to punish Ted for forcing Rupert to give up the paper in 1988, even though Murdoch got it back. At the *Daily News*, we were free of that agenda, but the Kennedys remained one of the most coveted species on the gossip safari.

We respected Ted—the Lion of the Senate—and younger members of the clan for carrying on the crusade for economic, social, and environmental justice. At the same time, it was sometimes hard to overlook their excesses and infidelities. Some of them could joke about their foibles. Once, at a party at Pat Kennedy Lawford's Sutton Place apartment, Joanna remarked on a pregnant guest who was smoking. "Please," said Lawford, "I smoked during my entire pregnancy and all my children turned out fine. Except the junkie, of course." (Her son, Christopher, an affable, self-deprecating actor, later wrote *Recover to Live* and other books about addiction.)

Virtually anything that Jacqueline Kennedy Onassis did was an item. One day, Joanna was walking in the East Sixties when she noticed an eerie silence had descended on the block. There was a construction site across the street, but she didn't hear the sound of a hammer or a saw. Instead, workers on its girders were standing still, mesmerized by something below. Joanna followed their gaze to a gray limousine outside a restaurant. A chauffeur had just opened the passenger door. Stepping out was Jackie, on her way to lunch. Such was the reverence that everyday New Yorkers had for the former First Lady, who was only thirty-four when her husband, President Kennedy, was cut down.

When Jackie was diagnosed with non-Hodgkin's lymphoma and a source told the *News* that "her longevity is not great," admirers held a vigil outside her Fifth Avenue building, where she was saying goodbye to family and friends. Two years after her death, John and Caroline put their mother's personal effects up for auction at Sotheby's. Our editor, Martin Dunn, recognized the regard that readers still had for Jackie. He came up with the idea of a contest where readers would cut coupons out of the *Daily News* in the hope of winning a piece of her jewelry. Martin got Mort to pony up $10,000 for Joanna to spend at the auction. She had trouble finding any jewelry that cheap in the catalogue. But there was one set of costume jewelry—a bracelet and two sets of earrings—that she thought the paper could afford. She ended up getting into a bidding war with a jewelry dealer. He kept going higher and higher. Joanna thought, "God, I won't get anything and readers will say the contest was a scam." At last, the dealer backed down. A photographer took a picture of Joanna sitting on top of a mountain of more than 53,000 entries. She put on long white evening gloves and picked out the name of a seventy-four-year-old lady. The lady had been reading the *Daily News* for forty years. Jackie had brought her luck.

Much has been written about the so-called "Kennedy curse." In reality, some in the younger Kennedys were simply trying to cope with the loss of a parent in the way many bereaved children do, with alcohol and medication. And they made bad decisions. One New Year's Eve, we were in the newsroom putting the last touches on our column when longtime source R. Couri Hay phoned us from the ski slopes of Aspen. He said that, at that moment, he was watching as several of the children of Robert and Ethel Kennedy were gathered around their brother, Michael, as he lay in the bloodstained snow beneath a birch tree he'd just hit with violent force.

"The Kennedys are on their knees saying the Lord's Prayer," Couri said.

Michael, who'd defied ski patrol warnings by playing helmetless ski-football in the dusk, died that night. The RFK siblings had already lost their brother, David, to an overdose. Michael's death dredged up hidden tensions. In the months before his death, Michael had been cheating on his wife, Victoria, the daughter of football great Frank Gifford. His fling with their sixteen-year-old nanny had caused the couple to separate. Michael had gone into rehab. As part of his sobriety program, he'd made a list of people he owed apologies—and why he owed them. After his death, sources told us, Victoria found the list. On it was the name of a Kennedy wife with whom, unbeknownst to Victoria, Michael had been having another affair. The woman and her husband came to Michael's wake at Ethel Kennedy's home in Hyannisport. We were told that, as soon as Victoria saw the woman, she screamed, "Get out! Get out, you whore!" Victoria's outburst mystified most at the wake. But the other Kennedy wife and her husband agreed to leave.

John Kennedy Jr.'s pedigree and beauty made him the prince not only of the Kennedys but, you might argue, of celebrities in his time. And yet he remained down-to-earth. New Yorkers would see *People*'s "Sexiest Man Alive" riding around on his bike or hanging from a strap on the subway.

His sister, Caroline, would run when we came close (despite her having worked as a copy girl at the *Daily News*). But John could always spare a couple of minutes. He'd been a few years behind me at Brown. We had some friends in common. We'd partied at his loft. Even in his younger days, he had a cool authority. We once were at someone else's party, where the neighbors were threatening to call the police about the noise. John got the party animals to go home.

After working in the Manhattan District Attorney's office, John started a magazine that integrated political and celebrity culture. He called it *George*, after America's first president. It made a big splash. John once told me that pundits on the left and the right "both kicked me in the shins, so I must have done something right." John's interviews showed he was smarter than some people suspected and we regularly picked up on them in the column. We also reported on the trouble behind the scenes at *George*, such as the time John got into a shirt-tearing scuffle with his cofounder, Michael Berman. Sometimes we gave the prince a break. Joanna once spotted him nuzzling a new brunette in between sets at a Beacon Theater concert. Having met him before, she asked him, "Should I get myself a great item here or let you have a life?" John put his arm around her shoulder and said, "Please, let me have a life." The item never ran.

We showed less mercy when he started dating a fetching blonde named Carolyn Bessette. She'd only been seeing John a few months when we heard Bessette was also dating Calvin Klein model Michael Bergin. The day the "Hunk Love Triangle" story came out, we were due to meet up with some people at Elaine's. When we got there, we discovered that one of our dinner companions was none other than . . . Carolyn Bessette.

Joanna wanted to spare everyone an awkward meal, so she said, "We'll just sit at another table." She sat down at a table with Elaine Kaufman. I hopped back and forth between tables. I thought we could get more information out of Carolyn if I sat with her. Elaine told Joanna she shouldn't be worried about Carolyn. Elaine said, "Carolyn can get over it. If she doesn't like attention, she should stay home!" But Joanna wouldn't move. She said, "I eat my prey, I don't eat *with* it!" So much for befriending the famous. Carolyn actually didn't seem that bothered by our story. In fact, we later found out that she loved it. It made John jealous.

For the next year and a half, John and Carolyn couldn't eat a salad without it showing up in somebody's column. But one Sunday in September, news broke that they'd pulled off a media-free wedding on Cumberland Island, Georgia. When we called longtime friends of John for details, they were equally shocked to hear about the nuptials—and hurt that they hadn't been invited. They blamed Carolyn for pulling him away from his old buddies. After the wedding, Carolyn had more and more trouble adapting to life in the public eye—especially since the public eye never seemed to close. Night and day, paparazzi camped outside the couple's home in Tribeca, four blocks north of our place. Many of our items dealt with skirmishes with photographers—John's swiping the car keys of one, Carolyn allegedly spitting in the face of another.

In the second year of their marriage, rumors began to fly that they were having some trouble. One of our editors pressed us into doing a story about their supposed heartache. We quoted friends who were optimistic about the newlyweds working it out. But John let us know he wasn't pleased. Exclusive interviews from *George* magazine went elsewhere; a coveted invite to a Kennedy-hosted cocktail party never arrived. One night John and Carolyn came to a Whitney Museum party. Joanna wanted to ask her about rumors that she was pregnant, but she started with the softball question, "Who did your dress?" Carolyn's ice-blue eyes looked right through her and walked away. But John never held grudges for long—he put his arm around Joanna and whispered, "Miuccia Prada."

When the news came on July 16, 1999, that their plane had disappeared off Martha's Vineyard, it felt different than other "Kennedy curse" stories. Teary-eyed strangers covered his doorstep with candles and flowers. We saw Spike Lee among those crying. Many people in our neighborhood—from the dry cleaner to the waiters at the Socrates diner—were aching. British reporters offered thousands of dollars to Fred and Mary Parvin to talk about the many afternoons when John would hang out in their magazine store, drinking wine and razzing them about not putting enough copies of *George* in their window. They wouldn't dream of taking the money. "His looks and privilege gave him every reason to be full of himself," we wrote in the column. "His family's misfortunes gave him every reason to be sullen. But that wasn't John F. Kennedy Jr." We recalled the last time we spoke with him, we asked about his plan to bring *George* to TV—whether he'd host the show. "If there's a need,'" he said, with typical humility. "But I think there are people who'd do it a lot better than me.'"

We eased up on the Kennedys for a few months after John and Carolyn's tragedy. But inevitably, there was another scandal. One July, Bobby Kennedy Jr. announced the "amicable" separation of his sister, Kerry, from her husband, Andrew Cuomo, former US Department of Housing and Urban Development (HUD) secretary and son of former New York governor Mario Cuomo.

"Amicable" it was not. The next day, Andrew's lawyer, Harriet Newman Cohen, announced: "Mr. Cuomo was betrayed and saddened by his wife's conduct during their marriage. Despite that, for the sake of their three daughters, Mr. Cuomo has been trying to keep their marriage together for some time. But he will try to accommodate Ms. Kennedy Cuomo's decision to leave the marriage." A friend of Andrew told us he'd walked in on Kerry during a tryst with a married man Andrew considered one of his closest friends. Some of Andrew's friends accused Kerry of jilting him because his political prospects had dimmed after he dropped out of the 2002 gubernatorial race.

We asked around and soon had the name (and a photograph) of the other man: Bruce Colley, a handsome, polo-playing hamburger-chain heir. Bobby and Kerry had been smart to announce the split right before the July Fourth holiday, when people would rather go to the beach than read the papers. But gossip never sleeps. A source told us that Colley was a member of the Mashomack Polo Club in Dutchess County. We headed upstate and *News* photographer Debbie Egan-Chin met us at the private club. We invited ourselves into the stables, where we lay in wait in the hay. After playing a few chukkas, Colley appeared on horseback. As Debbie snapped him in his jodhpurs, I peppered him with questions. The perspiring sportsman insisted the affair reports were "nonsense," adding, "I'm trying to be polite, but it's very upsetting." The front page of next day's *News* had Colley proclaiming, "I LOVE MY WIFE." That must have come as a surprise to Kerry, who'd left her husband for him. Despite Bruce's profession of devotion, Ann Colley, his second wife, divorced him by the end of the year. She should have seen the signs. Colley once told a friend of ours that he liked dropping his kids off at school. Why? Bruce explained, "That's when you meet all the sexy mommies!"

Kerry eventually figured out Bruce wasn't husband material. She showed what grit the Kennedys had when it came to surviving a scandal. Despite the mortifying things we'd reported, she couldn't have been more chipper when she and I wound up sharing a four-by-four during a dune-bashing expedition in Qatar. We went swimming together in the salty inland sea and shared a table at the emir's gala. Kerry soon put us to use, promoting her book, *Being Catholic Now*, her productions of *Speak Truth to Power*, and the human rights work of the Robert F. Kennedy Foundation. Don't get us wrong—we actually liked her book and believed in her cause. But Kerry was a black belt at media jujitsu: she knew how to convert an attacker's energy to her advantage.

Her brother, Bobby, also appreciated the mutual benefits of talking with us. Early on, we gave him a chance to respond to author Joe Kane, who claimed that Bobby had secretly negotiated with the Conoco oil company without getting the permission of Ecuador's Huaorani people. We also talked with Bobby about his environmental advocacy groups, the National Resources Defense Council and Riverkeeper. And so he returned our calls about things he probably didn't want to talk about—such as his voice box disorder (it was spasmodic dysphonia, *not* cancer) and calls to re-investigate his father's assassination (he didn't buy conspiracy theories).

We also heard at one point that he'd been having an affair with a well-known woman in Hollywood, and that he and his beautiful wife, Mary Richardson, were living apart.

I left a message at his office. Then I called his house. Mary answered the phone. We'd met Mary years ago and I'd gotten to know her better on that trip to Qatar. Honestly, I took no pleasure in making these calls. It was difficult. I said, "Mary, I'm sorry to have to ask you this, but we've heard that you and Bobby are having some trouble, that you're living apart." She immediately started crying. She said, "No! No! That's not true." I said, "So you're still together? Everything's fine?" She sobbed, "Yes! Yes! Who would say something like that?" I didn't even bring up what we'd heard about the other woman. I just said, "I'm glad to hear that. I'll let you go." She was obviously in such pain that I didn't feel like doing the story. A few minutes later, Bobby called back. I had a feeling Mary had called him. His voice sounded even more fragile than usual. I told him what I'd heard, mentioning the Hollywood woman. I said, "But I just spoke with Mary and she assured me everything's okay. So we're going to leave it alone." I've never heard a man so relieved.

Our leaving the story alone didn't solve their problems. As time went on, police came to their house in Westchester County to investigate domestic disputes. Bobby filed for divorce. He began seeing Cheryl Hines, who played Larry David's wife on *Curb Your Enthusiasm*. Mary was heartbroken. She was involved in two DUI incidents. She was due to go into rehab when Bobby sought custody of their four kids. In February of 2012, he told a friend of ours, "I have to protect myself and my children."

About two months later, three days after Mother's Day, Mary was found dead in a barn on their property. Mary, who was fifty-two was hanging from a rope. Everyone who knew her was shattered. One friend told me that Mary had said she was getting along better with Bobby, "but I think she was just putting on a brave face." We immediately heard about friction between Mary's family and Bobby—that Bobby had ordered two of her sisters out of his house when they had arrived at the news of her death.

Three days after her death, Joanna went up to Westchester for Mary's funeral. None of Mary's family was there. The Richardsons had been trying to stop Bobby from burying her on Cape Cod, among the Kennedys. Mary's siblings felt that, given the rift in the marriage, Mary should be laid to rest where they, and her children, could visit her more easily. They held their own memorial service at The Standard, her friend André Balazs's hotel. Kerry Kennedy, who'd been Mary's best friend in college, showed up but left early, distressed.

The Kennedys didn't want anybody thinking Bobby "drove" her to suicide by cheating on her, as some of Mary's confidantes contended. Soon after the funeral, *Newsweek* "obtained" the confidential affidavit Bobby gave when he sought a protection order against Mary. In it, he said that Mary had drunkenly beat him up, run over his dog, and repeatedly threatened to kill herself if he left her. Kerry helped with the damage control. The human-rights activist told reporters that Mary had been plagued by "lifelong demons." She wrote an op-ed calling on "all Americans to join the national efforts to address the causes of depression."

But the spinning didn't go quite according to plan. The same day Joanna wrote about the autopsy report, which said Mary's fingers had been between her neck and the rope, the *News* found out Bobby had illegally exhumed Mary's body and moved it to a lonely spot in the cemetery, far away from the Kennedys. Mary's family didn't know she'd been uprooted until they'd read it in the *News*.

The tragedy may have gotten to Kerry. That same week, she was arrested after smashing her Lexus into a tractor-trailer and then speeding off. At first, Kerry told cops she may have blacked out. She said she might have mistakenly taken an Ambien instead of her daily thyroid pill. Joanna pointed out that thyroid pills are usually a different color and shape than Ambien. (At her hearing, Kerry changed her story, say-ing her doctor now believed she'd had a seizure.) Joanna also reported that Mary's family and some of her friends didn't believe that chronic depression drove her to take her life. They argued that her philandering husband was to blame. (It was later revealed that Bobby kept a diary of his female conquests, even giving them grades.) Mary's defenders contended that Bobby had been "gas-lighting" her—making her believe she that she was going crazy.

Bobby and Kerry both called Joanna to defend themselves. Bobby said that he'd asked Mary for a separation three years after they got married in 1994. He claimed they were living apart when he was seeing the other women. And, he said, she would often exhibit manic behavior, such as inviting a large group of girlfriends to be her guests on a yoga retreat in Mexico, charging it all to his credit card, unbeknownst to him. Kerry said, "You've been very hard on me." Joanna told her, "You've been very hard on Mary." Kerry said, "I thought you and I were friends." Then she paused a moment and said, ". . . Well, not *friends*."

15

Diddy, Clef, And Hova

Back in the '80s, I never missed the rappers, DJs, and break dancers who came downtown to perform at the Roxy. White punks and painters and fashionistas got down with Harlem fly girls and B-boys while Grandmaster Flash, Afrika Bambaataa, and Run-DMC scratched and busted rhymes. One city under a groove.

Then the gangstas burned down Old School. We heard that somebody known as Puff Daddy was having a beef with somebody called Suge Knight, who ran Death Row Records. We were told that Puffy, a skinny wannabe record mogul whose real name was Sean Combs, was so fearful of Knight that he'd hired drug gang enforcers as bodyguards for his twenty-fifth birthday party. Knight's spokesman insisted he'd made no threats. At first Combs didn't call back. Then the hip hop radio stations started picking up our story.

"People are saying I'm scared," Combs told me over the phone. "I'm not afraid of anyone!" Combs said his bodyguards were off-duty cops. I told Combs that we'd heard one of his Bad Boy Records artists, Faith Evans, had been at Suge's L.A. home, and that she'd looked extremely friendly with somebody named Tupac Shakur. Combs claimed that was news to him.

Little did we realize the East-West crossfire we'd wandered into. We didn't know that Shakur suspected that Combs had helped orchestrate an attempt on his life the year before. Nor did we know that Evans's reported affection for Shakur was likely to inflame her estranged husband, Biggie Smalls, whom Shakur claimed had also set him up for the five bullets he took.

While no evidence confirmed these suspicions, Combs may have added us to his enemies list. After our conversation with him, a source told me he had called his bodyguard to say, "We have to chill for a while. Stay away from me. Press is trying to take me down."

Yet as time went on, we developed an unlikely rapport with the rapper. He invited us to his infamous summer "white parties," where scantily clad fire-eaters, acrobats, and belly dancers jumped in and out of the pool while Combs reminded everyone, "Don't disturb the sexy!" Best of all, guests could register to vote! (Election records later revealed Combs himself had never been much of a voter.) Combs's "Greatest Party of All Time" proved a little more difficult to penetrate. The invite had instructed all recipients to "pull the flyest shit in your closet." I believed my shit to be sufficiently fly, since Combs had complimented my linen suit a few weeks earlier at the Kentucky Derby. Nevertheless, one of Combs's fashion sentries turned me away with a single word: "Shoes!"

Shortly thereafter, Combs was arrested on weapons and bribery charges after he and girlfriend Jennifer Lopez fled a nightclub where gunfire had broken out. On the eve of his trial, facing up to fifteen years in jail, Combs gave his first sit-down interview to Joanna.

"They put [Jennifer] in cuffs," he remembered with outrage. "I don't think any woman should be put in cuffs. Me, you can throw in the dungeon till you sort it all out."

Combs beat the rap but Lopez dropped him.

He kept changing his name—from Puff Daddy to Puffy to P. Diddy to Diddy to (the quickly abandoned) Swag. We gave him props when he did things like send four hundred inner-city kids to his Daddy's House summer camp. Other times, we pissed him off—like when we caught him drinking vodka that wasn't Cîroc, the company that was paying him. We always had a lively conversation. Once he told us that in preparation for his movie role as Delta blues legend Robert

Johnson, "I'm going to work on a farm, learn about sharecropping and picking cotton." We told him we had a hard time picturing him picking cotton—unless he planned to plow through the fields on his Jet Ski, with his terrycloth robe billowing in the wind. Another time he told us that if they ever made a movie about his life, he wanted Brad Pitt to play him. We reminded him that Brad was white and blond. But Combs insisted, "I think he could pull it off. He would just have to get a deep tan. Put a scoop of butter on his behind and drop him off in Saint-Tropez for a month."

We stayed on top of Jennifer Lopez—pardon the expression—after her split with Combs. (She came away from their romance with a fur coat and enough memories to keep the chill off. A houseguest of Combs once told us he opened the wrong door and found the couple having sex on the pelt.) Every week we brought you another episode in the crazy telenovela that was her love life. There was her little-known 1999 hookup with future husband Marc Anthony, her rebound marriage to dancer Cris Judd, her "Bennifer" interlude with fiancé Ben Affleck. Plus there were her spats with her mom, Guadalupe, and her dependable diva snits (such as backing out of a mayoral appearance because the city couldn't afford a private jet, $9,500 hotel suite, hair, and makeup).

More and more, rap became a beat for us. We let Eminem know that his former bodyguard *and* his estranged grandma were peddling books about him. We also helped Mariah Carey serve notice to Slim Shady that he'd better not release those voice messages she left him, because, she hinted to us, she had recordings of him, too.

We shared some prison tales, reporting that starstruck correctional officers asked 50 Cent for autographs when he did a photo-op at a joint where he'd once done time. We also revealed that jailed rapper Lil' Kim worried that her breast implants were leaking. When a prison official told us Kim could be released if she needed to have her implants re-moved, we coined the rallying cry: "Free the Lil' Kim 2!"

We exposed a rapper who was pretending to be the only son of Colombian drug lord Pablo Escobar. We discovered Nelly and Ashanti's romance, Seal's plan to marry Heidi Klum in Mexico, and Eve's affair with the kleptocrat son of Equatorial Guinea's brutal dictator Teodoro Obiang Nguema Mbasogo. We announced the engagement of Ice-T to his pneumatic truffle Nicole (Coco) Austin, only to hear from a Vegas man who claimed she was still *his* wife. We hung on as Tameka Foster careened from being Usher's stylist to his girlfriend to his pregnant fiancée to his ex-fiancée (he called off their wedding as guests were arriving) to his wife and, finally, to his ex-wife.

I sensed my efforts to cover hip-hop might have been paying off when I got an unsolicited call from music impresario Steve Stoute.

"Do I *know* you?" Stoute asked. "I mean, have we met?"

We had written about that unfortunate day when Sean Combs and two bodyguards allegedly beat Stoute bloody with a phone, a chair, and a champagne bottle. But I said, "No, I don't believe we've met."

"Well, maybe we should," he said.

Stoute was a brawny, brainy man who'd gone from managing and producing artists like Will Smith, Mary J. Blige, and Eminem to being the foremost justice of the peace when it came to marrying white-run corporations with black consumers. He called his company, Translation, a "transcultural advertising agency." His partner and main man was Jay Z, aka Hova, aka Jigga, aka Sean Carter. Whenever I went out with Stoute, I got a peek into their world. Once, when Stoute and I were having some pasta at Cipriani Downtown, he got a call from Damon Dash, who'd founded Roc-A-Fella Records with Jay. We'd broken the news that Jay and Damon had drifted apart. Now here was Dash asking Stoute if he could get a lift on the corporate jet they were taking to the Grammys that weekend. Stoute told Dash he'd have to see if there was room. As soon as he hung up, Stoute dialed Jay to leave a message: "We got a 911! Repeat, a 911. Call me." It seemed they didn't want Dash on their plane.

We'd been reporting on Jay Z for a while. We'd written about his rift with rapper Nas and his stabbing of record exec Lance (Un) Rivera, whom Jay believed had bootlegged one of his albums. But only one story got him really mad. Joanna had heard about a 2000 concert documentary, *Backstage*, in which Jay Z appeared to strike a woman taking his photo. A few days earlier, Joanna had met him at a benefit where they'd had a good interview about his collaboration with the beautiful Israeli violinist Miri Ben-Ari. Joanna had found him quite approachable. But someone had posted the so-called "slap clip" on a blog and fans, especially women, were beefing about it. Joanna called Jay Z's people.

They didn't respond. We ran the story. The same day, Joanna heard from the man himself.

"I can't believe that we had a nice conversation and then you turn around and run that story," Jay said.

"I can't believe that you slapped a woman in the face and you think that's okay," Joanna replied.

"First of all, she's one of my best friends," he countered. "Her name is Chaka Pilgrim. She works for me. And secondly, I didn't 'strike' her—I gave her a 'smoosh.' It was all set up ahead of time. She was in on it."

"Well, that's not a true documentary then," said Joanna. "And I'm not the only one complaining about it."

"That blogger is a jealous guy," said Jay. "There's a lot of jealousy in this business."

Joanna granted him that much. "That's one of the reasons I think seeking fame is a bad thing," she said. "I would never want to give up my freedom, and my privacy, and have people constantly trying to bring me down."

"I've never sought fame," he argued. "I just wanted to express my-self. If I couldn't express myself, I would get sick."

That part resonated with Joanna. She talked to Chaka Pilgrim and *Backstage* director Chris Fiore. They both backed up Jay's story. They could have been towing his line out of loyalty or fear, but Joanna didn't think so. We ran their side of things in a follow-up story.

Many credited Jay Z's new relationship with singer Beyoncé Knowles for calming him down. But one night when we ran into him, he confirmed that he and Beyoncé were history. He wouldn't say what had gone wrong, but he seemed wistful when we mentioned their "03 Bonnie & Clyde" video.

"That's an old video," he said. "I've got a new video out."

And the new one doesn't feature Beyoncé?

"My point exactly," he said.

Within a few weeks, though, we saw them out together again. We asked her what was up. "Whenever people talk about their relationship in the press, they break up," she told us. "I'm not talking about my rela-tionships until I'm married." It took another five years, but the wedding did come off, amid much hugger-mugger. (Our MacGyver-like report-er, Evans, climbed onto a roof opposite their Tribeca penthouse to give us eyewitness dispatches of Beyoncé squeezing into her dress and Jay buttoning his shirt while puffing on a cigar. If only Sean read lips!)

Like Jay Z, more of the big hip-hop stars began renouncing the thug life and getting politicized. But they continued to provide us with fresh conflicts.

Russell Simmons had started the Def Jam label with Rick Rubin, who long ago had been Joanna's intern at a video-editing studio (where Rubin rarely showed up for work). Russell was continually searching for enlightenment through yoga, vegetarianism, Buddhism, and Democratic candidate Dennis Kucinich. None of these activities interfered with Russell's appreciation of beautiful women. His long-legged wife, Kimora Lee Simmons, was his partner in their clothing line Baby Phat and in baby-making. They'd been together for twelve years when we heard that they might be splitting. "Nah," he said. Then, to our amazement, he volunteered, "Some people say Kimora's into girls. Hey, if that were true, I wouldn't have a problem with it!" Despite his open-mindedness to love triangles, Russell and Kimora confirmed their separation the following month.

Argyle-addicted Russell was always so positive that we regretted bringing him down. Once, he told us he was heading to South Africa to meet the miners and laborers who worked for De Beers, his partner in a jewelry line. "I want to give my money back to the people in Africa," he told us. "We're starting the Diamond Empowerment Fund to teach Africans how to cut and polish diamonds on the continent." Russell had recruited supermodel Petra Němcová for his fact-finding mission. He returned from the trip with mostly positive impressions. But then we had to go and talk with director Ed Zwick, who'd dramatized the ruthless gem trade in his Leo DiCaprio movie, *Blood Diamond*. Zwick disputed Russell's findings and said he found it "embarrassing" that the big diamond companies were using Russell to polish their image.

"Dammit," Russell told us. "Why did he say that? . . . To suggest I'm a sellout is wrong. I'm not here to defend the past of these companies. I'm here to talk about the current reality. Diamonds pay for education and medical treatment in Africa."

Russell being Russell, he wasn't bummed for long—and we'd managed to have a debate about conflict diamonds in a gossip column!

Russell's social consciousness was rivaled only by Wyclef Jean. After speaking many times about his relief efforts in Haiti, the Grammy-winning cofounder of the Fugees invited me to join him on a visit to his homeland.

I knew Clef had a lot of fans in the States, but he was like a god in Haiti. His Yéle Haiti foundation provided everything from doctors to garbage trucks. I'd been all over the world, but Port-au-Prince was a new level of poverty for me. I did get inside the National Palace one night when Clef invited me and a few people to a small dinner with President René Préval. President Préval was a very approachable man. He told me that before he became an agronomist, he'd worked at the Ideal Toys factory in Queens. "I fabricated Donald Duck," he said. "That's why I hate Donald Duck." It was a very chill evening. Wyclef played acoustic guitar and sang Bob Marley's "Redemption Song." The next day, we stopped by the TV station Wyclef owned. He dressed up as Santa and gave out presents to six hundred kids. My Haitian artist friend, Jeffery Dread, and his photographer wife, Selma Fonseca, and I followed Wyclef to the coastal resort of Jacmel. Clef put on a free concert for twenty thousand people. It was one of most spectacular shows I've ever seen—as much because of the audience's appreciation as Clef's performance.

It was only when I got back to New York that I found out about the life-and-death drama that had been going on behind the scenes. The same day that he'd played Santa, gunmen had abducted one of his TV station's producers. The kidnappers wanted Wyclef to pay a $250,000 ransom. Wyclef wasn't able to speak directly with the kidnappers. But I remember that at the concert, without mentioning the producer, Wyclef said, "If we don't stop kidnappings, the country can't develop." The next day, the captors released the producer. No money was paid. One the captors, The Commander, told a local paper: "We freed the journalist after considering how much effort Wyclef is doing to help our sisters and brothers in the forgotten ghettos." I thought, "Well, why didn't you just leave the journalist alone then?" But Wyclef showed no bitterness. He told me, "I'm redoubling my efforts. Nothing is going to discourage me."

As much as we admired Wyclef's dedication, we didn't ignore his controversies. Those included the New York attorney general's investigation into mismanagement of his Yéle Haiti organization, another investigation into his use of steroids, opposition to his presidential candidacy in Haiti, and a nude photo of his pretty manager that his wife found on his cell phone. Even when he declined comment, Wyclef was a charmer. "Once it's sorted out," he'd say, "I'll gladly talk about it."

Our coverage of hip-hop also introduced us the Reverend Al Sharpton. Though he counted James Brown as his personal godfather, the Rev didn't dig many of the rappers. Once, Nas revealed to us that he planned to call his next album *N—r*. Only he wanted to fill in the blanks. The racial epithet had become a common greeting in the 'hood. But Sharpton told us: "I'm astonished by the psychological gymnastics some people perform to make that self-denigrating word acceptable. No other race does it. Why is it accepted?"

Some people thought Sharpton was a self-aggrandizing fraud and wouldn't forgive him for his role in the 1987 Tawana Brawley rape hoax. But we'd seen him grow as a leader (even as his waistline shrank). He continued to generate much-needed media attention for genuine victims of injustice. He certainly didn't back away from any of our questions. During one of his National Action Network conventions, we learned he was staying in the New York Sheraton's presidential suite—even though he had a home in Brooklyn. Sharpton, who'd had hotel bill issues during a past convention, said the Sheraton had comped his room. But why did he need the presidential suite?

"The question is why *wouldn't* I have the presidential suite?" countered the former presidential candidate.

He also rebuked those who wondered why he was spending as much time with his gorgeous National Action Network executive, Marjorie Harris, as with his wife, Kathy. "Kathy runs on her track and I run on mine," said Sharpton. "One minute I get blasted if I have all men around me. Then I get blasted if I have women."

Though he denied Harris was his girlfriend, four months later, Sharpton turned to us to announce that he and Kathy were separating after twenty-four years of marriage.

The Rev swore their split was "entirely amicable." Others couldn't say the same. Rush & Molloy became a kind of family court for baby mamas seeking support. Week in and week out, we'd hear the cases of women who shared tales of woe involving Black Rob, Island/Def Jam chairman L.A. Reid and others. We reviewed DNA evidence from DMX and RZA. The mother of three of Ol' Dirty Bastard's children scrambled to find a marriage certificate after the Wu Tang rapper died at age thirty-five, leaving an estimated twelve heirs. The testimony of Linda Sanchez, the mother of Ice-T's son Kevin, was typical: "[Ice] was a sweet talker when we met. He turned into a different guy."

LL Cool J admitted the temptation that lurked backstage after a show. A "nine-month-pregnant" groupie once "asked me to [blcep] her," he told Joanna. "Yeah, I did. I often wonder where that kid is now."

Roc-A-Fella mogul Damon Dash's custody battle hit closest to home: Dash lived right next door to us. Almost every day we'd see a $300,000 tricked-out black van arrive at his building. Out would jump his eleven-year-old son, Damon Jr. We found Dash's case especially egregious because he'd let Damon Jr.'s mother, Linda Williams, raise his son until Dash deemed him old enough party with. Then Dash hired an expensive lawyer to seek full custody. Williams testified that the luxe van transported Damon Jr. to "inappropriate venues," including "a Victoria's Secret runway show, discos, and adult nightclubs." Williams also claimed Damon Sr. had "engaged in highly offensive" behavior, including calling the child's godfather, Jay Z, a "Jew, for not spending money." Williams alleged that the boy told a teacher that he didn't approve of his father's marijuana consumption and that, in a novel bit of show-and-tell, he produced a bag of his dad's weed. (Dash's spokeswoman said he had "too much love and respect for his son to talk about him in the press.")

Our personal child services agency could sometimes bring us closer to the father. Though the first volley in producer Swizz Beatz's custody fusillade came from his estranged wife, Mashonda, we ended up sympathizing with Swizz. He dutifully handed the mother of his child a check for $334,000. He handed us the scoop that he was now madly in love with Grammy-winner Alicia Keys. And Alicia later handed him a son.

Twelve years after we first spoke to Sean Combs, he fessed up to us that he'd fathered a daughter, Chance, with Atlanta beauty Sarah

Chapman. Combs had been trying to keep Chapman's delicate condition on the down-low since his longtime girlfriend, Kim Porter, was simultaneously carrying his twins, D'Lila and Jessie—but his Atlanta fling's unexpected dividend had caused Porter to break up with him. But the father of five always had a lady waiting in the wings.

"I'm definitely getting to know somebody," Sean once told us.

What was her name?

"I can't tell you. You gotta catch me, baby. Otherwise it won't be fun."

16

Bubbalicous

Diddy was right. The chase was fun. But sometimes we wished it wasn't so easy to catch the president of the United States with his pants down. Like the Kennedys, Bill Clinton was a mixed blessing. His romps provided the paper with loads of copy. But it was kind of awful to see a man we admired—and the office he held—starring in this burlesque farce. The *Daily News* didn't work him over like Murdoch's mob at the *Post* did. Page Six was a favorite slingshot for Clinton-haters like Larry Klayman and Richard Mellon Scaife. But we didn't let him off scot-free. The month I started writing my solo column, the body of Deputy White House Counsel Vincent Foster was found in a Virginia park. I did one of the first stories on theories the FBI was checking out—including speculation that Foster had been having an affair with Hillary Clinton and that he'd been murdered. It took three years before independent counsel Kenneth Starr concluded that Foster had committed suicide.

Every few months, another woman would come along and claim that she'd either had sex with the president or that he'd come on to her. Gennifer Flowers, Paula Jones, Kathleen Willey, Juanita Broaddrick, Elizabeth Gracen, and Bobbie Ann Williams were among his accusers. We helped to cover their legal actions. We tried to be objective.

We reported that Kathleen Willey had at first tried to sell her tale to *Star* magazine. We also asked the president's lawyer, Robert Bennett, if it was ethical to raise questions about Paula Jones's sexual history. "It's ethical, legal, and proper!" bellowed Bennett. "Look at what Paula Jones's people have done [to the president]."

Privately, some of Clinton's celebrity supporters rued his behavior. Publicly, most of them supported him, though their reasoning may have caused him more embarrassment. "Who gives a damn who the guy has sex with?" Alec Baldwin told us. "I hate to say it, but sexual promiscuity has always been the medication of choice for the chief executive of the United States. What would you rather have him do? Take drugs? Drink?" Spalding Gray argued that Clinton's sex drive went with his musicianship: "Anyone who plays sax like that is going to pull his pants down." Dustin Hoffman admitted that when he was shooting *Wag the Dog*, he didn't have the heart to tell Clinton the movie was about a presidential sex scandal. But Hoffman concurred, "I prefer a president with a healthy libido, because I know that at least he is probably not going to sublimate it with a missile."

In late 1997, we began to hear about another impending "bimbo eruption"—this time, "a Jewish girl." Earlier that year, when we were in L.A. covering the Oscars, a mutual friend had brought a geeky guy up to our suite at the Chateau Marmont. His name was Matt Drudge. He was working out of a one-bedroom apartment with two computers. But his fedora hinted at his ambition to become the Walter Winchell of the World Wide Web. Getting his wish, Drudge was the first to air the name Monica Lewinsky.

It wasn't long before distinctions between "gossip" and "hard news" began to disappear. So-called "serious" reporters began to invade our turf—panting for salacious details about cigars and that stained blue dress. When we learned that book agent Lucianne Goldberg had tape recordings of Lewinsky's phone conversations with coworker Linda Tripp, we gave her a call. She'd been besieged by reporters. Goldberg said her favorite moment was when "my son came in and said, 'Mom, Tom Brokaw is on line one and he wants to talk about oral sex.'"

We also began talking regularly with Lewinsky's mother, Marcia Lewis, and her stepfather, Peter Straus. Apparently, they figured we were more trustworthy than Page Six, which dubbed Monica "the portly pepperpot." When Tripp's children dissed Monica, Lewis told us: "I feel sorry for Linda Tripp's children."

In 1999, after playing hide-and-seek with the media for a year, Lewinsky couldn't resist an invitation to attend *Vanity Fair*'s Oscar party in L.A. Some of her dinner companions were cool to her at first. But one by one, they found excuses to introduce themselves.

"Come on," we heard Ben Affleck tell Matt Damon, "we're all going to go over to meet Monica."

Lewinsky just about fainted when Affleck flashed his smile. They exchanged some banter. Later, we asked him what he'd thought of her.

"She was nice," said Affleck.

One of his pals chimed in: "She thought you were hot. She called him a 'hottie'!"

Affleck shrugged and said, "She blew the president. I don't know what she'd want with me."

At least for one night, Lewinsky had been the belle of the ball. A year later, designing handbags and hoping to meet a guy who could live with her past, Lewinsky told us, "I'm still trying to make sense of my life. [Someone said to me,] 'You'll never meet anyone who made more mistakes than I did.' I said, 'Maybe you made a lot of little mistakes, but I made one big one.'"

Though Clinton escaped impeachment, Republican candidates for president did their best to capitalize on his scandal in the 2000 election. More than ever, they had to present themselves as faithful husbands. But before the conventions, we heard that one member of the GOP field may have had a Clinton-esque problem of his own. We ran a blind item:

"What presidential candidate is praying that a former secretary doesn't go public with her claim that he's been having an affair with a twenty-something woman? Many on the married Republican's campaign staff are already jumping ship."

Putting the column to bed, we headed off for a week's vacation in Europe. Little did we know, as we toured Budapest and Prague, the trouble those two sentences would cause. When we returned, our frantic editors, who'd been trying to reach us, explained that Matt Drudge had picked up the item, fanning speculation about the candidate's identity. Defying all logic, Christian conservative Gary Bauer had called a press conference declaring himself the subject of the item.

"These rumors and character assassination are disgusting, outrageous, evil, and sick," Bauer declared, with his wife and three children at his side. "They are trash-can politics at its worst. . . . I have not violated my vows."

Bauer foresaw someone exposing him as a sinner. And he fulfilled his own prophesy. Instead of crippling the rumor, he made it walk! Praise the Lord, his news conference spurred two former members of his staff to reveal that they had indeed quit his campaign because of what they considered his "inappropriate" behavior.

Charles Jarvis, his former campaign chairman, and Tim McDonald, former chief of advance operations, told the *Washington Post* that Bauer had spent hours behind closed doors with a twenty-seven-year-old deputy manager and traveled alone with her—flouting the code of conduct they believed Christian married men should follow.

Bauer blamed operatives of rival Steve Forbes for spreading the rumor, prompting a denial from Forbes's camp. But the damage—much of it self-inflicted—was done. A few months later, Bauer dropped out of the race.

George W. Bush was more adept at deflecting the question of whether he had ever used cocaine, sticking to the line: "I learned from my mistakes."

"This is a game where they float rumors, force a person to fight off a rumor," he told the *Washington Post*. "And I'm not going to participate."

On election night, we ended up watching the returns at a party thrown by Miramax co-chief Harvey Weinstein, *Talk* magazine editor Tina Brown, and politically ambitious billionaire Michael Bloomberg. The crowd included Ben Affleck, Gwyneth Paltrow, Barbara Walters, Sydney Pollack, Sigourney Weaver, Chevy Chase, Jennifer Lopez, Barry Diller, Diane Von Furstenberg, Uma Thurman, and Ethan Hawke. Many of the guests had campaigned for Vice President Al Gore and for First Lady Hillary Clinton, who'd been elected to the Senate. Everyone was waiting for Hillary and her husband, the president, to turn up for a victory celebration. But as the night wore on, Gore's future remained very much in doubt. Just before 1 a.m., Weinstein announced that the Clintons wouldn't be making the party.

"They are working the phones right now for Gore," said the gravelly voiced mogul. He said that the Clintons were at the Grand Hyatt Hotel and had invited fifty people to join them. Somehow, we made the cut. At the Hyatt, we entered through a kitchen and rode up on a service elevator up to the thirty-fourth floor. A Secret Service agent waved his magnetic wand over Thurman, making her giggle. Inside a dimly lit suite, we found the Clintons.

Weinstein thanked Chelsea for sending him a thank-you note.

Affleck chimed in, "I thought I was the only one you sent thank-you notes!"

Hillary apologized for not making it to Harvey's party.

"We've been sweating out these races over here," she said. "Sweating and sweating . . . We couldn't leave. Bill is still trying to figure out what is going on—if there's any way of turning it around."

Having been shunned by the Gore campaign through much of the race, the president was now behind a closed door, feeding analysis of the election results to the vice president's organization.

Hillary, wearing a green pantsuit, told me, "He knows so much about what goes on in each state, what the different counties are. He just has a tremendous body of knowledge that everybody is drawing on."

The president finally emerged to greet everyone.

"The vice president is only twenty thousand votes behind in Florida now," he said. "He may wind up eking Florida out."

He blamed third party candidate Ralph Nader for sapping support from Gore.

"Nader has caused his defeat in Oregon," Clinton said. "Probably in Wisconsin. In Nevada. And in New Hampshire for sure."

The crowd moaned.

Harry Evans, the distinguished British editor and Brown's husband, said, "I want to kill Nader!"

"That's not a bad idea!" joked Hillary. *Joked*—the Secret Service was within earshot.

Dewy-eyed Thurman told the president how the first Bush-Gore debate "made me really miss you."

The president said, "The press was pro-Bush. They set an impossibly high standard, an absurdly high standard, for Gore. It was disgusting."

Addressing the room, the president continued: "I want to thank you all who helped Hillary. I'm really proud of her. She won bigger than anybody thought she would." The first couple held hands triumphantly.

The president then planted himself in front of a large television. When news came that deceased Missouri governor Mel Carnahan had defeated living Senator John Ashcroft, Clinton pumped his fist.

"Yes!" he cheered.

He put his palm on the TV set, on Carnahan's face, as though giving the departed Democrat a high five. He pointed a finger at Ashcroft's face and said, "He's a *mean* guy."

Asked about her Senate plans, Hillary said, "We have to figure out what we do now."

The president joshed, "You sound like Robert Redford in *The Candidate*."

At about 2:30 a.m., the president slipped away again behind that door to check in again with the Gore camp. "Gotta get back to work," he said.

As the butterfly ballots were counted in Florida, it became clear that even the master campaigner from Hope could do nothing to help his vice president move into his office. Clinton *could* still work some magic when it came to granting pardons. As we covered the celeb-sparse parties before Bush's inauguration, word spread that the departing president had forgiven fugitive financier Marc Rich of charges of tax evasion and illegal trading with Iran. A special prosecutor was appointed to probe whether Clinton had granted Rich's pardon because his ex-wife, Denise, had contributed more than $1 million to the Democratic Party.

We first met Denise a decade earlier at—where else?—Elaine's. Our superflack friend, Bobby Zarem, had told Joanna that high-class call girls regularly hooked up with clients at the restaurant. Looking around the room for suspects, Joanna fixed her gaze on two brassy babes with low necklines and high heels.

"Are *those* hookers?" asked Joanna.

"Yes, they are," said Bobby, who couldn't quite keep a straight face. In fact, the ladies were his friends Denise Rich and Jane Holzer, the former Warhol "superstar" who'd become a top real estate developer.

Bobby told them, "Joanna thinks you're hookers!"

Rather than being offended, Denise and Jane burst out laughing. Joanna apologized, but they actually seemed flattered.

Since then, we'd been to many parties that Denise had thrown at her twenty-room, twelve-thousand-square-foot Fifth Avenue apartment. Joanna had gone to the high-spirited bridal shower for Liza Minnelli, where Donna Summer made the *Cabaret* star a bonnet of bows and dueted with Natalie Cole on "You Are So Beautiful to Me." (The setting was perfect—kitty-corner to the Plaza Hotel, where Liza's youthful mischief had inspired her godmother, Kay Thompson, to create Eloise. Yet guests—they included Janet Leigh, Patricia Neal, Anne Jeffreys, and other friends of Liza's late mother, Judy Garland—quietly wondered how long Liza and concert promoter David Gest would last. A little over a year, as it turned out.) Denise also threw a winter wonderland party where she flooded her terraces so that figure skaters dressed as elves could whiz around outside. Denise always had a lively mix of drag queens, specious princes, blinged-out rappers, and the nervous politician, who, like many of the guests, desired some of the $365 million that Denise won in her divorce from Marc. Two months before her husband granted Marc Rich that pardon, we saw senate candidate Hillary Clinton get off the elevator, size up the overcrowded room, and say, "Oh, I can't stay here." She then turned on her heel and got back in the elevator. That the bash was in honor of former Soviet president Mikhail Gorbachev only made it more bizarre.

Denise had a ditzy manner, but she tirelessly raised money for Gabrielle's Angel Foundation for Cancer Research, named for her gorgeous daughter who died of leukemia at age twenty-seven. She was also in love with R&B, once telling us, "There is a black woman inside of me trying to get out." She admitted that, when they were married, Marc hadn't been the biggest supporter of her songwriting.

"I once worked a long time on a song," she told us. "When I played it for Marc, he said, 'That's the same melody that was on the radio when we were in the south of France.' The trouble was—he was right."

Denise had the last laugh. The "black woman inside" helped her win a Grammy nomination writing songs for Mary J. Blige, Diana Ross, and Aretha Franklin.

The End Of Gossip

Rudolph Giuliani was the man who'd made Marc Rich flee the United States. As a US attorney, Giuliani had built a reputation as an incorruptible, media-savvy crime fighter, which he used to get himself elected as mayor of New York City. But over the course of eight years, we discovered a different Rudy who despised the media and practiced deception.

We first endeared ourselves to Giuliani by reporting on some of his top officials. Joanna discovered that First Deputy Mayor Peter Powers was driving an $800-a-month luxury vehicle that was improperly leased with federal drug forfeiture funds. After I spotted Police Commissioner Howard Safir at a Hollywood party (at the height of a controversy over cops shooting the unarmed Amadou Diallo), the *News* revealed that Safir and his wife had accepted a $7,000 freebie trip from an executive working for billionaire Ron Perelman.

Giuliani's temperature started rising when we reported that he'd had a huge fight with Michael Greene, CEO of the National Academy of Recording Arts and Sciences. It was a hothead meeting a bighead. The bighead (Greene) threatened to take the Grammy awards show out of New York, potentially costing the city $40 million a year in revenue.

Asked about our column at a press conference, Giuliani told reporters, "The executive director of the Grammys acted in an abusive way toward a member of my staff. He used language with her that you shouldn't use and not only hasn't promptly apologized for it, but is lying about it." Giuliani added, "If they want to go back to L.A., they can. We could replace the [Grammys revenue] in about a day."

We really got under Hizzoner's skin when we started commenting on his close relationship with his communications director, Cristyne Lategano. We noted that when few City Hall staffers wanted to attend Lategano's thirtieth birthday party, the mayor phoned reluctant party-goers and encouraged them to go. We noted that Lategano had been wearing a custom-made gold shield with four stars, just one star short of the police commissioner. And we noted that Lategano no longer attended functions if First Lady Donna Hanover Giuliani was present.

In November 1995, we reported that "Mayor Giuliani spent a lot of time in hospitals this weekend." The curious chain of events began on Saturday night, when Lategano was treated for chest pains at Lenox Hill Hospital, prompting Giuliani to leave a banquet and rush to her side. He'd returned to Gracie Mansion late, only to return to another hospital the next morning as a patient. Giuliani required several stitches for an inch-long cut on his forehead. His aides said he'd hit his head on a shower door.

We noticed that the first lady's name was now missing from the mayor's official Christmas card. Her spokeswoman asked us to please refer to her from now on as Donna Hanover. The former TV anchor-woman was now pursuing an acting career, landing parts on film in *The People vs. Larry Flynt* and, much to her husband's distress, on Broadway, in *The Vagina Monologues*. We began calling her "The Artist Formerly Known as Donna Hanover Giuliani." When the mayor's beloved Yankees won the World Series, Joanna noticed that Giuliani and Hanover rode on separate floats in the victory parade. We'd been getting sightings of Giuliani and Lategano in the wee hours at a downtown steakhouse. We'd heard there was a bedroom in the basement of City Hall and that, one Mother's Day when Giuliani was AWOL, Hanover had gone down there and found her husband with Lategano. But we couldn't prove it.

The only people who really knew what was going on behind the scenes were the mayor's bodyguards and drivers. But they wouldn't talk.

Joanna wondered if pictures might tell the story. She found that the first couple hadn't been photographed together in four months. She also found that Hanover had attended few events in an official capacity. Our editors finally let us run an item asking, "Just what does Donna Hanover do as First Lady of New York—and why does it take four city staffers to help her do it?" City Hall spokespeople refused to say just how much of Hanover's time was devoted to the people of New York, who were paying for her Gracie Mansion office, her assistants, and her car and driver.

We knew a lot more about the mayor and his movements than we got in the paper. We sometimes had the sense that not all of our editors wanted us prying into his relationship with Lategano. We began to wonder if Hizzoner even had a spy in the newsroom. Two top editors had family members in the Giuliani administration. Anytime we were working on a Giuliani story, one of them would wander around to our cubicle and nonchalantly ask, "Whatcha guys got cooking for tomorrow?" We can't prove that the editor was leaking information. But inevitably, after we'd tell him something, Giuliani or Lategano or one of their lieutenants would call a managing editor to complain about our unwarranted invasion of his private life. Our managing editor would hold the item, saying we needed "to work harder on it." Yes, it was important to be journalistically scrupulous. But we also sensed that Giuliani would retaliate against our city hall reporters by cutting off access and information. And, of course, he would.

Vanity Fair didn't need to have a working relationship with city hall. The mag assigned writer Jennet Conant to look into the rumors about Giuliani's marriage. Conant called Joanna and, rather imperiously, told her how much she knew about a subject Joanna had been studying for two years. Conant declared, "Someone told me that you had a front page story that the mayor was having an affair and that Mort Zuckerman killed it!"

Joanna said, "That's not true." Joanna wished Conant had rephrased the question, as she did indeed have a deceased front-page story, but it wasn't Mort who'd killed it.

Conant, the wife of *60 Minutes* correspondent Steve Kroft, kept railing. "Yes it is true," she said. "Someone told me it's true!"

Joanna stuck with a "no comment."

Vanity Fair ended up reporting that the mayor and his communications director had an "intimate" relationship that was threatening his marriage to Hanover. Lategano and Giuliani denounced the story as "trash" and "fiction." In a dozen or so stories over several days, the *Daily News* detailed the *Vanity Fair* allegations and reactions to them.

Knight-Ridder columnist Sandy Grady asked, "Why did the hot-shot New York media, especially its two feisty tabloids, all but ignore Giuliani's rumored romance with top aide Cristyne Lategano and his shattered marriage, until *Vanity Fair* broke the story? . . . Maybe the real New York scandal is that editors, reporters, and TV producers coddled Giuliani. Easier to trash a US president than a mayor who pals around with your boss."

The *Daily News* defended itself in a long editorial that charged that the *Vanity Fair* article was "undermined by factual errors."

"What did happen at the *Daily News*," the editorial went on, "is that reporters chased rumors and reports and tips that didn't pan out. . . . No definitive story was ever written or published because no proof was obtained. . . . *Vanity Fair*, to judge from Conant's article, doesn't have proof either."

The editorial concluded that much of Conant's story was "based on facts printed in this newspaper and elsewhere. . . . A neat trick: crib facts from other publications, then say they're part of a vast conspiracy."

We continued to watch the movements of the mayor and first lady. Though Donna Hanover blew off her husband's reelection victory speech, we caught him celebrating with Lategano over dinner at Limoncello "as four bodyguards looked on." But Rudy grew impatient with Cristyne. Almost a year later, witnesses told us they'd seen Giuliani swearing at a tearful Lategano at a breakfast before the Columbus Day parade. In June 1999, it was announced that she was taking a leave of absence for family reasons. She never returned to her job.

In February 2000, we noticed that the mayor was not wearing his wedding ring. Photos suggested he hadn't worn it in two months. We shared our findings with Debby Krenek, the *Daily News*'s first female editor in chief. "Oh shit," she sighed. Debby explained that the paper had been trying to get the mayor, who was considering a Senate run, to cooperate with a profile. Since she owed him a phone call, Debby said she'd ask Giuliani about his naked finger. She did and reported back that the mayor had blasted through the roof: "He kept going on and on about how this had nothing to do with public policy. 'Why is it even worthy of putting in the paper?'" In quick succession, Giuliani called Mort, who called Debby, who read Mort the item (twice). Everyone agreed the story should run but, as a concession to Giuliani, we made it the second item. Nevertheless, it didn't go unnoticed. At a press conference, a brave reporter asked Giuliani what happened to his ring. "I respectfully suggest," said the mayor, "that that's none of your business."

Three months later, Giuliani called a press conference where he announced he was separating from Hanover after sixteen years. Incredibly, he hadn't told Hanover. Later in the day, she held her own conference outside Gracie Mansion, declaring, "Today's turn of events brings me great sadness. I had hoped that we could keep this marriage together." She added, "For several years, it was difficult to participate in Rudy's public life because of his relationship with one staff member." Hanover's spokeswoman confirmed the staff member was Lategano.

But by then, Giuliani had moved on. A few days before the dueling pressers, the *News* had reported that Giuliani had, for almost a year, been quietly seeing Judith Nathan, a twice-divorced drug company sales manager. As they began stepping out in public, we acquainted ourselves with her former boyfriend, Manos Zacharioudakis. The clinical psychologist, who'd dated her for five years, shared a copy of his autobiographical novel, which he admitted was "a sex book in many ways. . . . We're not talking about 'breasts, tender and sweet.' This is serious hard-core stuff. . . . Many people will drool over the book." He acknowledged that the main female character was inspired by Nathan, who he said, "is very much into passion." Though Zacharioudakis perceived Giuliani as "puritanical," the couples counselor said, "I share his taste in women." Hizzoner and his "very good friend" were thrilled with his analysis.

Our attitude toward the mayor, and the idea of fame, changed dramatically a few months later. On September 10, 2001, I'd just returned from Africa, where I'd gone to interview the King of Swaziland for, yes, *Vanity Fair*. (Relations with the magazine had warmed since its 1998

Giuliani article.) My bags were still packed the next morning when we heard the roar of a jet so loud it seemed as if it was about to crash on us. And then a thunderous *boom* outside. We ran downstairs to West Broadway where a few people were staring at a smoking hole in the north tower of the World Trade Center, eight blocks south. A workman said it had been made by a low-flying plane that had barely cleared the Western Union building across the street.

As we stood there gaping, a ball of flame erupted from the south tower. As fire ate across the north tower, Joanna grabbed our three-year-old son, Eamon, and headed for safety. I began interviewing people who were making their way from downtown. By 10:28 a.m., the mighty giants that Eamon had called "the Twinnies" were gone. Several of our *News* colleagues had close shaves. Reporter Greg Smith was nearly killed on Vesey Street. The legs of photographer David Handschuh were shattered. Fellow lensman Todd Maisel found an unconscious fireman covered in debris and dragged him to safety.

I went to a nearby First Aid center set up to receive the injured. But few injured arrived. Feeling more and more useless, I joined a team of volunteers that an army ranger was training in CPR. I boarded a bus bound for Ground Zero, only to be told by police that the area was now off-limits; other buildings might fall. A few minutes later, 7 World Trade collapsed. A typhoon of debris hurtled down the streets, sending first responders—including Joanna's cousin, federal cop Danny McFadden—fleeing to the McDonald's on Chambers Street. Customers inside wouldn't open the glass doors. "Are you crazy?" yelled manager Lloyd Frazier, who leapt over the counter and unlocked the doors, rescuing Danny and the other blackened rescuers.

After dark, we reunited. We slept at the home of our friends Karen Duffy and John Lambros—along with some firefighters from Gary, Indiana, whom Duff had found sleeping on the sidewalk. We ended up staying for eight days, when police let us back into our neighborhood. Joanna joined the overnight shift of volunteers at David Bouley's Michelin-starred restaurant, preparing meals for workers on "The Pile." For a short time, hatred seemed to disappear. In the inner city, the distrust of cops that had festered in the Giuliani years abated as we witnessed their bravery. We forgave Giuliani his previous sins as he rose to the challenge of running a shattered city and reminded the world that we were New Yorkers, and we would go on! His marital indiscretion seemed such a puny issue now. In fact, pretty much everything pertaining to famous people seemed trivial. When I heard that Anthony Perkins's widow, actress Berry Berenson, had been aboard American Airlines Flight 11, I fondly remembered talking with her and her two little boys when I'd interviewed Perkins years ago. But even the celebrities recognized things had changed. Their Hollywood dramas meant nothing next to the 2,977 innocent people who'd died that day. Real heroes—firefighters, cops, salvage workers breathing the fumes at Ground Zero—replaced people who were merely famous. Humbled stars just about genuflected before first responders and soldiers.

Rush & Molloy the column was suspended as we contributed to the paper's disaster coverage. After about a week, the column resumed. The mantra about anything entertaining, from shopping to baseball, was that if we didn't keep doing it, "they win." Celebrities had, after all, played a role in World War II. Our first post-9/11 columns chronicled Kathleen Turner pitching in to help harried staffers at St. Vincent's Hospital . . . Daniel Day-Lewis lugging boxes of ice at a blood center . . . Paul Simon singing at a memorial service . . . Alec and Billy Baldwin and Creative Coalition members launching an art therapy program for traumatized children. Naturally, actors put on plays and musicians held concerts to raise money for the families of 9/11 victims. On stage, Madonna swapped her tartan kilt for one made of an American flag.

Vestiges of the former culture of fame remained. Police wouldn't let most concerned citizens anywhere near the disaster scene. But actors such as Matthew Broderick, Sarah Jessica Parker, Steve Buscemi, and Michael Imperioli were allowed to help pass out food. Unaccustomed to the reverse idolatry, some firemen fell back on their fan instincts and asked Parker to sign their helmets.

While some celebs learned modesty, others couldn't help being themselves. Just when it looked as though 9/11 would put an end to gossip, we began hearing amazing tales of self-absorption.

On the morning after the attacks, Tommy Hilfiger called a West Village antiques store to put in an urgent order for Lampe Berger room fresheners for a friend—Sarah Ferguson. (Hilfiger later donated

$10,000 to the Duchess's 911 Fund.) Organizers of the Salute to Heroes telethon invited Michael Jackson to perform, but they rescinded the offer after the Gloved One refused to donate a track to a CD benefiting the victims' families, according to our sources. Paul McCartney, Mick Jagger, Jay Z, and The Who put their star power to work at the Madison Square Concert for New York. (Wracked with food poisoning, David Bowie had to be helped onstage at the Garden.) It was an unforgettable show. But, later, we heard that backstage Bill Clinton blasted VH1 chief John Sykes for having Hillary address the over-served cops and firemen in the front rows. After they heckled her, Hillary was practically in tears when she walked offstage," said a witness. Monologist Spalding Grey was depressed that he was out of town on 9/11. "I could have gone for hours [onstage] about it," Grey told us. When Grey shared his misery with Susan Sarandon at a 9/11 panel, she told him: "Snap out of it!" Alas, he couldn't—eventually taking his own life by jumping off the Staten Island Ferry in the dead of winter.

The attacks ignited other celebrity controversies. Charlie Sheen hooked up with conspiracy theorists who alleged the US government was behind the attacks, that the collapse of the towers was "controlled demolition." We learned that Tom Cruise was quietly funding Scientology-linked "detox" clinics that claimed to be helping 9/11 rescue workers suffering from smoke inhalation. New York Fire Department officials said the "cleansing" program was "medically unproven." We called out rapper KRS-One for asserting that he and other African Americans "cheered when 9/11 happened. . . . When the planes hit the building, we were like, 'Mmmm—justice.'" Parker later claimed we'd "quoted him out of context." A tape proved we didn't. We also questioned Oliver Stone's assertion that rogue Ground Zero workers had stolen jewelry from victims' bodies—even cutting limbs off to get it—and that "a man walked off with $132 million." As usual, Stone claimed there'd be an official cover-up. But when I pressed him, he admitted he had one source. "I can't give you the name," he said. Pressed further, the *World Trade Center* director conceded he couldn't vouch for the tale, weakly adding, "I think it *could* happen."

The aftermath of 9/11 also brought us face-to-face again with our neighbor Robert De Niro. Teaming up with his producing partner, Jane Rosenthal, and her husband, Craig Hatkoff, De Niro announced in 2002 that he was creating the Tribeca Film Festival in an effort to bring business back to our hood. We thought it was a great idea and heartily trumpeted the fest in our column. But by then, we'd given De Niro new reasons to hate us. Foremost among them was our story about the joint birthday party he and Sean Penn threw at De Niro's penthouse. The story was innocent enough, but we ran a photo of the birthday boys cutting their cake. Never before had a paparazzo penetrated De Niro's lair! Feeling violated, he filed a $1 million lawsuit against the photo agency that provided the snap.

Despite his outrage, we received an invitation to a festival kick-off party that De Niro was cohosting at the New York State Supreme Court Building on Centre Street. The steps of the temple of justice were lit with more than eight hundred tealights. It was a perfect spring night. Mingling on the open-air portico were David Bowie and Iman, Elvis Costello and Diana Krall, Kevin Bacon and Kyra Sedgwick, Jerry and Jessica Seinfeld, Caroline Kennedy and Edwin Schlossberg, Ralph and Ricky Lauren, Norah Jones, Paul Rudd, and on and on.

I was waiting for one guest—Angelina Jolie. The publicists had said she might come. But as the cocktail hour wore on, I'd given up hope. And then, just as the dinner bell chimed, she appeared! She'd climbed the courthouse's endless steps in a long gown. And she was alone. Not wasting a second, I dove over four men to get to her first. My musketeer leap seemed to make her smile. Brushing myself off, I asked her my standard question of the night—whether, since we were in a court-house, she'd ever served jury duty.

"I've wanted to serve," she said. "But if someone like me walks in, they don't want you."

I could think of a few guys who'd gladly be sequestered with her. Not wanting to lose her, I steered the conversation to her recent trip to refugee camps in Asia and Africa. She began to brief me on the conditions. As serious as the topic was, Jolie kept smiling. I sensed she found me amusing. Then she started laughing. Perhaps too amusing.

Suddenly De Niro appeared, putting his hand around her waist and whisking her away.

Joanna, who'd been watching our exchange, told me later that De Niro had been standing behind me, signaling Jolie to stop talking to me.

We moved inside to the rotunda, where dinner tables had been set up under the ceiling mural of Hammurabi, Moses, Justinian, and other judicial stars handing down verdicts. I made my way to De Niro's table. Summoning my nerve, I said, "Hi, Bob. Congratulations on the festival. Seriously. I think it will help the neighborhood come back."

"Here he is!" said De Niro, beckoning the attention of his wife. "Grace, didn't I tell you he was lurking around?"

De Niro seemed to have had a couple of cocktails. I hoped they might finally loosen his tongue.

"Bob, this is your festival," I said. "Do you have any films you're looking forward to? Anything you'd recommend?"

He hemmed and hawed.

"They're all good," he said. "You have a tape recorder?"

He seemed ready to pat me down, as if searching for a Glock. I showed him that I was holding a small recorder.

"I don't want to misquote you," I said.

"Listen, turn that off," he said. "I don't like those things. Let's just talk."

So I turned it off. We talked. Not a lot. But we managed to converse about his coming projects and his latest facial hair, a long pointy beard he'd grown to play the Grand Inquisitor in Thornton Wilder's *The Bridge of San Luis Rey*.

"I based the beard on a painting by Velazquez," he said.

By then, the waiters had given him the excuse that he had to eat.

When we'd all reached dessert, his cohost, *Vanity Fair* editor Graydon Carter, offered a toast, during which he likened De Niro's beard to a certain 1960s variety-show host.

"I told Bob he looked like Mitch Miller," Carter announced. "I thought he might lead us in song."

The crowd roared, then looked toward the actor who'd played sax-man Jimmy Doyle in *New York, New York*.

De Niro stood up.

"Not likely!" he bellowed.

Bushwackers

September 11th presented Republicans with a new political crisis: those loathsome Hollywood Democrats were actually praising them. After listening to President Bush's address to Congress, actor Matthew Modine told us how impressed he was with "his wisdom. I'm encouraged by him. He is our nation's leader, and, like it or not, you have to stand behind him." Woody Allen allowed that, even though "I was certainly very critical of him before he was elected," Bush "has got a good grasp on the problem [of terrorism]."

But after the first anniversary of the attacks, celebrities grew bolder again. Many began to question their commander in chief's claim that Iraq strongman Saddam Hussein had weapons of mass destruction, and that we needed to get them.

Kevin Spacey and I were talking in the wood-paneled library of the Hudson Hotel one night in November of 2003. Spacey could see Bush's political motive in invading Iraq.

"There's no clear victory in Afghanistan," Spacey said. "There is a clear victory in Iraq in about eleven days. I think [US armed forces] can pull it off. And President Bush knows it."

The Greek chorus of peace-seekers grew louder—and funkier—in the beginning of 2003. Launching into a Bob Marley anthem, Wyclef Jean told the crowd at one rally, "Tell Mr. President we don't want war."

After the song, we asked Clef why American soldiers shouldn't oust Saddam if he didn't mind them evicting "Baby Doc" Duvalier from his homeland of Haiti.

"The United States and Haiti always had a relationship," he argued.

Saddam had long forbidden any mention of Madonna in Iraq—apparently because her song "Like a Virgin" advertised a woman's disgrace. And, besides, the dictator preferred ABBA. But now the Baath party's newspaper saluted her Madgesty for her antiwar single, "American Life."

Not every star wanted to be part of Saddam's human shield.

"Why is everybody trying to stop the war?" Kid Rock told me as he swigged a beer one night. "George Bush ain't been saying, 'Y'all make shitty records.' . . . [Musicians] ought to stay out of it."

With a little prodding, though, I persuaded the millionaire redneck to share his foreign policy critique.

"We got to kill that motherfucker Saddam," he said. "Slit his throat. Kill him and the guy in North Korea."

On another night, in the bar of the Royalton Hotel, Bruce Willis told us he'd been seriously considering joining the US armed forces, "but my friends told me I was too old. I called the White House, called President Bush, and asked what I could do." Dubya suggested that the forty-seven-year-old movie star could better serve his country in other ways.

Harrison Ford was also reported to be in Bush's corner. But when we asked him if that was true, the *Air Force One* star said he actually detested Bush's military strategy.

"What I'm for is a regime change on *both* sides," Ford quipped.

The claim that Ford had opposed an antiwar statement signed by 104 actors and directors had originated—not surprisingly—on Fox News. Rupert Murdoch's network carried so much water for Bush, you could fill the White House pool several times a day. No one at Fox was better at sneering at Bush's celebrity critics than Bill O'Reilly.

Initially, O'Reilly had found Rush & Molloy's coverage fair and balanced. In 2001, Joanna uncovered a lawsuit he'd filed against a Long

Island neighbor whom O'Reilly claimed had been harassing his family. We'd also had a pleasant conversation when he denounced Pepsi for signing an endorsement deal with Ludacris, a rapper he branded as "a subversive influence on children." But then we got our hands on an advance copy of the lad mag *Stuff*. In it, mischievous editor Greg Gutfeld had Photoshopped animals posing his questions. A bobcat asked O'Reilly which country had the ugliest women.

"The most unattractive women in the world are probably in the Muslim countries," the jowly pundit declared. That was why "[they're] dressed head to toe in black and I can only see eyebrows."

We took it upon ourselves to see what Muslims thought of O'Reilly's dig at their women.

"It's an extremely offensive and racist statement," said Rania Masri, of the Arab Women's Solidarity Association. "If he really believes this, then he probably needs his head examined," said Hussein Ibish, of the American-Arab Anti-Discrimination Committee.

We called O'Reilly for comment. Around 6 p.m., when our column was on its way to the presses, O'Reilly called back. I told him that we'd found some Arab Americans who didn't agree that their women were repellant. O'Reilly accused us of "stirring up" controversy—something he surely would never do.

"Do not run this story," O'Reilly demanded.

"Why, Bill? Did they misquote you?"

"I'm telling you not to run this story," he repeated.

O'Reilly claimed he had sneered at the flowers of Islam only in "jest." But he wasn't about to apologize. Instead, he threatened to sue us and have his boss, Roger Ailes, call Mort Zuckerman.

I promised to include O'Reilly's comments but said I didn't see why we shouldn't report something that was going to be on every newsstand in a couple of days.

The next day, the story ran under the headline: "A NOT-SO-VEILED INSULT FROM O'REILLY." The story described the interview as "jokey" and "playful" and quoted O'Reilly as saying, "There was no malice intended." Nevertheless, when we got to work, we found that O'Reilly, whose syndicated column ran in the *Daily News*, had already called our new editor in chief, Ed Kosner. He wanted a correction. Kosner declined, remarking, "I thought you lived in the 'No Spin Zone,' Bill."

That evening, O'Reilly began his show with a "Talking Points Memo" devoted to the subject of "creeping evil." He said that Osama bin Laden, The Unabomber, and the Beltway Sniper were all obvious villains but that, sometimes, evil is less "well-defined." The previous evening, he said, "I was on the phone with a gossip writer who was printing something that was distorted and would be dangerous to the person involved. I laid out a case to that writer that was undeniable. His response? 'I don't care.' Evil."

O'Reilly never told his viewers that he was "the person involved." He never told me that the article could be "dangerous." And I never said, "I don't care." Only later did a Fox News spokesman divulge that Muslims had been writing angry letters because evangelist Pat Robertson said on Fox that the prophet Muhammad was "a robber and a brigand." But I was flattered to have Bill O'Reilly consider me "evil."

Little did we know how much O'Reilly revealed when he told *Stuff* that his *favorite* women were Scandinavian and Thai. Twelve years later, a thirty-three-year-old producer filed a $60 million sexual harassment suit in which she claimed the married O'Reilly had regaled her with descriptions of Thai sex shows and bragged about threesomes with Swedish flight attendants.

By the third week in March 2003, thousands of American troops were poised to invade Iraq. Inconsiderately, Bush and Congress paid no mind to the long-planned Academy Awards. Arriving in Los Angeles, we found that almost every pre-Oscar party had turned into a prayer vigil. At an AmFAR fundraiser, Sharon Stone asked for a moment of silence for the families in Iraq. Stylists told their actress clients to dress in black and tone down the jewelry. Chauffeurs were told to leave their stretch limos in the garage and drive more military-looking Escalades.

The night we got to town, we headed to the Beverly Hills home of Black Sabbath rocker Ozzy Osbourne and his wife Sharon. For months, they and Elton John had been planning a charity dinner for their foundations. But in the last few days, they'd debated whether to call the benefit off.

"We decided to continue because, war or no war, we are all fighting the war against AIDS and cancer," Sharon told the crowd of about one hundred gathered in a garden twinkling with candles.

By now, even Bush's harshest critics were voicing their support of the troops. But some of the party's older guests remained strident.

Tony Bennett remembered "the horror" he saw as an infantryman in World War II. "That was a good war—it had to be done," he told us. "This isn't a good war. . . . I'm hurt by what's happening in this country."

Guest of honor Elizabeth Taylor was fighting a stomach virus, but she told me that what really "sickens me beyond belief" was Bush.

"I was a refugee when I came to this country because of World War II," she said as we walked with her to the door. "I listened to the radio all the time and thought, 'Why don't the Americans do something?' Now I think, 'What the fuck are the Americans doing by saying [to Saddam], "Pack up your bags, mount a camel, and get out of town!"' What if someone said that to Bush?"

She went on: "You don't think [terrorists] are going to retaliate? You don't think they're going to bomb the shit out of us? It's going to be terrifying."

Elton, who wore a diamond peace symbol on his lapel, said, "I'm not for the war. I love America. [But] you can't say you're against the war without being called a traitor."

Elsewhere in Beverly Hills, art dealer Larry Gagosian found shade under the war clouds. Gagosian barred reporters from his usual pre-Oscar gallery show, claiming that, in light of Iraq, he "didn't feel media coverage was appropriate." His press ban probably had more to do with a $26.5 million federal tax evasion indictment filed against him two days earlier.

Ed Limato, one of Hollywood's top talent agents, didn't need an excuse to bar the media from his annual pre-Oscar party. Reporters were always persona non grata, which was why the party drew the biggest stars. Nevertheless, a friend of Rush & Molloy said he'd bring one of us as his "plus one."

"The only thing you have to promise," said our friend, "is that as soon as we get there, we go in separate directions. If you get caught, I don't know you."

I agreed to the deal. As soon as my friend and I got past the sentry at Limato's Coldwater Canyon estate, I peeled off. I wandered around the seventy-thousand-square-foot grounds, taking in the spa, the tennis court, the marble statue of Hercules in the buff, and the *tableau vivant* of hunky young men in Limato's pool house.

The real action was at one end of the rolling lawn, in a sprawling tent decorated with carpets and antiques. No wonder the party was said to cost Limato's agency $1 million. Our Page Six competitor, Richard Johnson, had predicted that most of Hollywood would boycott the fete because the father of Limato's client Mel Gibson had recently claimed the Holocaust never happened. But inside the tent were enough famous faces to perform at a charity telethon *and* answer the phones. As Rush & Molloy reported afterward:

"Hollywood apparently doesn't hold Mel Gibson's agent responsible for the sins of the star's father. . . . Barbra Streisand, sporting a beret, arrived with James Brolin and chatted with director James Brooks and designer Donna Karan. Leonardo DiCaprio huddled with Adrien Brody—giving the Best Actor nominee a good-luck soul shake. Winona Ryder chain-smoked and wobbled around in shoes that looked too big. Mike Myers joked with Tim Robbins. Sly Stallone talked acting with Salma Hayek. . . . Paris Hilton trained her blonde beam on Nicolas Cage, but the *Adaptation* star eventually turned his attention elsewhere (prompting Paris to impatiently check her rhinestone-encrusted cell phone)."

We listed a dozen other stars. Limato secretly must have loved the item.

The day after Limato's party, we headed to the Independent Spirit Awards, where I spotted Brad Pitt nibbling on his lunch. It had been a few years since Pitt had gallantly apologized for wrongly accusing us of printing his address. He was now a much bigger star. But he greeted me with a hearty handshake. Once again, the conversation turned to Iraq. What did Pitt think of the impending invasion?

"We can't go back now," said Pitt, who was wearing jeans and a white shirt with a buckle pattern. "We're in this together as Americans. We're going to have to go in and get the job done as soon as possible."

Pitt didn't buy Bush's linkage of Saddam and Al Qaeda and wondered, "Why attack now?" But he respected Bush for "pushing the issue, so people were forced to take a stand." Now that we've reached a diplomatic dead end, Pitt said, "We have to be productive instead of concentrating on what we should have done. Where do we go from this day forward?"

When the Spirit Awards ended in the late afternoon, we moved on to the Beverly Wilshire Hotel for the Miramax party. In light of the war, the usual star-studded vaudeville revue was jettisoned. Instead, guests, including Salma Hayek, Bono, and Richard Gere, were invited to join Michael Feinstein in singing "God Bless America."

"Everyone has to find their own way," the taciturn Daniel Day-Lewis told us afterward. "I think many people have ambivalent feelings."

But not Day-Lewis. We asked what his murderous, flag-bandaged *Gangs of New York* character, Bill the Butcher, would think of the approaching bloodshed in Iraq.

"Oh, he'd be all for it," said the actor. "He'd be the perfect poster boy for Bush."

After hitting a few more parties, we headed back to the Standard Hotel. Early the next morning, the day of the Oscars, the phone rang. It was Brad Pitt's publicist, Cindy Guagenti.

"I've been calling every hotel in L.A. trying to find you," she told me. "Brad said he talked to you yesterday."

"That's right," I said.

"About Iraq."

"That's right. Is there something wrong?"

"Well, he can't remember exactly what he said."

I began to suspect why Pitt had kept his sunglasses on inside.

Guagenti went on: "Would you mind telling me what you have him saying?"

I read her his quotes. She agreed that Pitt's remarks were measured and respectful of the troops. Was he worried about being branded a traitor—as Elton had warned? Or did he fear that, by Hollywood standards, he hadn't been hard enough on Bush?

Pitt's comments led the column under the headline "SOME STARS ARE GIVING WAR A CHANCE." At the Academy Awards that night, a number of people onstage injected antiwar messages—no one so much as *Bowling for Columbine* director Michael Moore, who declared, "Shame on you, Mr. Bush. Shame on you." Despite some booing, Moore told us at the Governor's Ball that he found the audience reaction "wonderful."

Elsewhere at the party, agent Ed Limato ran into Richard Johnson. Riled by Page Six's prediction that his Oscar bash would bomb, "Ed the Angry," as Richard always dubbed him, threw a vodka martini in Richard's face, calling him a "lowdown motherfucker." Limato asked Richard if he wanted to fight back. The younger and brawnier Richard declined. "I'm too well-mannered," he told us later. (Richard did not hesitate to run at least nine nasty Limato items in the ensuing weeks.)

As the death toll in Iraq mounted, Hollywood liberals became more vocal again. A year after Brad Pitt told me that America had to "get the job done," we spoke at the premiere party for Pitt's sword-and-sandal epic, *Troy*. Pitt agreed that Bush's search for weapons of mass destruction had turned out to be a Trojan horse.

"There was a line in *The Iliad* that sticks in my mind," said Pitt, "where Achilles asks, 'What are we doing here, afflicting the Trojans and afflicting their land?'"

Others were more blunt. In July 2004, we covered a fundraiser for John Kerry and John Edwards at Radio City. Chevy Chase called President Bush "dumb as an egg timer." John Mellencamp branded him "just another cheap thug." Whoopi Goldberg riffed on how she liked "bush" but not "Bush." The Republicans used the comments to tar Kerry. His campaign especially disavowed Whoopi's shtick and advised her to stay away from the Democratic National Convention.

Democratic celebs saw that mouthing off could hurt their candidate, that middle Americans distrusted "Hollywood values." So, once again, they began minding their tongues.

Though he later excoriated Bush-think in his song, "Sweet Neo Con," Mick Jagger wouldn't weigh in on the 2004 race. "I'm from the school that considers it impolite to comment on other people's elections," the British rocker told us at Tao one night.

James Gandolfini believed we should either pull out of Iraq or bring back the draft. "We should shit or get off the pot," the *Sopranos* capo told us at the premiere of *Alive Day Memories*, his heart-twisting documentary about vets who'd been physically and mentally maimed in

Iraq. So did Gandolfini think Bush's troop surge was working? "I'm not going there," he said, putting a finger to his lips.

At a small screening of his western, *Open Range*, Kevin Costner admitted being bothered by Dubya's squinty-eyed, Dead-or-Alive posturing.

"We're supposed to evolve from frontier justice," he told us. "[The Old West mythology] is a good thing to have in your spine. But it shouldn't operate your brain." Costner was obviously keeping a few bullets in his revolver. He mentioned that he'd voted for another candidate, not Bush, in 2000. He asked us to leave that part out. He explained that he'd played golf with the first President Bush and been to the Bush house in Kennebunkport.

"I don't want to turn my back on that family," he said. "They've been gracious to me."

We granted him a retroactive off-the-record at the time. We understood his dilemma. Bill O'Reilly may have called us "bad people." A right-wing blog may have branded us the "loyal lapdogs" of MoveOn.org, the liberal advocacy group. But we actually did have Republican friends. We had riotous arguments over drinks with law-and-order cops and private eyes. We had a great rapport with Representative Peter King, head of the House Homeland Security Committee, and with former senator Alfonse D'Amato, who seemed to revel in our reports on his love life. Lifelong Republican John Hendrickson called Joanna a "granola cruncher" when she pleaded with Hendrickson and his wife, social empress Marylou Whitney, not to allow development on their vast Adirondack spread. After they nobly sold nearly fifteen thousand acres to the state for public use, we shared a few juleps with them at the Kentucky Derby. (We also came to see that Hendrickson was right to fear an invasion of fishermen who nearly decimated the Little Tupper Lake brook trout.)

A gossip columnist had to be able to infiltrate different circles. If a liberal wanted to find out what conservatives were up to, you had to wade in among them, "dress in mufti," as my friend, Watergate burglar G. Gordon Liddy, used to say. But we, too, sometimes found it hard to hold our tongues. Henry Kissinger returned our calls because we had a mutual friend. But then came the Four Seasons party for Kissinger's book, *Crisis*, based on recorded White House conversations. I apparently asked the former secretary of state too many pointed questions about alleged war crimes and whether he'd pruned the White House transcripts to make himself look more sympathetic. Soon after, Dr. K took our mutual friend aside to ask, "Are we sure Rush is on our team?"

19

In Bed With the Flesh Peddlers

The last scraps of New York's old newspaper world were blowing away. Back when the *Daily News* was in the Daily News Building, we used to go to the international newsstand in what was then the Pan Am Building to pick up copies of the British papers flown over the night before. Later, the fax machine allowed a London stringer to send us copies of the columns there—the *Mail*'s "Baz Bamigboye," the *Mirror*'s "3 a.m. Girls," the *Sun*'s "Bizarre"—the same day they ran. But now we could find them instantly on the Internet—usually with items the Brits had nicked from us. We hadn't thought much of it when Matt Drudge had offered to "link" to our column from his Drudge Report. Little did we know the fedora-lidded aggregator would help bring Rush & Molloy a huge new audience. We'd considered it an achievement when Tribune Media started syndicating our column. But syndication was becoming superfluous; readers could get the column faster online and for free.

Initially, the *Daily News*'s website was a half-hearted affair. You could find some of the stories from the paper. But the *News* resisted giving away its news. Any important story was saved for the next day's print run. The *Post* did the same. To find out what the competition had, the *News's* editors still had to send a copy kid down to South Street to buy the first edition of the *Post* from a driver. Our runner would sometimes cross paths with a *Post* copy kid dispatched for a copy of the *News*. If the *Post* had a scoop, an editor would call and ask us to "match it"—ideally, within the next half hour in the middle of the night.

We learned that holding stories for print could cost us. One time, we had some good intelligence that Cynthia Nixon, who played Miranda on *Sex and the City*, was seeing another woman. As before, we tried not to yank people out of the closet. But we did sometimes give clues. We once ran a photo of 'N Sync's Lance Bass with Jamie-Lynn Sigler and Shannon Elizabeth as they picked out free stuff at a hospitality suite. Bass's then-secret partner, Reichen Lehmkuhl, was with them. In the caption, Joanna mischievously wrote: "What Rhymes with Swag Bags?" It was naughty, but it got a lot of pick-up. One blogger wrote: "I thought that was really wrong of [Rush & Molloy]. But hilarious." A few weeks later, Bass came out. We let one Oscar winner continue to wear his fig leaf, even after a handsome straight friend told us the actor had once put his hand on his thigh at Joe's Pub. Our friend said to the star: "I thought you told [a men's magazine] you weren't gay?" The smirking actor said, "They always ask the wrong question. I'm *not* gay. I just like having sex with men."

In the case of Cynthia Nixon, we called her publicist to see if she'd confirm her relationship with education activist Christine Marinoni. To our surprise, Nixon's publicist, Carrie Ross, said she was ready to declare her love, but asked if we'd hold the story for a day so her client wouldn't face a barrage of coming-out questions during a previously scheduled press conference the next day. We agreed. While we waited for the presses to roll, Gawker.com, a new website that reveled in media gossip, posted an item asking, "Wouldn't it be funny if *Sex and the City* alum Cynthia Nixon, like, came out as a lesbian . . . in the next twenty-four hours??!" The *Post* immediately jumped on the story, meaning we had to run it for the next day, meaning that Nixon was confronted with more reporters than ever at her press conference.

This was also the dawn of Internet radio. Bob Meyrowitz, who created the King Biscuit Flower Hour and cofounded Ultimate Fighting Championship, hired us to host a daily two-hour Rush & Molloy talk show on eYada.com, a streaming radio network that predated Sirius and XM. Besides gossiping, we interviewed Mel Brooks, Heath Ledger, LL Cool J, Michael Caine, and many others. Our producer, Tim Reid, was a pop culture sponge we continuously squeezed for questions to ask. Unfortunately, at the time, most computer owners had dial-up connections and *one* phone line. The noble experiment expired with the burst of the Internet bubble.

Once we only had the *Post* to compete with. Now we had to battle everyone on the Internet: not only the ruthless, source-paying Brits and supermarket tabs, but also a metastasizing number of dot-coms. Harvey Levin, an attorney and veteran TV legal reporter, had the smart idea of creating a website, TMZ.com, that aggressively tracked celebrity lawsuits, arrests, and divorce filings in Los Angeles's byzantine maze of courts and police departments. Whereas our West Coast stringers once stood a chance of finding something exclusive, TMZ now seemed to have the court clerks and cops there locked up. TMZ reported Mel Gibson's anti-Semitic tirade within minutes of his 2006 DUI arrest. Levin admitted that TMZ did "sometimes pay sources for leads on stories," a practice forbidden at the *News*.

Niche gossip sites sprang up on the web—specializing in rumors from the worlds of art, fashion, finance, tech, whatever. And, just as the Scoville scale grades the amount of capsaicin in peppers, the measure of what was "hot" gossip kept rising—driven up by bloggers who wrote whatever they wanted, usually in their pajamas. You often couldn't find out whom these bloggers were. In one case, we tracked down a twenty-eight-year-old Dayton man, Tim Hughes, who'd built a site titled "Walter Cronkite Spit in My Food!" Hughes alleged that he and his wife had met a crotchety, drunken Cronkite at a Disney World restaurant where the former CBS anchor insulted his former colleagues, bragged about bedding one of their wives, and hurled a loogie into Hughes's dessert. The site cautioned that "actual events may differ substantially from those depicted here."

But when we brought the site to the attention of "the most trusted man in America," he was furious.

"I want to file a libel suit," the eighty-year-old news legend told us. "It's a major abuse of this wonderful new medium. I'm not doing this for myself alone. This is a serious infringement on personal liberties. I don't expect to win any damages. But I'm going after this guy. If I have to go to the Supreme Court, I will."

Hughes, who considered himself a satirist, told us he'd created the site because "tearing down someone everyone loves is very appealing to me." But he soon tore down his site.

Cronkite had no idea what personal liberty infringements awaited us on the World Wide Web.

Blogger Mario Lavandeira, a frustrated actor who called himself "Perez Hilton," repeated unchecked rumors he heard about successful entertainers. He claimed Michael Jackson's fatal cardiac arrest was a publicity stunt and pronounced Fidel Castro dead when he was alive. Lavandeira posted photos without paying—claiming it was "fair use" because he'd creatively altered the photos. His creativity amounted to drawing white drops around the lips of actors he decided were gay. And yet Lavandeira admitted wanting to hang out with celebs and wanting to be a celebrity. He'd write us long whimpering emails when we made fun of him.

The Parisian car chase that killed Princess Diana in 1997 had made us see the dark side of the madcap pursuits of our paparazzi pals. Hearing of the tragedy, we remembered the line we'd used the year before in describing Di's arrival at the Costume Institute Ball: "Most people gawked as if she were a traffic accident." Times were changing. New York paparazzi actually knew something about photography. But cheap, point-and-shoot cameras, combined with the money paid by TMZ and X17online.com, lured more and more punks into the game. Veteran photogs told us some of the stalkerazzi in L.A. were Crips and Bloods who thought nothing of provoking celebs. Scarier than the gangbangers, according to the old paps, were lead-footed, club-hopping starlets. One photographer sued Lindsay Lohan for injuries *he* suffered in a car accident. A photo agency head told us it was now "too dangerous" to follow one singer: "I tell my guys now, 'don't speed, don't chase, and stay away from Britney Spears!'"

Among the celebrities spawned by the Internet was Paris Hilton. During the Great Depression, the average working-class *Daily News* readers—sometimes called "Sweeney and Mrs. Sweeney" by the editors—followed the antics of Park Avenue swells in the same way that they escaped from reality through movie comedies like *Poor Little Rich Girl* and *My Man Godfrey*. As the years passed, Mr. Sweeney, and our new readers, Mr. Sanchez and Mr. Singh, lost interest in socialites. But Paris Hilton was a kind of throwback to those days. It gratified working men to see a privileged nitwit get into so much trouble. What gratified them even more was seeing her having sex on a homemade tape you could pay to watch on Sexbrat.com. Who knew socialites did that?

The hotel heiress's representatives initially denied the tape's existence. Then they tried to block its distribution, claiming that her ex-boyfriend, Rick Salomon, took advantage of an incapacitated, naive girl when he shot it. But when Salomon slapped her with a $10 million defamation lawsuit, she leaned back and began to enjoy the profits from the DVD *One Night in Paris*. Hilton not only survived the tape scandal, she capitalized on it to win appearance fees, TV and movie roles, and her own fashion and fragrance lines.

Sex tapes and nude photos allowed thousands of people to pull up chairs around a celebrity's bed. Pam Anderson and Tommy Lee, whose wedding we'd revealed, made one on their honeymoon, becoming pioneers of the genre. The foremost broker of these graven images was David Hans Schmidt. Schmidt had negotiated *Playboy* and *Penthouse* pictorials of Clinton accuser Paula Jones; Olympic skating bad girl Tonya Harding; and Hugh Grant's pleasure-giver, Divine Brown, among others. His latest score, we heard in September 2003, was a trove of twenty-seven nude photos of Amber Frey, the former mistress of wife-killer Scott Peterson. Looking to confirm the story, I tracked down Schmidt at a Nevada whorehouse. Mustachioed, fast-talking, and muscular, the former paratrooper said, yes, he did have the Amber pictures. He also crowed about the fantastic sex he'd just had.

Two months later, we again heard from Schmidt, who lived in Phoenix. He now had saucy barracks pictures of Private Jessica Lynch, the twenty-year-old soldier recently taken hostage in Iraq. Schmidt had Larry Flynt interested in publishing them in *Hustler*. But the porn baron admitted to us that his wife, Elizabeth, had told him, "America is going to hate you for this!" Patriotically, Flynt had decided to buy the shots "to take them out of circulation." The *Daily News*'s front page story—headlined AMBUSHED TWICE—spanked Schmidt for trying to embarrass the war hero. But Schmidt loved the publicity. And so he kept coming back to Rush & Molloy with more celebrity skin exclusives.

He brought us photos that showed Jamie Foxx having sex with a woman—and, um, himself. A construction worker told us he'd "found" the photos in a dumpster next to Foxx's Vegas home. The construction worker said that, later, several goons had beaten him up in an effort to recover the photos. Foxx's reps denied that he had anything to do with the attack. Schmidt ultimately returned the photos to Foxx, who professed that he thought they were "nice." Perhaps because they proved he was indeed one of Hollywood's biggest stars.

Schmidt offered Colin Farrell and ex-girlfriend Nicole Narain the chance to share in the booty from their videotaped booty call—just as Hilton and Salomon had done. Schmidt pointed out that rocker Fred Durst had stalled on giving him approval to sell his sex tape, which "got on the Internet anyway." Narain, a former Playmate, was game. But Farrell hired legal bruiser Marty Singer—ironically, the same attorney who'd helped Salomon bring *One Night in Paris* to market. Singer filed suit to crush Schmidt's deal. I asked Singer if Farrell might still agree to release of an authorized version. "Absolutely not!" he said.

But others would. The world had largely forgotten Dustin Diamond, who played nerdy Screech on the sitcom *Saved by the Bell*. But when Schmidt told us that he'd obtained a forty-minute tape of Diamond romping with two women, nostalgic voyeurs started shelling out for a peek. Diamond claimed he was shocked—shocked!—that the tape had found its way to the Internet, and he began bad-mouthing Schmidt in TV interviews. Offended, Schmidt said he was tired of Diamond's "charade" and told us, "Dustin was in on this deal from the start." Schmidt showed us what he vouched was Diamond's signature on a contract. Schmidt suspected Diamond of being doubly deceptive. "I have reason to believe that is not Dustin's [manhood] in the movie," he said. "If, in fact, he used a body double, I'm going to sue him for defrauding me and the American public." When Schmidt challenged Diamond to prove he didn't use a stunt organ, Diamond stopped his complaining.

We suspected more skullduggery when Schmidt began hawking what he purported was a tape of O. J. Simpson getting it on with two women. Simpson's lawyer, Yale Galanter, told us that though his client did appear fully clothed in portions of the tape, the man having sex "is an imposter."

Five years earlier, Galanter had acknowledged to us that Simpson had accompanied then-girlfriend Christie Prody and former pinup model Patty Kuprys to a Florida hotel for a "nightcap." *Globe* magazine reported at the time that Simpson was in on a sex-tape scheme—that he knew a porn director had outfitted the room with hidden cameras. The supermarket tab also alleged Simpson was due to get one-third of the film's profits—deposited in an offshore bank account so he wouldn't have to give his cut to the families of his alleged murder victims.

Galanter told us it was the *Globe* that had set up the videotaped honey trap, that his client "never undressed," and that he "high-tailed it out of the room" after noticing a tiny camera.

"This tape is garbage," said Galanter.

Schmidt told us: "O. J. is welcome to say that's not him on the tape, just like he said he didn't murder Nicole Simpson and Ron Goldman."

Schmidt called us every week—sometimes every day—with another deal he was cooking up. Once, he claimed he'd discovered "a King Tut's tomb of scandal" when one of his clients bought the contents of Paris Hilton's storage locker after she neglected to pay the warehouse bill. Schmidt said he had photos and videotapes, "sex toys," lingerie, and eighteen diaries in which the heiress supposedly divulged her sexual adventures. As usual, the P. T. Barnum of smut was aiming high. He got nowhere near the $10 million he was looking for.

In 2007, Schmidt flew to Berlin, where some shadowy Germans claimed they represented a "foreign head of state," whose intelligence service believed Saddam Hussein was alive and well. Schmidt promptly began peddling "forensic evidence" that one of Saddam's body doubles had been hung the previous year in Iraq and that the real Saddam was living in a foreign country under an assumed name. Schmidt said he even had Saddam's "new home address." We ran the conspiracy theory past the Pentagon and several Middle East experts, all of whom called it preposterous. To our knowledge, Schmidt never closed a deal. But the story got global pick-up.

Detestable as he could be, Schmidt grew on me. The tireless huckster gloried in being called "the Sultan of Sleaze," once donning a bath-towel turban for a TV appearance. We had a symbiosis. He was what we called "a heavy lift"—a source that required constant attention. He was bipolar. One minute, he'd be trying to bully me; the next, he'd be in tears. His income swung like his moods. But in the summer of 2007, he was jazzed about his latest score: hundreds of stolen photos from the wedding of Tom Cruise and Katie Holmes. There was nothing scandalous about the photos, but they'd never been published. Following his usual MO, Schmidt first offered to sell them to the couple, promising he wouldn't shop them around if they paid him $1.3 million. One of their handlers said they'd be willing to negotiate. Schmidt flew to L.A. for a meeting. As soon as he presented his terms, FBI agents burst through a door and arrested him.

He pleaded guilty to extortion. The feds put an ankle monitor on him while he awaited his hearing. He was getting more and more depressed. He faced up to two years behind bars. He'd once served a few months for violating a restraining order that his ex-wife had taken out. He told me, "I can't go back to prison. I can't."

He was phoning me every other day. One Saturday, I got a call from him. He said, "I did something really stupid. I put a belt around my neck in the shower. Fortunately, it didn't work."

I told him he had to get some new medication. I tried to tell him how much he had to look forward to. I said he could use his jail time to write his memoir.

I took it upon myself to call Tom Cruise's lawyer, Bert Fields. I asked Bert if Tom might show Schmidt some mercy. Schmidt had cooperated; he'd led the FBI to the data recovery expert who'd downloaded the photos from a wedding photographer's computer. The world had seen that nobody shakes down Tom Cruise. I asked Bert if Tom would be willing to recommend to the sentencing judge that Schmidt get probation.

Bert said, "Sorry, George, it's out of my hands. It's up to the prosecutors now." He said that neither he nor Tom wanted to see Schmidt kill himself. What's more, Bert said, Schmidt might be crying wolf—"he likes to be dramatic."

A few days later, *Phoenix* magazine ran a profile of Schmidt in which his estranged father, a Minnesota farmer, was quoted as saying he didn't love David. His father said, "The farther away I can get, the better off I am."

I got a voice message from Schmidt. He said, "I'm trying to stay positive. But time's running out. The sand is trickling through the hourglass."

The next day, police found him hanging in his shower. This time he'd succeeded. He was forty-seven.

I called Bert again. He picked up and said, "You were right, George. Perhaps the scathing article pushed him over the edge. I've told Tom what happened. In any event, it's very sad."

Schmidt's suicide didn't end our dealings with the skin trade.

Among our acquaintances was Dimitra Ekmektsis, a high-priced escort whose clients included Aaron Sorkin, Oscar-winning writer of *A Few Good Men, Moneyball,* and *The Social Network.* She felt a little burned by him. It wasn't that he didn't pay her enough. (In fact, she said, she'd fallen in love with him and turned off her meter.) It was that he based his call-girl character on *The West Wing* on her. "He asked me to tell him in minute-per-minute detail about my life as a call girl," she told us. "Who knew then he was gathering information?"

We ourselves gathered some information the week that Eddie Murphy gave a late-night lift to a transsexual Samoan prostitute, Atisone Seiuli, known as Shalomar. Stopped by L.A. police, Murphy claimed he'd offered Shalomar a ride as an act of kindness. But some were skeptical. Since Murphy had spent time in New York, we decided to see if we could find any drag queens who'd also met the *Beverly Hills Cop* star. Our friend, club promoter Chip Duckett, gave us a tour of Manhattan's transgender subculture. All though the night, we hopped from one drag club to another. Arriving at "Trannie Chaser" night at Nowbar, we found a large sign at the curb that read: "This Space Reserved for Eddie Murphy." Inside, the club was plastered with posters of the actor. Had any of the sashaying, six-foot divas in size 12 high heels ever met Eddie Murphy? We couldn't find one who hadn't—or so they claimed. It was hard to get any of them to break out of character long enough to admit her/his real name was not Cassandra Chardonnay, so we gave up any hope of verifying their fantastic tales. And given that Murphy's lawyer was the ferocious Marty Singer, we called it a night. The club-crawl did produce one accidental celebrity sighting: a once-cherubic, now-obese former child star with someone's face buried in his lap. We wished we hadn't seen that.

Jason Itzler, the self-proclaimed "King of All Pimps," would call from jail to tell us how Jeremy Piven was going to play him in a movie. Itzler was such an incorrigible self-promoter that it was hard to believe much of what he said. But we worried when a friend of his claimed on Facebook that Itzler had killed himself in Miami. His Wikipedia entry also reported him dead. Police eventually found him alive in his apartment, but he was in such a delirious state that they committed him for twenty-four-hour psychiatric observation. Itzler later told us his friend made up the suicide claim because he thought an angry club owner wanted to kill Itzler. In any case, Itzler loved the dozens of concerned calls and emails he received. "I went to heaven," he told us, "but I didn't know anybody there!"

Another sex education counselor was Paul Barresi, a master double agent in the war between celebrities and the tabloids. Barresi started out as a star and director of porn films. In 1990, the *National Enquirer* reportedly paid Barresi $100,000 for a story in which he claimed he'd had a two-year love affair with John Travolta. Barresi later recanted his story, attesting in writing to Travolta's attorney that he'd never engaged in homosexual activity with the actor. Barresi worked both sides of the scandal fence. He supplied gossip, but he also became an unlikely investigator for the lawyers of some major stars. Tom Cruise's lawyer, Bert Fields, confirmed to us that Barresi had helped him head off a fabricated claim by a porn actor—known as "Big Red"—that he'd been intimate with Cruise. Barresi also revealed to us how nefarious private eye Anthony Pellicano hired him to find dirt on celebrities, who were sometimes Pellicano's own clients. Pellicano would then ask his client for $25,000 or more to put out the fire he himself had started. "Anthony would prey upon the doubts of his clients," Barresi told us. "He'd make them feel insecure so they'd need him to solve their problem."

Dennis Hof, owner of the Moonlite Bunny Ranch, a legal brothel near Carson City, Nevada, was also an invaluable source of salaciousness. Hof was a huckster as good as or better than his late friend Schmidt. The star of HBO's *Cathouse* reality series, he offered free sex to returning GIs and presented a "Trainee" bathrobe to Diane Sawyer.

Even we were shocked when he called us one night to announce that he and Howard Stern planned to auction a young woman's virginity. "I don't have a moral dilemma with it," the twenty-two-year-old beauty in question told us. "We live in a capitalist society. Why shouldn't I be allowed to capitalize on my virginity?"

Hof usually relied on his employees to satisfy his carnal desire. His only deviation was when Hollywood Madam Heidi Fleiss, came to visit Carson City with an eye toward opening a high-end "sex resort." Hof graciously showed her around and, against all odds, the king and queen of American prostitution found something like love.

"We're banging every day," Hof told us. "This is so out of character for both of us. But Heidi has so much drive, she reminds me of myself."

"Dennis is romantically involved with every girl around him," said Fleiss, who'd recently escaped a brutal co-dependency with actor Tom Sizemore. "I'm always single."

Within a month, they were both sick of each other. Serving as a relationship counselor, we listened as Hof complained about Fleiss's ongoing drug use and she griped about his policy of bed-testing his would-be employees.

"I love Heidi," said Hof. "But we're like two tornadoes coming up against each other. She's a real handful."

"I *am* a handful," she said. "He should be able to handle me. If he can't, he's not a very good pimp."

Dennis returned to dating younger women. The next time I saw him in New York, I invited him to lunch at Michael's, the swank midtown media fishbowl. He arrived with Becca Brat, a halter-harnessed porn actress who'd just completed a Larry Flynt production that required her to have sex at various national landmarks, including the Alamo, Dallas's grassy knoll, and Oral Roberts University.

Heads turned as Hof swaggered through the restaurant introducing himself as "Dennis Hof—I put the 'ho' in HBO."

"I just saw one of my customers," Hof whispered to me. "He looked like he was about to die."

Hof was nothing if not generous. On another trip to New York, he invited me to join him for a steak at Smith and Wollensky. I had to send my regrets.

"Too bad you didn't come," Hof said, revealing that he'd brought me a "little present"—one of his curvaceous ranch hands. "I thought I'd give you one on the house."

20

Old Grudges and Fresh Feuds

The *New York Observer* may have called Rush & Molloy the "fairest" gossip column, but plenty of people would put up an argument.

My very first interview with a famous person—as a freshman in college—was with William F. Buckley, the father of modern conservatism. Even if you didn't agree with his politics, you had to love his erudition and wit. Later, I became a fan of his son, Christopher Buckley, the brilliant author of *Thank You for Smoking*. I interviewed Chris about several of his hilarious novels. But then we found out he'd fathered an out-of-wedlock child. Chris wanted to seal the court papers. The mother's lawyer said, "It's the height of hypocrisy that Christopher Buckley, who makes his living from his political satire—humiliating people—now seeks to be protected." Two years later, we reported that "friends were saddened" to hear Chris and his wife, Lucy, had separated. When Bill Buckley died, I called Chris to express my condolences and ask if he wanted to comment on a scathing epitaph that Bill's old foe, Gore Vidal, had written. Chris hung up as soon as he heard my voice.

I felt less bad about offending Taki Theodoracopulos, a Greek shipping heir who made Bill Buckley look like Che Guevara. Back when

I was working at *Esquire*, I helped Taki research some columns for the magazine. We met at his townhouse. He seemed like a charming rogue. But when I got to the *Daily News*, I came across a column he'd written for Britain's *Spectator* about New York's Puerto Rican Day Parade. Taki called the parade's participants "dirty," "ugly," and "semi-savages." I reported his remarks. Outrage ensued. Geraldo Rivera called him a "snot-nosed, trust-fund suckling." Mayor Giuliani denounced Taki's hate speech. Taki insisted he was just making a "joke"—that people took things "too seriously." A decade passed. Our mutual friend Chuck Pfeiffer, a dashing Green Beret-turned-movie-producer, invited me to a Christmas brunch. When Taki found out I was coming, Chuck had someone call me to say, "Chuck is sorry but he has to disinvite you. Taki won't come if you're there."

We also proved nettlesome to Madonna. Once, her publisher threw a party for her porn book, *Sex*. The party was going to be at an industrial warehouse. Word was that it was going to be wild—like an orgy. No photography would be allowed. One of our TV producer friends heard we'd been invited. He suggested we sneak a video camera in. This was before cell phone cameras. I figured, "Why not?" So I tucked a little camera under my raincoat. Inside the party, Madonna had freaky, pierced performers in leather engaging in all sorts of bondage and domination. Whenever I stumbled upon some kinkiness, I'd open my raincoat and film a little of it. I was sort of a flasher/voyeur. The next day, I brought my footage in to *A Current Affair*. They loved it. But a rival tabloid show producer snitched to Madonna's spokeswoman, Liz Rosenberg, that Rush & Molloy smuggled a camera into the party.

For some reason, Liz blamed Molloy. "She wouldn't talk to me for years after that—only to George!" says Joanna. "I'd met Madonna years before at a small party. She was wearing a corset covered with bangles, beads, and charms. I said, 'What a gorgeous dress!' She said, 'It's Dolce e Gabanna.' She turned, bent over, and flashed her thighs at me. 'Look,' she said, 'practically no cellulite at all!' Maybe Liz still had her eye on me because of a different incident. There had been a party under an atrium in midtown for k.d. lang. Most of the guests were lesbians. Madonna was there, sporting a butch look that included a gold tooth. At one point, I was searching for the ladies room. I peaked around some shrubbery and—hello!—stumbled on Madonna and her pal Ingrid Casares *in flagrante*. Madonna was sitting on a chair. Ingrid was standing between her spread legs, kissing her, while Madonna squeezed her ass. I guess Madonna came up for air long enough to spot me, even though I immediately scrammed. She must have told Liz I was spying on her."

Other vintage vendettas needed tending.

Bill O'Reilly was always happy to talk—or, rather, snarl. In February 2008, the right-wing carnival barker denied the existence of homeless veterans in America. In protest, a group of vets came to Fox News headquarters with a petition signed by seventeen thousand people who wanted O'Reilly to apologize. Our reporter Sean Evans went along to witness their confrontation with a camera crew O'Reilly sent outside. That day, O'Reilly admitted homeless vets "may be out there, but there's not many out there." We suggested in the column that the "sheltered" pundit "get out of his limo" more often. O'Reilly did not let this affront go unanswered.

"Now I feel sorry for those [vets]," he said on his show, deeming the protest a "foolish brouhaha." "But it is a damn shame they are being used by bad people. Like Rush and Molloy, notoriously dishonest, who printed a hatchet job about the situation today."

Sometimes we found ourselves in feuds we didn't know we were having. One night at the Tribeca Grand Hotel, we were having a pleasant chat with Javier Bardem when Julian Schnabel interrupted the conversation.

"Don't talk to these people!" Schnabel told Bardem, who'd starred in Schnabel's *Before Night Falls* as Cuban poet Reinaldo Arenas. "They're vile! They print lies and distortions!"

Bardem was confused. So were we. We asked Schnabel what he was talking about. He claimed that we'd reported that he'd broken promises to Lázaro Gómez Carriles, the Cuban artist whom Olivier Martinez had played in his film. Schnabel said he couldn't have been more generous to the guy, and that we hadn't called him. He went on and on. Neither Joanna nor I could remember writing the story. But Javier Bardem was staring at us like we were the scum of the earth. So, taking Schnabel at his word, we apologized. Finally, he calmed down and we all ended up laughing. The next day, I went online and found that the *New York Observer* and Page Six had written stories about

Carriles. Not us. But by then, Joanna had bought Schnabel a $100 bottle of wine—as a peace offering—and left it with a note at Julian's studio. I called his assistant and let him know we were innocent. Julian kept the wine anyway.

The ancient grudges weren't as stressful as the sudden falling-outs. An incendiary story could instantly set a sturdy relationship ablaze.

Our bonhomie with Mariah Carey took a turn for the worse when we reported that she'd accepted $1 million to perform at a New Year's Eve party thrown by Moammar Khadafy's son Moatassem-Billah. Taking the Libyan dictator's money apparently wasn't something she wanted to advertise.

Publicist Lizzie Grubman, whose attorney dad represented the biggest stars in the music business, had always been a pleasure to gossip with. But when she backed her Mercedes SUV into sixteen Hamptons club goers (allegedly shouting, "Fuck you, white trash!"), all bets were off. It was a class warfare drama we couldn't ignore.

Likewise, we'd been friends with Lee Daniels, the Oscar-nominated director of *Precious*. When we heard he might direct a biopic about Dr. Martin Luther King, we got our hands on the script. Then we dutifully called Dr. King's family to see what they thought of a scene depicting one of his extramarital trysts. "Why did you have to tell them about that?" said Lee, who vowed to cut the sex scene.

I always liked talking with Police Commissioner Ray Kelly. We often talked about Haiti, which I'd visited with Wyclef, and where he'd served as director of the multinational police force in 1994. One night, at the end of a party, I was chatting with Kelly about my friend Ed Conlon, a Bronx narcotics detective whose memoir, *Blue Blood*, became a movie. Kelly said that Ed was being posted to Jordan as a member of the NYPD's elite intelligence unit that monitored terrorist hotbeds. The conversation was on the record. When we ran an item, Ed's boss, former CIA operative David Cohen, came down on Ed, demanding to know if he'd planted the story. We let Cohen know that, no, our source was *his* boss, the commissioner. From then on, Kelly kept us at arm's length.

Meanwhile, Joanna developed a rapport with New York's mafia nobility. In elementary school, she became friends with Joanne

Petri-zzo, a Michelle Pfeiffer lookalike whose father, Thomas, was a brilliant builder who shaped the steel for Battery Park City and numerous buildings on the city's skyline. Joanne always said, "My father is a businessman." The federal government said he was a capo in the Colombo family. Joanne grew up to marry Michael Persico, a son of Colombo godfather Carmine (Junior) Persico. She was madly in love with him, and he had their names entwined in stained-glass on a canopy above their bed. They had two children. In the 1990s, with Carmine Persico and his older son Alphonse (Allie Boy) in prison, Vic Orena tried to take over, and war broke out within the family. Joanne's father and father-in-law were on opposite sides. It tore her marriage apart and she was heartbroken.

Joanna wanted to write about Joanne's experience as a woman inside the fractured family. Joanne didn't seem to know anything about the business. But just the prospect of her speaking to a reporter prompted a visit to the *News* by two Colombo emissaries. They wanted to know what Joanna wanted to know. The muscular gentlemen were pleasant enough. But no sooner had the reverse interview begun than one of them yelled, "Hey! Is that Capeci?!" The other man jumped up. The duo squinted across the newsroom at Jerry Capeci, our fearless "Gang Land" columnist, one of the country's top authorities on organized crime. One man barked, "I'm gonna go over there and fucking flip his desk over on him!" Joanna begged him not to, saying that could get her fired. They sat back down and continued their interrogation in a distracted way. That night, Joanne called Joanna to say now might not be the best time for the story.

Later, Joanna brought Joanne to a season premiere of *The Sopranos* at Radio City Music Hall. As she watched Carmella Soprano trying to understand her husband Tony, Joanne whispered, "This is my life!" At the party afterward, bodyguards blocked fans trying to get near star James Gandolfini, who was with his father. Gandolfini gave the nod for Joanne, who was dressed to the nines, to pass the velvet rope. "I just want you to know that your portrayal is 100 percent realistic," she said. "Thank you," said Gandolfini as he signed autographs for her children. She didn't give her name. But he knew.

Joanna met Gambino boss John Gotti's daughter, Victoria, at a book party at Le Cirque. Her literary agent, Frank Weimann, had sold Victoria's novel, *The Senator's Daughter*, on the strength of her realistic portrayal of an Italian union boss's murder. At the party, Joanna said, "I grew up with Joanne Petrizzo. Do you know her?" Victoria replied, "Yeah, she's a great girl." They exchanged numbers.

Victoria called Joanna a few days later. They chit-chatted for a while before Victoria came to her point. "Hey, you know that friend of yours?" she said. "What was her name, Joanne Petrizzo? I was mistaken. I don't know her at all."

Joanna found the unprompted correction a little strange. But they kept talking. Long before her reality show, *Growing Up Gotti*, Victoria would regale us with the lavish Christmas preparations she planned for her Long Island mini-mansion. "My kids say they don't believe in Santa anymore," she sighed. Not Victoria—she never lost faith in Santa, just as she never doubted (publicly) that her father was a plumbing supply salesman. (She also vouched to us that her husband, Carmine Agnello, ran a "100 percent aboveboard" scrap metal business—that is, until he wouldn't stop fooling around with his *goumada* and they divorced. Agnello was later convicted on racketeering charges.)

Joanna also talked with Victoria about her health. Victoria wrote a book, *Women and Mitral Valve Prolapse*, in which she described the heart ailment that required her to undergo four surgeries and wear a pacemaker and a defibrillator. One day in 2005 when Joanna and Victoria were talking, Victoria started to cry. She had breast cancer, she said. Please don't write about it, she said. At one point, Victoria confided that she had had a double mastectomy. As a survivor herself, Joanna respected her privacy and wished her well. Finally, Victoria said she was ready to talk about her ordeal. In a long interview, she told Joanna that she'd kept her grueling treatments, during which she lost twenty-five pounds, hidden from her sons. "[I didn't want them] to think that Mommy is dying," she said.

But Victoria apparently had forgotten that she was once a column-ist for the *New York Post*, where they don't like turncoats. It wasn't long after Joanna's exclusive that the *Post* gunned Victoria down with the front page headline: "Gotti's Sick Cancer Scam." The *Post* accused her of exaggerating her condition to promote the third season of the show.

Victoria's diagnosis was ductal carcinoma in situ (DCIS). An American Cancer Society spokesman told Joanna that "DCIS is can-cer" and that "some women need a mastectomy [or] chemotherapy" for it. Victoria maintained on *Good Morning America* that "what I have is considered by most to be cancer."

But she began to waffle, calling it "noninvasive cancer." And, in a flip worthy of her father's betrayer, Sammy (Bull) Gravano, Victoria told the *Post* that Joanna had "browbeaten" her to do the interview and even gave the *Post* personal emails Joanna had sent her.

Joanna told Victoria, "Lose my number."

We started out on decent terms with Daniel Day-Lewis. Our Irish friend, Terry George, who wrote *In the Name of the Father* and *The Boxer*, had told him we were okay. So Daniel was usually obliging at premieres where we'd try to unravel the incredible screen silk he spun as he molted from one character into another. Still, how could we overlook his private life? A friend of Isabelle Adjani, the ethereal French beauty he'd dropped while she was pregnant with his son, Gabriel, told us he hadn't sent any support—at least at first. He wasn't much sweeter to Deya Pichardo, a Dominican-born physical trainer. They'd been living together. Then she opened the paper and found out he'd eloped with writer-director Rebecca Miller, daughter of Arthur Miller.

"He must have been cheating on me," Pichardo told us. Daniel must have read the item. Soon after, Pichardo said, "He asked me, 'What are you doing talking to the media?' I said, 'How else am I supposed to know you got married? *You* sure didn't tell me.'"

We further endeared ourselves to Day-Lewis when we found out that, on the day after Arthur Miller died, Rebecca had evicted his much younger fiancée, Agnes Barley, from the playwright's Connecticut estate. Our airing of Bailey's story caused Daniel to cancel an interview with the *Daily News* respected film writer Graham Fuller.

Liam Neeson was easier to know. We'd become friendly with Michael Caton-Jones, who'd just directed Liam in *Rob Roy*, about the Scottish folk hero. One night over dinner, Joanna asked Caton-Jones about the truth of the legend: not of Rob Roy but of Liam Neeson—whether he was indeed well-endowed.

"Put it this way," the director said. "We were filming the scene where Liam doffs his kilt to bathe in a lake. It early in the morning. The water was absolutely freezing. When Liam emerged from the water, the crew fell silent for a moment." It was as if they'd just glimpsed Nessie.

"After Liam was out of earshot," Caton-Jones went on, "my cameraman said, 'Aye, that's a fine bit of rope on that lad. And not a wee bit of shrinkage on him!'"

We talked regularly with Liam about Ireland's troubles after he'd played freedom fighter Michael Collins. "On one level, the movie is depressing," he admitted, knowing too well that his northern homeland was still a war zone. "But there's a lot of spirituality in [the movie], and a lot of good." The week that the Oscar nominations came out that year, I ran into Liam and his wife, Natasha Richardson, at a party at Patroon. I told Natasha that I couldn't believe the Academy hadn't nominated him for *Michael Collins*, especially after he'd been denied the Best Actor prize for playing Oskar Schindler the year before. Natasha admitted she was angry and vented at some length, on the record. A few minutes later, she cornered me and asked if she could take back what she'd said. She feared that her spousal support would hurt Liam. I suddenly caught amnesia.

But the Academy's snub may have stung Liam. Three years later, he told me he was quitting acting. "It's not a decision I made overnight," he said over a cocktail at Il Cantinori. "I've been thinking about it for the last ten years." Even though he was about to star in George Lucas's latest Star Wars installment, *The Phantom Menace*, Liam contended that Hollywood stunted creativity. "I don't fit in anymore," he said. Natasha told me he was just having a mood. "I don't take it too seriously," she said. A year later, he was involuntarily sidelined when his motorcycle collided with a deer near their upstate farm (and our own weekend place). Liam underwent major surgery. Four months later, at a benefit for the Christopher Reeve Paralysis Foundation, Natasha told me, "I just thank God that, by a small piece of luck, Liam isn't sitting where Chris is tonight—or that he isn't dead." Liam's wit was unscathed. He declared victoriously that the deer "was sliced up into sirloin steaks."

In 2009, at a party thrown by the French consul general, he and I chatted about his habit of taking roles—*Gangs of New York, Kingdom of Heaven*—where he's killed in the first act. "Yes," he said, "but then they talk about me the rest of the movie!" He said he was about to fly to Canada to film *Chloe*, in which he promised he'd stay alive till the credits. Three weeks later, Natasha suffered a catastrophic brain injury while skiing in Canada. Two days after her fall, her family took the forty-five-year-old actress off life support as Liam and their two young sons stood at her bedside. That Sunday, Joanna and I drove upstate to cover the funeral in Millbrook, where they'd been married. We kept a respectful distance on the roadside when Liam and his children arrived. Snow began to fall as he lifted the coffin of the woman who'd always worried so much about him.

We weren't always so well behaved at funerals. At the memorial service for Atlantic Records cofounder Ahmet Ertegun, Mick Jagger, Oscar de la Renta, and other eulogists told what a rascal the music man was. (One of my first Page Six items dealt with a shapely personal trainer who complained about what lusty Ahmet considered "exercise.") So it felt fitting to inject a little mischief into our coverage. Speaking with Ahmet's socialite widow, Mica, afterward, we remarked on how open-minded she was to have invited several of his rumored mistresses. "I'm much more European than some people," Mica acknowledged, though she added, "I think a lot of [women] are dreaming that they might have been linked with him." We mentioned the name of one lady. "Please," Mica huffed, "she was a little nothing!" On a more serious note, we asked the great soul man Sam Moore about the struggle of Atlantic's early black artists to claim their rightful royalties. "I sometimes got mad at Ahmet," admitted Moore. "I once said to him, 'Give me those [hand-made] shoes! Take my money off your feet!'"

We'd met producer Brian Grazer years before, when his Imagine Entertainment partner, Ron Howard, had shot his film *The Paper* at the *Daily News*. Since then, Grazer and Howard had gone on to develop such films as *A Beautiful Mind* and *The Da Vinci Code*. But Grazer's real genius, we learned, lay in his painstakingly crafted pranks. His typical gag in Hollywood was to arrive at someone's house and to place a framed picture of himself alongside his host's family photos. His latest twist? According to several sources, the spiky-haired scamp had been leaving vials of his urine. For weeks, his spokesman kept us at bay by saying, "I can't imagine Brian doing that" or "I can't reach Brian." When we wouldn't go away, Grazer finally sent word that the story was "absolutely untrue." We ran it anyway, allowing Grazer to piss on the rumor. A few months later, he conceded to a mutual friend that . . . well . . . maybe it wasn't *absolutely* untrue.

Larry David often mined his life for material—but he didn't like us doing it. We sympathized with the *Seinfeld* co-creator when his wife, eco-activist Laurie, jettisoned him for Bart Thorpe, the hunky landscaper of their Martha's Vineyard estate.

Two years after their breakup, I saw Larry at a party in New York. I asked him if he was still going up to the Vineyard, where he'd gallantly ceded the couple's spread (known as Camp David) to Laurie.

"Yes, I'm still going up," said Larry.

Feigning off-handedness, I asked, "Is Laurie still seeing Bart?"

Suddenly, I found myself in an episode of *Curb Your Enthusiasm.*

"Can you *believe* this guy?" Larry asked loudly. Other people at the party started turning their heads. "Come on! That's out of line! Why do you think you can ask that?"

"Okay, okay," I said. "I withdraw the question. How about *you?* Are you seeing anyone?"

"Listen," said Larry. "My philosophy is to go out with anyone who will go out with me."

We loved talking with Elton John. You could always count on him unloading with both barrels—though we once got blamed when he shot himself in the foot. It was late in the night at his 2004 Oscar party in L.A. We asked if he and longtime partner David Furnish ever planned to wed. "I was on the fence about it for a while," Elton said. "I've been married before [to wife Renate Blauel]. I thought, why would I want to get married again?" But he said that right-wing measures to "defend" heterosexual marriage had helped make up his mind. "I'm totally for it," Elton told us. As soon as a parliamentary measure on civil unions became law in the United Kingdom, he said, "We're definitely going to do it. I would like to commit myself to David." For some reason, after our story was picked up everywhere in Britain, the usually resolute Rocket Man started to backpedal. His publicist claimed we'd misquoted him. Just to refresh his memory, we printed a transcript of our recorded conversation. Later, we heard that Elton had either neglected to run the idea past Furnish or, more importantly, past his financial advisers. In any case, Elton and David entered into a civil partnership the following year.

One of our favorite high-brow contretemps involved swinging political philosopher Bernard-Henri Lévy. (One critic summarized BHL's credo as "God is dead, but my hair is perfect.") We'd heard that, while in New York, the intellectual rock star had been cheating on his actress wife, Arielle Dombasle, with fashion icon and brewery heiress Daphne Guinness.

One morning, I called Levy at the Carlyle Hotel to see if he'd like to comment. A sleepy-sounding woman with an haute Irish accent answered the phone.

"Bernard's not here," she said.

"Is this Daphne?" I asked.

"Yes it is," she said cheerfully.

"Well, actually, you might be able to help me," I said. "We've heard that you and Bernard are dating now. Is that true?"

"Oh, crikey," Guinness sputtered. "This is a bit of a shock. I don't know what to say. This is awkward. George, I know we've just met, but would it be possible for you *not* to mention that you reached me here?"

"I'm afraid not, Daphne. But I'm happy to quote you any way you like."

"Well, you can say I never discuss my private life with anybody." The thrice-married Lévy never did get back to us.

A surprising number of our later tangles involved dogs.

Paper magazine once threw a lunch where guests were encouraged to bring their canine companions. Tatum O'Neal's Scottie, Lena, lunged at our dachshund, Pickle. Lena must not have liked our last item about her mommy, who'd left a snappish message on our voice mail. Pickle was also invited to a Very Important Pooch screening of *Must Love Dogs*. There was so much damn barking in the theater that you couldn't hear the movie. Pickle did get the chance to inspect the hindquarters of Bianca, a bulldog belonging to Howard Stern and his fiancée, Beth Ostrosky. Beth mentioned that, due to her peculiar anatomy, "Bianca can't reach her behind. So we have to clean it. Howard helps." Our copy editors gave the item a headline E. M. Forster would have loved: "Howard's End." Stern's fans went wild. Naturally, the King of All Media had to complain on his show. He said it wasn't Bianca's butt he cleaned, but rather her "folds." Oookay.

Then there was Martha Stewart. Her friend, Dr. Sam Waksal, hadn't billed his Fourth of July brunch as a canine event. But that didn't stop Martha from descending on his weekend home like a Valkyrie, surrounded by a trio of enormous black-tongued chow chows. None of the dogs was on a leash. One raced to the backyard, where it jumped up on Waksal's teenage nephew, Jesse, and sank its teeth into his thigh. Jesse writhed on the lawn, with two trails of blood trickling down his leg. Martha stood above the boy, her arms folded across her chest, tapping her foot, as Waksal tended to him. In a quintessential Hamptons moment, Lizzie Grubman's power-lawyer father, Allen, asked, "Is it the Lexus or the Mercedes that has the first-aid kit?" He and other guests tore off to their SUVs to find one. One wag at the party joked that, if the kid sued Stewart, her magazine might end up being renamed *Martha Stewart and Jesse's Living*.

The next day, we called Waksal to find out how Jesse was.

"The dog just jumped up on Jesse and frightened him," he claimed. "He never bit him. The dog was over affectionate."

Waksal, the founder of the ImClone biopharmaceutical company, must not have known we were *at* the party—that we'd seen the blood. Apparently, he was trying to cover for Martha—just as they tried to cover for each other when, three years later, federal prosecutors brought insider trading charges against them. Both of them went to prison, which took a bite out of their lives.

21

Reacquaintances

For a decade now, we'd been monitoring the separate heartbeats of Brad Pitt and Angelina Jolie. Having chronicled Brad's engagement and breakup with Gwyneth Paltrow, we noted in 1998 that he had his arms around *Friends* actress Jennifer Aniston at the Tibetan Freedom Concert in DC. "Maybe he was just helping her locate one of her chakras," we wrote. After the traditional courtship period where their publicists insisted they were "just friends," they got married. When the supermarket tabs bruited that something was afoot between him and costar Julia Roberts, Pitt assured us, "Jen and I couldn't be better."

Meanwhile, in the same column where we reported Pitt and Aniston's Tibetan canoodle, we asked, "Has *Girl Interrupted* star Angelina Jolie interrupted the romance between Billy Bob Thornton and Laura Dern?" Our L.A. spies had spotted Jolie bowling with Thornton, whose name was tattooed on her arm. It seemed like only yesterday that Joanna had seen Billy Bob rubbing Dern's thigh under the table where he sat with his fourth wife, Pietra. But soon he had a fifth wife, Jolie, who wore a vial of his blood around her neck.

Jolie and Thornton's marriage developed anemia after three years. Then she was cast opposite Pitt in *Mr. and Mrs. Smith*. They played married assassins. It wasn't long before rumors spread that Pitt's real wife, Aniston, had been a victim of this casting. At the premiere of his Homeric epic *Troy*, Brad and Jen did their best to vanquish rumors that their four-year marriage was already a piece of antiquity. They kissed and held hands on the red carpet.

There was a party after the *Troy* screening at Cipriani 42nd Street. It was loud and chaotic, but I managed to sit down with Brad on a couch in a corner. Jennifer was sitting a few feet away, but I asked him about the rumors regarding him and "Mrs. Smith."

"I read that you and Angelina ended up sharing a cold," I said.

"Everybody on the set was sick," said Brad. "The place was like a petri dish."

I asked about that quote he'd given *Vanity Fair*, where he'd wondered if "it really is in our nature to be with someone for the rest of our lives"?

"I was just trying to say, 'Let's see where this [relationship] goes,'" he said. "It's not like it's set in stone, that it has to be the perfect marriage. I was saying, 'Don't put all those expectations on it. Keep growing.'"

Three months later, reporters interviewing the stars of *Mr. and Mrs. Smith* had to sign his-and-her agreements, promising not to ask Pitt and Jolie personal questions. Five months after that, Pitt and Aniston announced their separation. Free to declare their love and adopt as many refugee children as they desired, Jolie and Pitt became Hollywood's Juno and Jupiter. Newsstand sales of the proliferating celebrity weeklies rose and fell based on whatever melodrama the mags could concoct about "Brangelina."

When they stepped out of their SUV at the premiere of her film *The Good Shepherd*, they detonated a blinding explosion of flash. I could see that a few other people wanted to talk with the couple. So I decided to place my bet on one playful question. Considering that Jolie portrayed a CIA wife whose son wanted to follow in his father's footsteps, would Pitt and Jolie mind if one of their own children joined the agency? Jolie had been lovely when I interviewed her in the past, but when I posed the question about her kids becoming spies, she was brusque.

"It's not going to happen," she said as she dashed down the theater's stairs.

I wasn't sure whether she was talking about the kids' spy careers or our interview.

We did our best to make stone soup the next day by writing the *Good Shepherd* story in the form of a "confidential memo" to CIA Director Michael V. Hayden. It began: "Re: Possible Recruitment of Brangelina Children . . . Son Maddox, now five, is a former Cambodian national skilled in handling all-terrain vehicles (based on analysis of recent [paparazzi] photos). His sisters, Zahara (eleven months old; born in Ethiopia) and Shiloh (six months; born in Namibia), come with perfect pretexts for future sub-Saharan missions." We reported that "Pitt seemed reluctant to discuss the matter in the public setting [but] acknowledged Langley's post-9/11 trend toward openness: 'I think [the agency is] redefining itself. It's hard to say how good [today's agents] are. If they're doing their jobs right, we never find out.'"

We'd had no falling out with Brad and Angelina. They'd just grown into superstars and we had to let them go—like parents sending kids off to college. Happily, there were a lot of celebs that kept moving back into the house.

After several years of not hearing from her, we reconnected with a more sober Courtney Love. We ran into her at an event where Venezuelan president Hugo Chavez talked with Oliver Stone. Courtney sensed that the leader really had his eye on her. "It was the third wink that sold me," she told us. "He's a sexy dawg. He invited me to visit his country and I'd like to go. I'll rock Caracas!" Our cell phones filled up with her texts. Her real romantic beam wasn't on Chavez but our old friend, hotelier André Balazs. André had been very tolerant of Courtney's late night hijinks at his hotels, The Mercer and the Chateau Marmont. And since he was between girlfriends Uma Thurman and Chelsea Handler, Courtney saw an opening. For a couple weeks, rarely a day passed when she didn't call to strategize about how to land the handsome and cultured "Mr. B." We got the sense that the affair was mostly in Courtney's mind. But her mind was still a fun place to hang out, at least for short visits. She brought us up to speed on her battles—financial and physical—with her beloved daughter, Frances Bean, then seventeen, who'd been placed in the custody of relatives. Courtney wished Frances was more stable but quickly added, "Look who her parents are! We were a little lax." She also was still claiming that her former employees had stolen millions from her. But, now, she had some heavyweight lawyers on her side. They alleged that as much as $250 million had been stolen from the Cobain estate. Listening to her latest evidence, she started to convince us. After all, if you were going to steal from someone, wouldn't Courtney Love make the perfect victim? Who'd ever believe her?

We also stayed in touch with Donald Trump. When French president Nicolas Sarkozy started dating singer Carla Bruni, Joanna asked Trump, who'd also dated her, what she was like.

"I don't kiss and tell," Trump said. "But I will tell you this—she has a great ass."

By now, Trump had started floating his own presidential balloons. He hadn't yet inhaled too much right-wing helium. Most of his ego was invested in *The Apprentice*. He brooked no challengers. When Martha Stewart announced she wouldn't do another season of *her* version of the show because she was too busy, Donald didn't sugarcoat it. "Martha and I are good friends," he told me "But—honestly?—she's not too busy. Her ratings stink. I wish Martha got better ratings. By the way, NBC loves my show." Stewart went on to claim she'd wiped her hands of *The Apprentice* because Donald wouldn't let her "fire" him. Rage instantly knitted his eyebrows. Pulling one of his signature moves, he wrote Martha a scorching letter—calling her a talentless liar—which he then slipped to the press. (In this case, *People* "obtained" the missive.) Stung, Martha went on daughter Alexis's radio talk show and branded Donald's behavior "juvenile," "evil," "unethical," and "immoral." I asked Donald if he cared to comment. "I thought she didn't want to talk about my letter anymore," he hissed. "But Martha has a record of lying."

Nothing pleased Donald more than hearing some dish about his ex-wife Ivana. Though he remained publicly cordial with the mother of his children, he seemed to resent her massive divorce score and her success in capitalizing on his name. When she dared to get into real estate development, he made sure we knew about her setbacks. (She claimed he was jealous of her proposed Vegas tower, The Ivana, because Donald's tower "can only go to fifty stories, while I can go to eighty.")

When reports alleged she'd gotten sloppy at parties, Donald offered to "help" her quit drinking. ("I have no problem with alcohol," she assured us.) Donald especially relished any new pratfalls in Ivana's farcical romances with younger Italian hunks. His six-year marriage to Marla Maples looked like an ancient sequoia next to his ex's sapling union with Riccardo Mazzucchelli, which never reached its second anniversary. When Ivana's marriage to gadabout Rossano Rubicondi, twenty-four years her junior, fizzled after six months, Donald told us: "This was inevitable. I told her, 'Why are you wasting your time with this guy?' Hopefully, she's going to get on with her life. She got a good prenuptial agreement—at my insistence."

Our status as conservative hate objects made some Hollywood progressives see us as fellow travelers. Now that we, too, were proud members of Bill O'Reilly's enemies list, we always had a good laugh with George Clooney about the latest ranting from the "No Spin Zone." We worried that there might be détente when O'Reilly endorsed *Good Night and Good Luck*, Clooney's compelling reenactment of the battle between broadcaster Edward R. Murrow and Red-baiting Senator Joseph McCarthy. When we saw it at the New York Film Festival, we told Clooney how much his footage of the hectoring McCarthy reminded us of O'Reilly. Clooney nodded but told us O'Reilly "sees himself as Murrow." Clooney added, "Unlike McCarthy, O'Reilly was never elected to public office. What's more, Joe McCarthy was never accused of telling one of his female staff members she should use a vibrator." Even though O'Reilly accused Rush & Molloy of being "notoriously dishonest," he apparently believed us when we quoted Clooney. The Fox News-hound advised his followers that, while he had recommended Clooney's film, "I don't recommend Clooney as a human being." Clooney told me, "I want to use that quote in an ad."

We started out on good terms with Anne Hathaway. At the Democratic convention in Denver, she and I were having a wonky talk about policy. But then I had to bring up her ex-boyfriend, Raffaello Follieri, who'd been arrested a few months earlier on fraud charges. We'd reported on speculation that Hathaway had helped the FBI trap the handsome Italian financier. Hathaway was in no mood to talk about Follieri. She quickly broke off the conversation when I asked if she'd like the

FBI to return her private diaries, which agents had confiscated at Fol-lieri's Trump Tower apartment.

I really pushed my luck with Hathaway at an inauguration party in DC when I jumped on an elevator she had just boarded.

"Did you just follow me?" she asked me with a scowl.

"I thought we might have a quick talk," I said.

"I don't give interviews on elevators," she said.

And so we rode down ten floors in dead silence.

The Follieri story did help bring Rush & Molloy into the orbit of ano-ther famous Democrat—William Jefferson Clinton. I had first spoken to the former president's top aide, Doug Band, when Band had tried to persuade me not to run that story on billionaire Ron Burkle's messy divorce. Now Band had some of his own unwanted media attention. Having introduced Follieri to Burkle and another investor, Band was getting calls about his role in the Italian's real estate deal. Band said he wasn't used to talking with reporters. But since we were already ac-quainted, he helped me gather some background on Follieri, with whom I'd once had a couple of Cipriani Bellinis. Clinton's handlers seemed to recognize that they could work with us. At one tsunami relief event, a witness told us that the former president's team wouldn't let anyone take a photo of him alone with swimsuit model Petra Nemcova—lest the picture become grist for a late-night comic, a supermarket tab, or a right-wing smear campaign. It made sense, but Clinton's spokesman, Jay Carson, didn't think this information was "newsworthy." We ran it, anyway, as part of a story on people gathering opposition research on Bill as Hillary prepared to run for president.

Carson must have seen that we didn't kill his guy. Knowing that nothing softens up a reporter like access, Carson was soon offering us prime seats at the Clinton Global Initiative, where we were within eaves-dropping distance of everybody from Barbra Streisand to Kofi Annan. One night we were invited to President Clinton's Harlem headquarters for an intimate book party for his former advisers James Carville and Paul Begala. By the end of the evening, a few of us were hanging out with Clinton in his book-lined inner office. Trim and tan, he wore a crisp three-button charcoal suit and a robin's egg tie. He was in fine form. When we asked him about Dick Cheney's accidental shooting of his friend, Harry Whittington, three days earlier, Bubba jawed like we were sitting on the porch of a shotgun shack. He reckoned that, if Cheney had been hunting wild quail, "a lot of times you can't see them on the ground, and you do turn [suddenly] and fire. Accidents happen." But if they were on a quail farm, "the quail are slow. . . . Then, the vice president shouldn't have done that."

The Arkansas country boy then turned into a classical scholar, discoursing on Caesar, Cicero, and Demosthenes. "The Roman senate wasn't like ours," he chuckled. "There were things one senator couldn't say about another. . . . I grew up in a world where people said all kinds of things about you. I learned to put some distance between myself and what [my opponents] thought I was. John Kerry fought some tough races in Massachusetts. But he waited twenty-one days to respond to the Swift Boat ads. John started addressing each point. Finally I called him and said, 'If you don't stop addressing every point, *I'm* going to vote for Bush. Why don't you hold a press conference tomorrow? Say that you'd like to hold a debate—to compare your Vietnam experience with that of Bush and Cheney.'"

"If I want to attack someone," Clinton went on, "I do it in public. The [Bush people] send someone to do their dirty work. [The Bush White House] won't release anything—its meetings with [corrupt lobbyist Jack] Abramoff, the Katrina phone calls, the NASA whistleblower. We'd release everything. I'll tell you the biggest mistake of my presidency. I appointed a special prosecutor to look at Whitewater. I've been punished for this and I deserve to be. I did it because of the whining of *The New York Times* and the *Washington Post*. And the Republicans in Congress. And because I was naive. I wanted the truth out.

"The [Bush people] are like local politicians I knew from the South. They appeal to the soft underbelly of people. . . . That's why they're afraid of Hillary. No matter how high her negatives are, they still know we're the only ones who've beaten them."

It wasn't every night that we got to hang with Bill. But our cast of recurring characters made sure we were never lonely. We also met others who discovered it could be useful to know a gossip columnist.

A major actor asked if we could find out how serious his ex-girlfriend was about the married director she was seeing. There were other capers. Several scorned women turned to us to avenge them. In 2003, Billy Crudup dumped Mary Louise Parker two months before she gave birth to their son William; he then quickly recoupled with Claire Danes. We thought that was cold, even by Hollywood standards. So every time we mentioned Crudup, in almost any context, we parenthetically reminded people what he'd done. He couldn't eat a hot dog without us mentioning that he'd once given pregnant Mary Louise Parker the heave-ho. Parker didn't ask us to do this, but she seemed to appreciate it. Any time there was a development—like when she agreed to let their son meet Billy's ailing father (provided Danes wasn't around)—a friend of Parker's would let us know. A little bird also told us when Danes and Crudup split up (boo-hoo) and when Parker found love again with her *Weeds* costar Jeffrey Dean Morgan.

For about a year we'd been noticing CBS Chairman Les Moonves's "special rapport" with his network's *Early Show* anchor Julie Chen. CBS spokesmen swatted away suggestions that the twenty-years-younger Chen owed her morning slot to Moonves. But when Moonves's wife, Nancy, finally filed for divorce after twenty-four years of marriage, she told us that she hadn't watched CBS "in years" because "I don't want to see [Julie Chen]. I hope to God I never will [meet her]." Later, after Moonves wed Chen, he was able to laugh about it, telling us: "You guys busted me."

More health scares brought new celebs into our clinic. The *National Enquirer* reported that Tony Sirico, who played Paulie Walnuts on *The Sopranos*, was battling "deadly" mouth and throat cancer. So we called Sirico in Bensonhurst, where, like his wise-guy character, he lived with his elderly mom.

"Those fuckers!" the snub-nosed, razor-coiffed ex-con blurted as we read him the story. "I had a dead saliva gland removed from my tongue. . . . I have no cancer. It's complete bullshit! . . . I have doctors who can ram it right up their asses. I'm a cool gabagool. There's nothing wrong with [me]."

We remained a department of corrections for other people who felt wronged. Once, *Advertising Age* ran a story slamming Bono's idea of selling fashionable red products to fight AIDS in Africa. The story contended that his RED campaign had raised just $18 million, while its corporate partners had spent as much as $100 million in marketing. We gave RED director Bobby Shriver a chance to do what *Ad Age* should have done—let him argue that those numbers were off. It wasn't a big thing. But one day an email showed up. Subject line: "A Note from Bono." We thought it was one of those lame fundraising pitches but, when we opened it, the email said, "Joanna George, George Joanna: Thanks again for setting the facts straight." He passed along an article he thought we'd find interesting and remembered that I'd told him about my *Vanity Fair* story on Swaziland's wife-collecting King Mswati III, who once suggested that his HIV-positive subjects be "sterilized and branded." Diplomatically, Bono concurred that the king "is, er, quite a character." We spoke with the U2 singer a couple of times after that. Even his off-the-cuff remarks had a precision. Once, at the premiere of *The Departed*, we asked him about a scene where Matt Damon's character tells his psychiatrist girlfriend: "Freud said the Irish were the only people impervious to psychoanalysis." Did Bono agree? "In a movie that's all about lies," said the Dubliner, "that is not one of them."

At a party one night, Joanna went up to *Saturday Night Live* comic Fred Armisen.

"Mr. Armisen," she started to say, "do you think . . . ?"

"I'm not Fred Armisen," interjected Armisen, who was standing with actress Martha Plimpton.

"Wow," said Joanna. "You're his doppelganger then. You look exactly like him."

There's no question he *was* Fred Armisen. Figuring he didn't want to talk, Joanna left him alone, though she wondered why he couldn't have just said that. But Armisen made up for it a couple of years later when Governor David Paterson complained about the actor's bumbling impersonation of New York's legally blind chief executive. A source had told us that NBC's Standards and Practices people were putting pressure on *SNL* producer Lorne Michaels to stop doing the Paterson bit. So Joanna talked with about twenty blind people, describing how Armisen crashed into cameras and what not. Every one of them laughed. Said one: "The governor needs thicker skin." Joanna wrote, "Maybe Armisen paid disabled folks the highest compliment of all with his no-pity chop-busting." Paterson eventually lightened up and even took part in a sketch. Lowering his own defenses, Armisen emailed Joanna a nice note.

Oprah Winfrey had appreciated our telling her that Bulgari had allegedly been overcharging her. Years later, when we saw her at a party, she thanked us for letting her know that her seventy-four-year-old father, Vernon, was working on a book about her.

"One of my assistants said, 'The *Daily News* is calling. They say they heard your father is writing a book about you.' I said, 'That's impossible. I can assure them it's not true.' But then my sister said, 'I think you should call your father.' I called him and it turned out he *is* writing a book."

"I was upset," Oprah acknowledged. "I won't say 'devastated,' but I was stunned. The last person in the world to be doing a book about me is Vernon Winfrey. The *last* person. I have a good relationship with him. The worst part of it was his saying, 'I meant to tell you I've been working on it.' . . . It would have been a nice gesture."

Kate Winslet became especially solicitous when she got herself into a sticky wicket. Winslet had given an interview to *Vanity Fair* in which she complained to writer Krista Smith about the looks she got from other mothers when she dropped off her young son and daughter at their private school in Greenwich Village. "When I walk into that classroom in the morning," she said, "I'm being checked out. And some of them will even say to me, 'Okay, what's the secret with the skin?' At which point I'm like, 'Oh my God, there's no secret. I have makeup on.'"

We heard that, when the article came out, Winslet went into a panic, fearing that those same jealous mommies would devour her. So she sent out a letter to parents, claiming that she'd been misquoted and invited all the children to a private screening (possibly to remind everyone about the perks of having a movie star parent around). A source tipped us to the letter. We called Winslet's spokeswoman. The actress was now in a jam, because she knew we would call *Vanity Fair* for comment and that its reporter would stand by her story and back up the quotes with a tape recording.

Through her people, Winslet begged us not to write about the letter. Since children was involved, we didn't run the story. A few weeks later, we were invited to the Plaza's Oak Room for a lunch promoting Winslet's film *Revolutionary Road*. Winslet thanked me profusely for giving her kids a break. As if compensating me for my trouble, she gave a delicious interview in which she told what it was like to have her husband, Sam Mendes, direct her sex scenes with Leonardo DiCaprio. "Initially, I was very worried it would be difficult to concentrate [on the sex]," she said. "But Leo was fine with it, which relaxed me. And I never sensed Sam feeling awkward. Quite the opposite. He'd yell [pointers] from the other room: 'Press your hand into her back more!'"

Another actor had even more reason to ask for clemency. We'll call him Dash. One Sunday night, Dash was out partying in New York with an Oscar winner with a history of bad behavior. We'll call him Butch. It was after midnight when they hit a downtown club. It obviously wasn't their first stop. The inebriated pair began to ask strangers—quite loudly—how they could score some coke. The dynamic duo was soon down in the club's kitchen tooting up.

The snow-capped movie stars made quite a spectacle of themselves, which is why we heard about it. We called their publicists. They checked with their clients. The two flacks, who worked together, wouldn't officially confirm the coke binge, but their clients had obviously copped to it. Butch, famous as a libertine and an a-hole, didn't seem particularly worried. But Dash, who'd been through rehab, was mortified by his "slip." His rep begged us not to write the story. Both Dash and Butch had been nominated for Oscars that year. Dash feared older Academy voters wouldn't cotton to his drug use. Butch didn't seem to give a damn. Much as we would have enjoyed nailing Butch, we considered Dash an upright guy. And, since none of our witnesses would go on the record, we shelved the story. When it didn't run, Dash sent us a note, thanking us for what he perceived as our kindness. Butch's note must've gotten lost in the mail.

By that time, we knew well that life could be unfair. But it also delivered some pleasant surprises. Many people lied to us. Yet, sometimes, talent handlers got fed up with their talent.

Star Jones, the legal "expert" on *The View*, expected those around her to go along with her deceptions. They were to repeat her claim that she'd lost 160 pounds thanks to diet and exercise—until Star herself finally admitted she'd had a gastric bypass operation. Shortly after she and investment banker Al Reynolds announced their engagement, we began to hear some curious things about the groom. One source recalled seeing Al at an all-male Halloween party—dressed in a little Speedo swimsuit and carrying a bone. A female reporter came up to us in the newsroom and said, "Um, my hair stylist says that he went out with Al Reynolds." A nearby gay reporter hollered, "So did I!" We asked one of Star's people whether there was anything Reynolds wanted to tell his future wife. The mouthpiece said, "I'm in a difficult position. I'm friends with a guy Al went out with. I don't know what to say anymore!" Soon after, Reynolds said in a statement: "My fiancée and I have discussed all relevant parts of our personal histories. We are satisfied that we know everything we need to know about each other's pasts and are looking forward to our future together." Star and Al went ahead with their media-saturated, sponsor-underwritten wedding. But, four years later, they divorced.

For years, one of Whitney Houston's alibi dispensers told us the singer was suffering from "a cold" or "jet lag." When Houston's drug use became inescapable, the professional denier fessed up about the parasitical friends and family who depended on keeping Whitney out of it. But flacks could be enablers, too. One spokesman justified taking a fat check from his client by telling himself that he was the star's last tie with reality. But even the best-paid apologists had their limits.

Once, I called the publicist for an actress I'll call Lorelei, a once promising, supposedly rehabbed young star. I briefed the spokeswoman on the alleged activities of her client and her client's boyfriend, "Duncan," the night before. "According to our sources," I began, "Duncan ordered some booze delivered to his hotel room. When Duncan opened the door, the delivery guy saw a girl who wasn't Lorelei on the bed. There was also money and coke on the bed. Duncan asked the liquor store delivery guy, who'd been there before, if he wanted to hang out. Then another delivery guy arrived with some coke. Duncan told them both to tip themselves with some of the money on the bed. He said, 'It's Lorelei's money. I don't care.' Around 4 a.m., Lorelei came back to the hotel. She was drunk and screaming that Duncan was cheating on her. She wanted to find him but she couldn't remember his room number. She walked up and down the hallways calling for him. Other guests complained. One of the managers had to escort her to her room." Taking a breath, I asked the spokeswoman, "Any comment?"

"Go ahead and write it," said the publicist.

"Huh?"

"Write it," she repeated.

"The part about the coke?"

"I'm sure that's true."

"The money?"

"Sounds like Duncan. This guy is such a shit. He's just using her for publicity. I've given up. I'm so tired of dealing with this. She's a lost girl. She needs a mother who does some mothering instead of giving interviews to *Us Weekly*."

"Well, maybe she'll wake up someday," I said.

"Maybe," said her exhausted mouthpiece. "Or something worse."

We printed a version of the story. Since the publicist wasn't on the record and wasn't a witness to the illegal activity, we could only say so much. It took the publicist more than a year to part ways with her client. But we had new respect for the spokeswoman.

The passage of time brought us closer to a number of former adversaries.

Jamie Foxx may have called out his lawyers after skin-peddler David Hans Schmidt showed us those photos of the Oscar winner's own upright little man. But the ebullient actor forgot the episode when we talked to him about *The Soloist*, in which he played a mentally ill street musician. Foxx recalled that, in college, "someone slipped me PCP. I thought I was losing my mind. I had a roommate, Mark Provart, who got me through those nights. I hope he reads this and contacts me. He saved my life."

Billionaire Ronald Perelman was the last person we'd expect to embrace us. Once the richest man in New York, the five-foot-seven financier had a nitroglycerine temper that we regularly jiggled. We listened to third wife Patricia Duff's tearful accusations of his legal bullying during their epic custody battle over daughter Caleigh. We also aired the grievances of the fourth Mrs. Perelman, Ellen Barkin, who told us, "I wasn't free to work." (After their divorce, Barkin sold every piece of jewelry he'd given her, reaping $20.3 million.)

Throughout these marital hurricanes, the press-phobic Perelman never spoke to us. So I was surprised when, in between wives, he invited us to a party at his East Side mansion. I couldn't resist seeing his fabled art collection. At the party, I was mingling when Perelman approached, extending his hand. It looked like a peace gesture. But with barely a word, he pulled me close, strapped a headlock on me, and inflicted a wicked noogie. I guess that was Ron's idea of a hug.

22

The Threadbare Red Carpet

Come the holidays, we received small gifts from people grateful for coverage or hopeful for better coverage. Most sent stuff like caramel corn or scented candles. But some people believed in bigger gifts, even when it wasn't Christmas.

Nello Balan was a beefy, bleached-blond Romanian who owned a Madison Avenue restaurant. He claimed to be descended from Vlad the Impaler, which we could believe, considering that he gouged you $275 for a plate of pasta.

Sightings of celebrities at Nello's had been showing up on Page Six for years. One day, Nello emailed us the names of some stars who'd dined recently at his place. They were good names, so we ran them as Surveillances (as we called our sightings). The next morning, the manager of Nello's called to ask if I'd be in the office around lunch. I figured Nello was sending over some food. Around noon, Nello's delivery guy arrived. I was expecting some tortellini. Instead, the messenger handed me an envelope filled with *arugula a la Treasury*—seven $100 bills.

I called Nello to tell him I was messengering the money back to him.

He said, "I just wanted to send you some money so you could come to my restaurant."

"It's not necessary," I said.

"I didn't mean any offense," said Nello, who later pleaded guilty to attempted assault on his girlfriend. "I sent it honestly."

Another time, I was speaking with the head of a music company. I said I was sorry to hear that the CEO's daughter was in drug rehab—though I made it clear we were not planning to write about her.

The executive thanked me for respecting his child's privacy. A few minutes later, he called back to ask if I'd tell him who'd told me about the rehab. When I balked, the CEO said he'd pay for the name.

"I'd be very grateful," said the exec. "Like, you could buy a house with my gratitude."

"I can't," I said. "You understand."

Checkbook journalism usually referred to the controversial practice of reporters paying for interviews. But apparently, some journalists expected the checks to come their way. We learned that female columnists at other papers had long been receiving furs and jewelry. Aileen Mehle (*Women's Wear Daily*'s "Suzy") was baffled when I called to confirm that Fendi had been sending her furs for years. Mehle—whom Joanna had read since she was a girl—didn't see what the problem was.

Rare was the critic or columnist who didn't accept free entry to a play, movie, concert, or sports event. Otherwise, the paper couldn't afford to cover those events. We also wrote travel stories, so we were invited to check out new resorts. Rather than being complete spongers, we usually paid a reduced media rate. Even when we accepted an invite, we tended to bite the hand offering us the room key.

Just as I'd angered our Atlantis hosts by repeating Michael Jordan's diss of the Washington Wizards, I instantly wore out my welcome at the Ritz-Carlton on Grand Cayman. I'd flown down with a bunch of celebs and reporters for the hotel's grand opening. Sheryl Crow was the headliner. It was a lovely hotel. Every employee continually said hello. But then I had to remind readers that, during his presidential campaign, "Sen. John Kerry blamed [Grand Cayman]—where Enron hid its massive debts—for America's tax-evasion problem. Though she campaigned for Kerry, [Sheryl] Crow wasn't about to knock her host country, especially since the Ritz-Carlton had treated her to a week of scuba diving and piña coladas."

We were once invited to Burma, or as it was now known, Myanmar. We were due to travel up the Irrawaddy River on a small Orient Express cruise called "the Road to Mandalay." Once again, our hosts got more than they bargained for when we devoted our entire Sunday page to the trip. Yes, we saluted Orient Express chairman James Sherwood for building day-care centers and restoring medieval monuments in Myanmar. But we also took gossip readers into the Orwellian land where billboards commanded citizens to oppose foreign "stooges" who "jeopardize stability of the state." We observed that the message of the three ruling generals had "the subtlety of Moe, Larry, and Curly. The generals, who took power in 1988, perform under the name of the State Law and Order Restoration Council—SLORC. . . . Sounds a bit like James Bond's old adversary, SPECTRE, doesn't it?" We noted that the junta's newspaper, the *New Light*, treated readers to thrilling photos of Secretary 1 and Secretary 2 meeting with ambassadors of other pariah nations, as well as to complete details of Bill Clinton's scandals and such TV listings as: "4 a.m.: Martial music . . . 4:15 p.m.: Songs to uphold national spirit . . . 5:45 p.m.: *I Dream of Jeannie*: Jeannie learns to cook."

Sanitized for our protection, the *New Light* didn't mention that riots had caused martial law to be declared in the city of Mandalay. Our cruise director informed us we would therefore not be visiting the destination of our trip. The news blackout made us appreciate the press freedoms we took for granted. All we had to go on were rumors. We were used to dealing in rumors but here, they were about bloodshed. The people who whispered them clearly feared they could wind up imprisoned or killed. When we returned to the capital of Yangon, we were determined to see the house where the junta held Nobel Prize winner Aung San Suu Kyi captive. We asked a taxi driver to take us there. He begged us to take another taxi. We said he could just drop us off near her house. But even when we were a few blocks away, armed soldiers jumped out of the bushes to turn us around.

We noted in our column that, as long as Suu Kyi remained a prisoner, "travel to Burma will remain a guilt trip."

We'd gone on junkets with Richard Johnson and his Page Six team. Once we were away from New York's gossip battlefield—in a demilitarized zone—we could joke about the nonsense of it all. But our collegiality was shattered in 2006 when the *Daily News* learned that the FBI was investigating Page Six reporter Jared Paul Stern for allegedly trying to shake down Ron Burkle for $220,000. Burkle's globe-trotting lifestyle and friendship with Bill Clinton had made him a frequent subject of Page Six. The *News* reported that Stern had written to a Burkle associate offering to help the tycoon "regulate" his Page Six coverage. Stern arranged several meetings with Burkle. Unbeknownst to Stern, Burkle's security team was videotaping him.

During one meeting, Stern outlined the "levels of protection" he could provide Burkle. Level One would require him to feed the column stories about his celebrity friends, so Page Six would go easier on Burkle.

Page Six, Stern explained, was "a little like the Mafia. A friend of mine is a friend of yours."

Then again, Stern cautioned, "Being friends with Richard is fine, but that will not stop your problems."

"We know how to destroy people," Stern said. "It's what we do. We do it without creating liability. That's our specialty."

For maximum protection, Stern advised, Burkle would need to pay.

"How much do you want?" asked Burkle.

"Um, $100,000 to get going," Stern stammered. "And month to month, $10,000."

At their final meeting, a federal agent and an assistant US attorney were present to monitor the recording. At the same meeting, Burkle agreed to make a wire transfer to Stern. Within a week, our Pulitzer Prize–winning colleague, William Sherman, broke the "Page Fix" exposé. The *Post* had long harangued *The New York Times* for its liberal positions (a photo of Arthur Sulzberger Jr. with a black eye was the *Post*'s go-to headshot of the Gray Lady's publisher). The *Times* now dove on the Stern story with gusto. An investigative team of half a dozen *Times* reporters produced day after day of coverage.

We only knew Stern from parties, where he drew attention with his double-breasted suit, fedora, and spats. He was a clever writer, but his boasts about his scoops quickly wore on you. Was Stern's boss,

Richard Johnson, in on his scheme? We doubt it. On the tape, Stern made no mention of paying Richard; in fact, he discouraged Burkle's idea of hiring Richard's wife, Sessa, as a publicist. Page Six had gotten stronger since Paula Froelich had become Richard's second-in-command. But some of his staff had become arrogant. They slashed away with impunity at people like Burkle, who eventually slashed back.

Prosecutors ultimately decided not to file criminal charges against Stern. (For some reason, Burkle didn't lock the trap by making the wire transfer Stern kept asking for.) Initially, Stern apologized for embarrassing the *Post*, which suspended him until the investigation was resolved. But when he wasn't invited back to work, he began hatching a lawsuit. His former Page Six colleague, Ian Spiegelman, provided a damning affidavit. Among other things, Spiegelman alleged that he'd been ordered to kill a Page Six item about a Chinese diplomat visiting a New York strip club because it would have "endangered Murdoch's broadcast privileges" in China. He also testified that Page Six had killed unflattering stories about Bill and Hillary Clinton as part of a "favor banking system." Stern's lawyer, Clinton-hater Larry Klayman, gave the affidavit to the *Post*, apparently in the hope that it would scare the paper into re-hiring Stern. Instead, the *Post* preemptively printed the "smears and lies" on Page Six. One charge *Post* editor Col Allan didn't deny: that, in 1997, Nello Balan had given Richard $1,000 in cash. Allan said he'd reprimanded Richard "after he informed me of his error in judgment." (The *Times* reported that, since 1997, the *Post* had printed about two hundred mentions of Balan and his establishments.)

It was hard to resist a little schadenfreude as the fearsome Page Six took its licks. Rush & Molloy's lame asses looked good by comparison—though we were a little insulted that Balan thought we were only worth $700.

Day to day, the *Post* didn't deliver as much *tsuris* as we found in our own newsroom. Like all reporters, we served at the pleasure of a succession of editors who each had ideas of how our job should be done.

We were saddened, in 1996, when ingenious editor in chief Martin Dunn returned to London to run the cable and new-media operations of Viscount Rothemere's Associated Newspapers. But Mort Zuckerman had impressed even his detractors when he persuaded fabled columnist and novelist Pete Hamill to edit the paper. When Joanna was sixteen, she'd sent Pete a fan letter and he'd taken the time to send back a letter of encouragement. No one cared more about writing than Pete. He once invited some younger reporters, who he felt "were sounding too much like each other," to his house to read some of his favorite writers. When Mike McAlary didn't appear, Pete asked McAlary's friend, Mark Kriegel, if they should wait for him. "I don't think he's coming," said Kriegel. "He thinks we should be studying *him*."

What other tabloid editor but Pete would run a nineteen-part serialization of his friend Norman Mailer's new novel? Pete knew a lot of famous people. He was the last person to interview John Lennon. His liner notes for Bob Dylan's *Blood on the Tracks* won him a Grammy. He was on a first name basis with Frank Sinatra, whom he remembered in *Why Sinatra Matters*, one of Pete's twenty-one books. He *dated* Jacqueline Kennedy Onassis. He singlehandedly broke the barricades of Farrell's men-only bar when he brought girlfriend Shirley MacLaine in for a drink. Once, we mentioned a sighting of Czech Republic President Vaclav Havel at a Lou Reed concert. Pete casually remarked, "Oh, Vaclav's in town?"

At the same time, Pete fundamentally disdained celebrity worship. He wanted the *Daily News* to get back in touch with its blue-collar roots and to reach out to new immigrants. He said he didn't believe people in Bensonhurst cared about Princess Diana. One of his first reforms was firing Wendy Henry, who'd been running the *News's* Sunday entertainment section with Dick McWilliams. Wendy was the first woman to edit a British national daily. (Buckingham Palace pressured Rupert Murdoch to fire her after she published photos of a urinating Prince William, then five, with the irresistible headline, "The Royal Wee.") At an office party after her firing, Wendy walked up to Pete, declared, "I've forgotten more about editing a paper than you'll ever know," and threw her drink in his face. Pete also decided the *News* didn't need two gossip columns. Fortunately for us, he chose to extinguish "Hot Copy," ably manned by future E! host A. J. Benza and GossipCop.com cofounder Michael Lewittes. We shared Pete's aversion to celebrity writing where, as he put it, "we have our noses pressed against the window of the party." But we sometimes felt Pete underestimated the blue-collar appetite for gossip. Our own informal polling of maids and taxi drivers indicated that new immigrants were fascinated with Donald Trump, whose hubris Pete couldn't stomach. Sadly, after just eight months, Pete got tired of hearing Mort say the paper wasn't lively enough and he left. (Among Mort's last complaints: Pete had buried a story about a Princess Di gown auction on page 34.)

By contrast, Ed Kosner was a connoisseur of well-done gossip. The product of Washington Heights and City College, Ed had scaled the palisades of power. But he sometimes seemed to forget where he worked when he regaled his metro editors with tales of his weekend quail hunt. As Joanna knew from working for him at *New York*, Ed's taste ran toward insider dish about media, real estate, society, and politics. He brought in Deborah Mitchell and later, Michael Gross, to do Sunday columns about the people he and Mort knew. Ed permitted our mainstream celebs. But from time to time, he'd decree that some overexposed rapper—Diddy was one—should be banished "to the island" for a while. Having also edited *Newsweek* and *Esquire*, he had an admirable allergy to clichés. But some of his dictums felt snooty. He outlawed the slangy noun-verbs that had long been part of the tabloid argot. Our celebs could no longer "party" in Miami, "host" an event, or "ankle" a job. To us, it was like forbidding the use of slide guitar in country music.

Most of the *News*'s reporters were a pleasure to work with. We had a great rapport with the police shack and the bureaus—Washington, Albany, City Hall. They were a huge help, even after we didn't have the budget for tip fees. Sometimes, when we were nosing into the love life of a star jock, we'd ask one of the sports guys for guidance. They'd always assist, usually adding, "Just keep me a million miles away from this, or I'll never get in the locker room again!" A rare instance of resistance came when someone at a Toronto Film Festival screening told us that *Post* movie reviewer Lou Lumenick had smacked esteemed critic Roger Ebert with a rolled-up binder. Ebert had merely tapped Lumenick on the shoulder. Since cancer had rendered him speechless, Ebert had been trying to get Lumenick to move a little because he was blocking the movie's subtitles. Incredibly, said our source, Lumenick hadn't apologized. Even though Ebert had called our account "truthful," *Daily News* film critic Elizabeth Weitzman didn't want anyone to think she'd told us about the incident. The daughter of shoe mogul Stuart Weitzman, she sent an emissary who asked us to cough up our source, so she could share it with festival organizers and clear her name. Maybe she'd never reviewed *All the President's Men* or heard of "Deep Throat." We told her emissary she should know better.

Diplomatic relations with our fellow *Daily News* gossip columnists could get tetchy. Many times we were chasing the same stories. And every day, media critics—professional and self-appointed—would compare our column with the other guy's. We'd developed a good system of divvying up parties with Mitchell Fink, a *haimish* guy who'd written *People*'s "Insider" column before coming to the *News*. But after three and a half years, Mort bid him farewell. For more than a year, we had the luxury of having all the parties to ourselves. But Mort liked to hire almost as much he liked to fire. As a pundit on DC's political talk shows, Mr. Zuckerman had become a regular reader of Lloyd Grove, who wrote the *Washington Post*'s "Reliable Source" column. Seeing Lloyd at an Oscar bash, Mort asked, "Have you considered plying your trade in New York?"

We'd always gotten along with Lloyd. He was an arch and artful writer. But soon *Washingtonian* magazine was speculating "whether Zuckerman will keep Rush & Molloy." Mort had reportedly offered Lloyd a salary greater than that of *Washington Post* executive editor Len Downie. *The New York Times* heralded Lloyd's arrival with a front-page profile of "the new prince of gossip for the *Daily News*." The story noted that though we'd been writing for the *News* for a decade, "Mr. Grove's column will appear at least one page before Rush & Molloy." Ed Kosner told us Mort had ordained the new batting order. Speaking to the *Times*, I tried to put a positive spin on it: "In television, when you have a strong show like *Seinfeld* and you try to introduce a new show, you put the new show before the established hit. I still think people will find the strength to turn the page."

Once his Lowdown column set sail, Lloyd was at his best writing wickedly about Washington players. He had many enviable items about politics and media. But the demands of filling a page every day in a bigger city with many competitors began to show. He started doing items about Foxy Brown and Lindsay Lohan and other people he admitted he didn't give a fig about. Once, out in L.A., Lloyd and I both attended an Oscar party at the home of New Line cochairman Bob Shaye. Conferring the next morning, Lloyd said he'd heard that Paris Hilton had fallen into Shaye's fish pond. She had. In fact, I had witnessed her sloshing among the koi and interviewed her as she wobbled out. But Lloyd said he had nothing else to lead with. So I let him have the story.

Paris became less desirable to Lloyd a few months later when he came up with the shrewd idea of publicly banning her from his column. He said she wasn't worth anybody's attention. His own "craven play for attention," as Lloyd called it, got him on the *Today* show. But that didn't stop rumors—fanned by Gawker.com—that his days were numbered. Mort stood by Lloyd, telling one reporter: "I think, over time, he'll be the dominant columnist in New York." Yet, three years after arriving in New York, Lloyd confirmed to the *Times's* David Carr that Mort was letting him go. Writing a gossip column in this cutthroat town, Lloyd concluded, "is not for sissies, not for the faint of heart."

The mere fact that we'd survived this long had made us a stubborn stain on the media scene. I'd figured that my alma maters had long ago written me off as a disgrace. But the Columbia Journalism School asked me to join legal eminence Floyd Abrams on a First Amendment panel. It was a sad commentary on the decline of our educational institutions. We tried to remain suspicious of our growing notoriety. Whenever somebody said, "I love your column," I'd say, "You shouldn't be reading that trash!" Yet here was Salman Rushdie—whose courtship of Padma Lakshmi we'd unveiled—name-checking us in his novel, *Fury*. Producer Ismael Merchant offered to make an Indian dessert in our honor—*ras malai*. As if our caricatures on the wall of Tribeca's Palm steakhouse weren't causing enough appetite-loss.

Martin Dunn had returned from London to become the *Daily News's* editorial director. He insisted that we take part in Bravo's reality show about the *News's* battle with the *Post*, called *Tabloid Wars*. Joanna was reluctant. She'd just been big-time sick and thought she looked like hell. Plus, she's shy. But the producers, Belisa Balaban and Ted Skillman, were serious documentarians and seemed like they wouldn't turn us into shrieking Bravo monsters. Their camera crews followed us—and some truly great reporters—for weeks.

One of the show's minor characters (in every sense) was our son, Eamon, then seven years old. He'd sometimes show up at the newsroom. The logline for one episode: "Rush and Molloy balance family life and work when their son's sudden injury leaves Rush to cover a Gotti family party solo!"

For better or worse, Eamon had grown up in the gossip world. He was three when he went to the premiere of *Harry Potter and the Sorcerer's Stone* at the Ziegfeld. Richard Harris was there, wearing the wizard's robe of Albus Dumbledore. Children gaped at him in wonder. When we had to flee the theater with another boy who'd gotten scared, Harris was outside having a cigarette. Seeing Eamon and his friend approaching, he dropped the cig, so the lads wouldn't see Dumbledore smoking—a disappearing trick we'll always remember. Another time, we were invited with a lot of other media types to watch the Yankees from George Steinbrenner's box. The reporters were all wondering if the team's irascible owner, who was rumored to be suffering from dementia, would make an appearance. Eamon, who was in kindergarten, was more interested in the huge buffet of desserts. Suddenly, the Boss burst out of nowhere and grabbed Eamon by the shoulders. "Try the chocolate cake!" he whispered. We only saw the back of his head, like on *Seinfeld*.

Gradually, Eamon become aware of what we did. On the subway one day, he noticed a lady who had the *Daily News* open to the page with our pinhead pictures.

"Look, Dada," he said, "she's reading your story!"

"It must not have been too interesting," I pointed out. "She's sound asleep."

Once, he picked up the phone when I called home and said, "You better hurry up. Page Six will get the scoop!" Another time, when we were debating whether to publish a true but potentially libelous item, Eamon, then about five, asked, "Why don't you run it as a blind item?"

Our tiny fame could sometimes lead to delusions of grandeur. Columnists liked to sit around in bars crowing about who was on the A-list and who was a "has-been." After all, hadn't Winchell's biographer, professor Neal Gabler, said, "The thrust of almost everything in American life is toward celebrity. . . . [Gossip] columns don't report on celebrity. They make celebrity"? Hadn't the coverage of Brad and Angelina's romance been credited for *Mr. and Mrs. Smith's* opening weekend gross of $51.1 million?

But, more often than not, I'd look in the mirror behind the bar and see a bottom-feeder. Gossip columnists did not create albums or movies or laws. We just wrote about the private lives of successful people who did.

I was feeling a bit worthless one night at a small party at the Harvard Club, where I got into a conversation with Bill Murray. Over the years, we'd heard that Murray could be a jerk. But we'd also heard he had another side. An old friend of Joanna told her she'd been out shopping with her two kids one Christmas eve when her little boy called out, "Mama, mama, it's Ghostbusters!" At the end of the store's aisle was Bill Murray. "Oh, Mr. Murray," she said. "Could I take a photo of you with my children?" "No!" he snapped. The mortified mom grabbed her kids and left. She'd just loaded the children into her Jaguar when Murray came knocking on the window. He let himself into the car, sat down, and apologized. He said he'd just had an argument with his wife. As it happened, Joanna's friend had just had a fight with her husband. Murray asked if he could make it up to everyone by taking them to dinner. The kids yelled, "Yes!" So they all went off to the Tribeca Grill. He was quite entertaining. "I hope you're not sore at me anymore," Murray said. "I'll let you live," joked the attractive lady as they went their separate ways. Murray smiled. Little did he know that the woman who'd spared him was Joanna's pal, Joanne Persico, the Colombo mob princess.

I'd never met Murray, but we shared Chicago roots. Over a few drinks, we talked about the woebegone characters that had become his specialty. I complimented him on the way he'd conveyed the internal life of miserable Herman Blume in *Rushmore*.

Murray then said, "You seem like you're a very internal guy."

Graciously, he hadn't said, "for a gossip columnist." I said, "You mean what am I doing this for?"

"Yeah," said Murray, sticking another swizzle stick in his jacket pocket.

"I don't know," I answered. "I'm trying to find an escape hatch."

"Don't do that," said Murray. "Don't deny what you have going. You have this possibility. I've seen the column and I go, okay, sometimes it's flip, but look at the forum you have. You have the opportunity to go off more than you do. Just go and do it, will ya? Make us proud for Chrissakes! You're from Illinois—the Land of Lincoln!"

A Change Of Pace

It was nice of Bill Murray to cheer us on—as though I were some star, like Liam Neeson, brooding about whether to leave the stage. But the job was getting to us: the libel letters, the back-biting with the *Post*, the conflicts in our own newsroom. Rare was the weekend when we weren't pulled in to help with a story. I'd missed half our son's childhood because of the evening events. When he was three or four, Eamon asked Joanna where I was. "He has to work late to make money," she said. Eamon went to the window and called into the night, "Come home, Dada! We have enough money!"

The daily race to fill the column with *something* had left us feeling a little empty. The deadline demanded we follow up on the tips that promised instant results. We didn't have time to chase a lead that didn't pay off within a few hours. We also didn't have space for complicated stories. A three-paragraph item would prompt an editor to say, "This is running on a bit." And forget about having the leisure hours to take on outside magazine stories or books.

But maybe there was a middle way. We asked Martin Dunn if he'd let us appear just one day a week—on Sunday—while developing longer news features and doing breaking stories as they arose. We'd take a pay cut of course. Martin said no. He claimed the Rush & Molloy "brand," which he'd invented, was too valuable. And what would go in our place the other days? Our former R&M reporter, Ben Widdicombe, a supremely witty gentleman from Australia, had created a weekend gossip column called "Gatecrasher." Though Ben, sadly, had left the paper, we suggested that his former assistant, Laura Schreffler, team up with our intrepid reporter, Sean Evans, to resuscitate "Gatecrasher." After more than a year of nagging him, he gave in—on one condition.

Martin had toyed with the idea of Joanna writing an "occasional" opinion column where she could, shall we say, draw on her reservoir of emotion. It would give her a chance to, as Bill Murray put it, "go off more than you do." And, believe me, Joanna could go off!

Martin and Managing Editor Stuart Marques would always be thinking of some fresh hell to send Molloy into. When the Yankees were due to play the Phillies in the 2009 World Series, they suggested she go down to Philadelphia to draw some "impressions" of the city that hoped to rob New York of its rightful championship rings.

"I had to plunge into a rally of rabid Philly fans, admit I was from New York, and ask them what was so great about their city," says Molloy. "The people I spoke to actually seemed pretty nice. They liked New York—they came up to the Manhattan clubs on weekends. Stuart growled, 'We don't want 'nice!' Naively, I wrote a tongue-in-cheek column ribbing the Phillies fans, one of whom once attacked Santa Claus, or a guy dressed as Santa Claus."

Stuart and Martin gave it the headline:

DELUSIONS RUN WILD IN CITY OF BROTHERLY LOVE

JOANNA MOLLOY STIRS IT UP! "PITY SILLY-DELPHIA FOR THINKING THEY CAN BEAT NY! CHEESE STEAK-STINKIN' TOWN POSES PHANTOM MENACE TO YANKEES"

From 6 a.m., hate mail streamed in. Many of the fans were particularly upset that the *News* had called their team's mascot, the Phillie Phanatic, "a green, pig-nosed monster." The comments were vicious. One guy said the Phillies "will make the Yankees crumble faster than the Twin Towers." Charming. The subject line of another email was: "You ignorant c—." Joanna had to lay down a couple of times. It was nice to get the front page play. But the blowback was fierce.

While Joanna's opinion pieces became more than "occasional" (sometimes running four times a week), I handled much of the carpentry on our Sunday column. Naturally, the conversation pit was built around show biz exclusives: Penelope Cruz's engagement to Javier Bardem . . . Phil Spector's prison beat-down . . . Jack Nicholson's improv insertion of a dildo into a scene in *The Departed* ("I'm planning to market a line of them on the Internet," Jack told us, "in Day-Glo colors!") . . . Billy Joel's secret trip to rehab and his divorce from wife Katie Lee . . . and Sean Penn and Robin Wright's on-off-on divorce. (Hey, I tried to warn Robin about him years ago.)

The column still had political planks and shingles. Connecticut election officials probed conservative pundit Ann Coulter after we determined she'd voted in the Nutmeg State while living in New York City. . . . We got Mayor Bloomberg to declare his support for Senator Kirsten Gillibrand when insiders claimed Bloomberg's aides were trying to unseat her. . . . We asked Sarah Palin what her beloved "everyday Americans" thought of her $100,000 speaking fees and Lear jet demand. ("We live in Wasilla, Alaska," she insisted. "You can't get more grounded than that.") . . . Exposed CIA operative Valerie Plame hissed when we told her that Kate Beckinsale was playing a character inspired by jailed reporter Judith Miller. (Plame, who blamed Miller for her exposure, told us: "For [Miller] to be the heroine of such a movie is really quite a stretch.") . . . And we made former White House spokesman Ari Fleischer squirm when former Christian Coalition mouthpiece Lisa Baron recalled performing oral sex on him.

Moguls remained ensconced among our luminaries. We revealed Virgin Atlantic billionaire Richard Branson's bid to poach US Airway's hero pilot Chesley "Sully" Sullenberger. We also heard that, in addition to screwing his investors (including Mort Zuckerman) out of billions, Bernard Madoff had cheated on his wife, Ruth. Madoff's lawyer said, "I'm told that's not accurate." But later, ABC News correspondent Brian Ross reported that our story opened Ruth's eyes. "Ruth seethed for days," Ross recounted in his book, *The Madoff Chronicles*. "She had been warming to the role of the lonely, devoted wife until she picked up that *Daily News*. Now she was experiencing the overpowering sense of betrayal." Madoff mistress Sheryl Weinstein confirmed her years-long affair in her memoir. "I don't know how far back his other affairs went,"

Weinstein told us. "When we ended ours, he led me to believe it was his last. He was going to stick to [erotic] massages." Weinstein, whose lover devoured her savings, tearfully asked us for advice on rebuilding her life. In spite of the evidence, Madoff insisted he'd been faithful to Ruth. "I think he still wants Ruth to visit him in jail," Weinstein surmised. "I guess no one else is."

Tiger Woods blessed us with almost a year of stories. One blonde after another kept jumping out of his golf bag. Former stripper Cori Rist initially declined comment when I'd learned about her arrangement with Woods. (On the PGA tour, Woods would put her up in a luxury suite adjoining his, a friend said, but eventually Rist felt "like a bird in a gilded cage.") Rist later told Joanna she wouldn't have hooked up with Tiger "if he'd told me the truth about his marriage." Even worse, Rist said, he didn't always use protection, exposing her—and his wife, Elin—"to health risks."

Joanna got to know another Tiger mama, porn star Joslyn James, when they both wound up in Georgia while Woods was competing in the Masters.

"Joslyn agreed to pose for our photographer, Debbie Egan Chin," Joanna recalls. "I thought it would be fun to shoot her wearing a green blazer, like the Master's jacket Tiger was hoping to win in Augusta. I searched high and low for a damn green blazer. Finally, I found a shop that *rented* me one for a few hours. We met Joslyn at a hotel room where she bounced on a bed in this blazer and lacy black lingerie."

We also got wind of a wild evening Woods allegedly had with two women in Arizona. Woods was said to be in the middle of, um, the rough, when he realized that one of the girls was taking pictures. "Tiger goes ballistic," our source said. "He starts chasing the girl around. She runs out the door. He runs out after her. I don't know how much clothing either of them is wearing, but Tiger finally catches up with her and grabs her cell phone or camera." We were told that Woods later bought the women's silence. Tiger's agent didn't return our calls, but Michelle Braun, a madam who allegedly staffed his romps, later concurred that "he liked three-ways." Braun told me: "He could go for days. The girls would talk about his stamina." Guess he ate his Wheaties (that is, before General Mills kicked him off the cereal box).

Madams had always been good to us—going back to Heidi Fleiss and Sydney Biddle Barrows. Our latest friend in the sex trade was Kristin Davis (not to be confused with the *Sex and the City* actress). Kristin had worked as a vice president for a Wall Street hedge fund before she fell on hard times and opened an escort agency. Kristin worked the tart look—cascading yellow hair, plumped-up lips, and radial-belted bosoms. But she had a natural gift for management. In 2008, she was swept up in the tide of arrests coinciding with the exposure of New York Governor Eliot Spitzer as the client of another escort agency. Kristen had just spent four months on Riker's Island when I got a look at a list of her alleged clients.

Now that I had more time to spend on stories, I waded through the thousands of names, finding several well-known actors, sports stars, Middle Eastern diplomats, a famous jeweler, a best-selling novelist, one of Hollywood's biggest directors, and many executives. Some had notations about their likes and dislikes.

I started calling the clients. Some *plotzed* when I said why I was calling. Naturally, most denied being clients. They couldn't imagine how their cell numbers got on Kristin's list. Some didn't return repeated calls. You couldn't allege they were johns just because they were on the list. Kristin would only help up to a point. Her code of honor kept her from publicly talking about her clients. Fortunately, some of her former employees had fewer qualms about spilling to us.

One of Kristin's former girls—whom we called "Annie" in the story—opened up to us about a session she'd allegedly had with Spitzer.

"He wanted a scenario where I was supposed to say I had just been to a self-defense class," Annie claimed. "He was supposed to respond, 'Let's see if you learned anything.' . . . He was holding me down. He pinned me to the bed. That didn't bother me. But when he grabbed my throat that was too much. . . . Finally, I pushed him away and got up. He hadn't finished. But I'd had enough."

A lawyer for Spitzer called the account "outrageous and defamatory"—but did not use the word *false*.

In another story, Annie told us about three "dates" she had with the chief executive of another state. Kristin corroborated that he was a client, but a spokesman for the prominent governor hung tough, insisting he'd never hired a hooker. Still, it was hard not to be intrigued by Annie's highly detailed story. She recalled how one of her clients, "Michael," had booked a date but, when she opened the door to greet him, there stood the governor. "He was smiling. I knew what was happening. I was okay with it. He didn't take the full hour. . . . He was very appreciative, like I was giving him a sort of affection he wasn't getting elsewhere. Later, I found out his wife is quite prominent in her own right."

Annie and Kristin said the governor could rightly say he hadn't paid for sex, since his friend "Michael" took care of the bills. We ran the story, anyway, calling the politician "Governor X." A sirocco of speculation blew around the web. Political writers offered their best guesses as to Governor X's identity. One female journalist friend pegged him immediately—perhaps because, while she was interviewing him in the back of his limo, he'd made a pass at her. When she threatened to mention his advances in the story, he laughed, "Go ahead. I'll deny it."

Kristin later made good use of her gubernatorial experience. She'd gotten to know Roger Stone, a GOP strategist who'd worked for Richard Nixon, Ronald Reagan, and George H. W. Bush. The platinum-haired Stone had engineered Governor Spitzer's downfall by tipping off the FBI to his use of prostitutes. Stone was able to supply the investigators with Spitzer's quirks—like his supposed habit of keeping his knee-high black socks on—because Stone himself was a client of the same prostitutes.

One night, I had dinner with Stone and Kristin at Hotel Griffou in the West Village. They told me that Kristin was going to run for governor. Stone admitted that initially he'd encouraged her to go for Spitzer's old job to make sure Spitzer didn't try to get reelected. "But now that it looks like he won't run," Stone told me, "Kristin still wants to use her celebrity to highlight a reform agenda." He saw her as an ideal Libertarian Party advocate for the repeal of income tax and legalization of prostitution and marijuana. Kristin and Stone announced her candidacy in our column. Some took it as a passing prank. But with a switch to a more conservative suit, Kristin got onto the ballot and took part in the official debate.

Earlier, Kristin landed on the *News's* front page when some of her agency's former employees told me that Yankee slugger Alex Rodriguez had been a client. They said Kristin herself had dated him (free of charge). Kristin would only say officially that "our paths have definitely crossed personally and professionally." According to sources, the then-married A-Rod sent Kristin flowers, jewelry, and heated emails. In one missive, he allegedly told Kristin: "You have been playing hard to get for a year now, your [sic] killing me."

Rodriguez's spokesman never denied the story. By then, his wife, Cynthia, had already claimed in her divorce action that he was a serial adulterer. Among the beauties that had turned his head, she charged, was Madonna.

I had seen how cozy A-Rod and Madge were at a United Nations benefit for Madonna's Raising Malawi charity. I happened to be standing near Madonna's table when the slugger came over. Her daughter, Lourdes, was sitting next to her.

"This is Alex," Madonna said to Lourdes. "He's a baseball player."

A-Rod smiled. "Maybe you can come and see me play sometime," he told the eleven-year-old. She was clearly underwhelmed.

"She's not that into baseball," explained Madonna.

Rodriguez, whose mother was named Lourdes, had grown closer and closer to the singer, even visiting her Manhattan pad shortly after Cynthia gave birth to their second child. Madonna, whose own marriage to director Guy Ritchie was on its last legs, denied that she had anything to do with the Rodriguez split.

"I believe he was having an affair with Madonna," Cynthia told a friend in one of our front-page stories.

The divorce battle raged for weeks. The mix of celebrity, sex, betrayal, and baseball pleased almost all of the tabloid taste buds. Alas, the spouses eventually agreed to stop dissing each other.

The A-Rod divorce had the added attraction of Cynthia's claim that Madonna had "brainwashed" her husband—using the mystical teachings of the Kabbalah. We'd always been fascinated with sects that lured celebs—particularly the Church of Scientology. Once, after a screening of *Phenomenon*, I tried—sincerely—to get a better understanding of the church's beliefs from its disciple John Travolta. In the movie, Travolta played a dim, small-town auto mechanic who said his thinking became "clear" after seeing a mysterious flash of light. "Clear" is a Scientology term. But Travolta said that, in Scientology, it had "a technical definition that's different. It refers to the erasure of painful incidents in your past." I asked about the church's "Incident II" theology—wherein Galactic Confederacy dictator Xenu blew up billions of people in volcanoes, creating "thetans." Did Travolta take that story as literal truth? Or did he see it as mythologist Joseph Campbell saw all religion, as "a metaphor for a mystery that absolutely transcends all human categories of thought"? Little did I know how I'd overstepped. The Incident II story—concocted by science fiction writer L. Ron Hubbard in 1967—was part of the secret OTIII Advanced Technology that Scientologists only learned if they'd paid a lot of money. Travolta shut down the conversation. He told me, "Most of what's been reported about our beliefs is inaccurate. I can't go into it here."

Yet Travolta, who'd never heard of Campbell, seemed intrigued. His publicist said later, "What did you say to John? He enjoyed talking with you." Scientology officials weren't as fond of us. Whenever we looked skeptically at the church (like when it sent "ministers" to give "grief counseling" to shell-shocked students after the 2007 Virginia Tech shooting), Scientology's media harpies swooped down us. We'd be grateful if we only got an angry voice mail. Sometimes they arrived uninvited at the *News's* front desk. If we didn't come out, they'd leave a couple of slabs of proselytizing materials. Once, as a peace gesture, they invited us to the Midtown branch of their Celebrity Centre.

Joanna went with our fearless reporters Jo Piazza and Chris Rovzar. The lobby had a big oil portrait of founder L. Ron Hubbard and a Maoist-style painting of laborers walking away from a rising sun. People were coming in to get "audited." The Rush & Molloy contingent sat down for tea with the Centre's director. Chris asked if it was true that Scientology does not accept homosexuals—since Hubbard had called them "perverts" who were "dangerous to society." The director said that, if someone wanted to change, Scientology merely gave him the tools. Chris, who went to Yale and became a Fulbright Scholar, found the answer "pretty disingenuous. Why would you want to change being gay if the church didn't have a problem with it?" The highlight of the visit was the exact replica of Hubbard's office. The Scientologists said it was simply a historical display, but Chris said, "I'm pretty sure it's in case he *comes back!*"

Taking on a Scientology story was always a bear. But now I had the time to delve into a dramatic Reformation in the church—brought about by high-ranking officials who'd defected. One, Amy Scobee, claimed that supreme leader David Miscavige had "snooped" in confidential confessional files and that he'd pressed members to snitch on famous Scientologists "deviating" from the church's "moral code." Another, Marty Rathbun, once one of Miscavige's most trusted lieutenants, told me about a visit Tom Cruise paid to a Scientology compound where three disobedient members were allegedly held captive. Rathbun shared a letter that he'd sent to Cruise's lawyer, Bert Fields. In it, Rathbun claimed that "Miscavige berated [the compound's managers] for being far too light in their demands for confessions [from the three traitors]. Miscavige said that Tom . . . had vowed to . . . personally 'beat the living shit' out of [the trio] if the managers failed to do so. . . . In response, the mob rushed at the three, [pounding them until] each had two black eyes."

I called church spokesman Tommy Davis, the son of actress Anne Archer, for comment on both accounts. As usual, Davis first asked if he could record our conversation. He said that, in response to her "disgusting allegations," the church was "preparing a lawsuit" against Scobee. "Nobody in the church has ever violated the priest-penitent privilege." As for Rathbun, he said that the so-called traitors had all made sworn affidavits stating they were not assaulted and that Miscavige never invoked Cruise's name. Bert Fields said he doubted Rathbun's claims and promised that Cruise would sue Rathbun if he revealed the confidences the actor had shared with him during "audit" sessions. "I would never reveal what Tom told me," Rathbun told me. "Unlike the church, which does, I actually hold those secrets sacrosanct."

Our Sunday column also turned into a nursery for famous love children.

Bassinet #1: We'd always admired Richard Parsons, a Bed-Stuy kid who became one of the country's most prominent African American executives. We liked our Tribeca neighbor's independence and sly sense of humor. Even when he was chairman and CEO of Time Warner, he'd get twelve-dollar haircuts at the Russian barbershop on Chambers Street. But one day we got a tip: the married, sixty-one-year-old Parsons had fathered an out-of-wedlock child. The mother was said to be

MacDella Cooper, a thirty-two-year-old former model and founder of a charity for children in her homeland of Liberia.

I called Cooper and asked if Parsons was the father of her eleven-month-old daughter, Ella. "My private life is private," she said. But she added with an audible wink, "I'm sure you can draw your own conclusions." I got the sense that she wanted Parsons's paternity out there—that, once again, we were being used in some behind-the-scenes drama. I called Parsons for comment at Citigroup, where he was now chairman of the board. It wasn't long before Parsons called on Mort Zuckerman, who owned the Citigroup building. He asked Mort to kill the story. To Mort's credit, he deferred to our editor, Martin Dunn, who knew that if we didn't do the story, someone else would—certainly before Ella was too much older. We tried to put a positive spin on it—reporting that the "widely admired executive" had agreed to support Ella and set up an educational trust for her. I continued to see him around the neighborhood with Laura Parsons, his wife of forty-one years. But I steered clear of his barbershop.

Bassinet #2: Jeffrey Toobin had long been a big wheel on the media scene. His reporting on CNN and in the *New Yorker* had made him arguably the foremost legal analyst in the country. But over the course of nine months, we learned that Toobin himself was party to some delicate litigation. For nearly a decade, the married father of two had been having an off-and-on affair with attorney Casey Greenfield, the beautiful, ginger-haired daughter of political pundit Jeff Greenfield, a former colleague of Toobin's. In 2008, when she told Toobin she was pregnant, he questioned whether he was responsible. A source told us he also offered her "money if she'd have an abortion." When she refused, Toobin "told her she was going to regret it, that she shouldn't expect any help from him," claimed another source. (This was around the time Toobin wrote a *New Yorker* piece on a woman's right to choose.) A DNA test ultimately proved he was the dad of her son, but Toobin wouldn't give Greenfield the support she requested.

Toobin didn't look too pleased when I showed up at a morning hearing in Manhattan Family Court. "Respectfully," he said, "I have nothing to say." He sat glumly as other attorneys recognized CNN's famous analyst and wondered what case he'd come to analyze.

Our stories about Toobin spurred some prominent women in the media to recall their experiences with him. Our friend who'd dodged

Governor X's advances said Toobin had left a startlingly crude message on her voice mail when she declined his date offer. Another well-known woman in the media told me that, at a party in Washington, "He came up behind me and whispered in my ear. . . . [What he said] was so disgusting. At the time, I never even knew people *did* that." We also obtained some graphic emails Toobin had sent. We couldn't consider repeating his alleged language in a family newspaper. But media bloggers were eager to post his come-ons. They pleaded with us to leak what he supposedly said. We had no particular affection for Toobin. But we imagined how the raunch would permanently stain the memories of his children if they ever Googled them. We used to scoff at celebs who used the child defense—until we became parents. The bloggers could accuse us of being wimps, but were Toobin's sex fantasies really vital information?

Even without disclosing the steamiest allegations, our stories gave ammunition to Toobin's critics. When conservative gadfly Andrew Breitbart accused Representative Anthony Weiner of sending sex texts, Toobin said he was embarrassed that CNN had given credence to Breitbart. To turn the Weiner story "into something more than a mild prank," said Toobin, "seems really excessive." Breitbart countered that Toobin was no one to take the moral high ground. Of course, Weiner's "mild prank" ultimately resulted in his resignation from Congress.

Bassinet #3: During the 2008 Presidential race, we watched Richard Parsons—yes, the same Richard Parsons—interview candidate John Edwards. At a reception after the interview, we asked Edwards about the *National Enquirer*'s claim that he'd had an affair with a female campaign staffer, Rielle Hunter. We shared some mutual friends with Hunter, who used to call herself Lisa Druck when she was a coke-Hoovering party girl. The *Enquirer* had promised a follow-up story. But seven weeks later, we were still waiting.

"The story disappeared," Edwards told us, "because it's made up."

Much later, Edwards admitted to the affair, but his lies continued. After Hunter gave birth to a daughter, Quinn, she and Edwards claimed the father was Edwards's aide Andrew Young. A friend who'd seen the baby told us: "She looks like John Edwards in a onesie."

Then Young turned on Edwards, admitting Edwards was Quinn's father. We revealed that Young had a sex tape Edwards and Hunter had made. Hunter had been hired to videotape Edwards's campaign, but we reported that this tape apparently showed "him taking positions that weren't on his official platform."

Around the time Edwards finally admitted he was Quinn's daddy, I heard that his wife, Elizabeth, had been branding Hunter as a blackmailing gold digger in blog comments where Elizabeth used the pseudonym "Cherubim." I also heard that Elizabeth had been investigating whether her twenty-eight-year-old daughter, Cate, could become the legal guardian of the younger Edwards children, Jack and Emma, should, God forbid, Hunter became their stepmother.

After Elizabeth lost her cancer battle, Hunter dared to say in her memoir that Elizabeth had gone "bonkers." Joanna came to the dead woman's defense, asking why Elizabeth might not be herself under the circumstances. "Could it be that you [Hunter] started to have sex with her husband just fourteen months after she had been diagnosed with terminal breast cancer? . . . You call Elizabeth 'venomous.' . . . You call Elizabeth a 'witch on wheels.' Yet it is you who was driving around in a BMW . . . part of $900,000 paid for your silence. If only we could get that now."

24

Rush & Molloy Split

Joanna's *picante* commentaries worked well with my slow-cooked Sunday barbecue of celebs. In the fall of 2009, I fired up the smoker for another story. This one was about math teacher-turned-billionaire Jeffrey Epstein. The fifty-six-year-old money manager had come from humble beginnings in Brooklyn; now he owned the largest private residence in Manhattan, as well as homes in Paris, New Mexico, and Palm Beach, and his own Caribbean island. He'd given generously to scientific research and education. But there was some mystery as to how he made his money and what went on behind the doors of his mansions.

Four years earlier, a woman had told Palm Beach police that her fourteen-year-old daughter had been taken to Epstein's home by an older girl and that her daughter had been paid $300 to strip and massage Epstein. After hearing more and more similar stories, the cops started an eleven-month undercover investigation. Epstein hired a legal dream team that included Alan Dershowitz, Roy Black, Gerald Lefcourt, and later, Kenneth Starr. They argued that many of the girls had told Epstein they were eighteen or older, and that many were already prostitutes. After two years of wrangling, Epstein signed a sealed

Non-Prosecution Agreement in which he pleaded guilty to reduced state charges involving the procurement of minors for prostitution. Former circuit judge William Berger, who represented one accuser, called the secret arrangement a "sweetheart deal." Epstein served just thirteen months of an eighteen-month sentence—spending nights only in the Palm Beach County Stockade.

Epstein was still on probation when I started looking into the civil suits filed in Florida against the silver-haired mogul by women who alleged he'd sexually abused them as minors. One plaintiff, "Jane Doe 102," alleged that Epstein's ex-girlfriend, Ghislaine Maxwell, the daughter of late, disgraced *Daily News* owner Robert Maxwell, had led the plaintiff "up a flight of stairs to a spa room [where Epstein] was lying naked on the massage table. . . . Ms. Maxwell then took off her own shirt and left on her underwear and started rubbing her breasts across Defendant's body, impliedly showing Plaintiff what she was expected to do. . . . The encounter escalated, with Defendant and Ms. Maxwell sexually assaulting, battering, exploiting, and abusing Plaintiff."

I allowed that some of Epstein's accusers might be exaggerating their trauma. But two dozen? Jane Doe 102's charges had never been reported in New York. Maxwell, whom we knew casually, was a *marchesa* among the city's socially conscious social set. I learned that the attorney for several Epstein accusers, Brad Edwards, had just served a subpoena on Maxwell as she was leaving the Global Initiative summit of her friend Bill Clinton.

Naturally, I reached out for comment to Ghislaine and Epstein's lawyers. I didn't hear back from them for several days. But a few hours short of our deadline, Martin Dunn heard from Mort Zuckerman. I'd been afraid this would happen. Ghislaine and Epstein had known Mort for years. In fact, Epstein had been Mort's partner in a couple of publishing deals. They'd called Mort. Ghislaine had vigorously denied that she'd been Epstein's procurer. I was told my story was not dead, but that I should hold off on it because Mort had arranged for Epstein to speak to me the following week. Epstein had given few interviews in his life, so this was an opportunity.

A few days later, I went into Martin's office for our phone conference with Epstein, who was under house arrest in Palm Beach. His first sentence was: "Can we keep this off the record?" I had a long list of questions. But he dodged most of them, on the advice of counsel. After about twenty minutes, I could see we weren't getting anywhere. There was nothing usable. To me, it seemed Epstein had promised an "interview" just to stall my story.

I kept digging for new stuff on him. I was talking to lawyers for other accusers, private eyes, cops, and other journalists. There were people in Palm Beach who believed Epstein was still preying upon young women. A couple of these people had been great about sharing information and documents. One night, I got together in New York with three of these sources—a journalist, an activist against child sex trafficking, and an attorney who'd been following the Epstein case. I told them I'd talked with Epstein. They asked if they could hear my recording. They agreed to keep it confidential. Since they'd been helpful to me, I played them three or four minutes. Even though he was just repeating his usual denials, they were riveted. It was like they were hearing Mephistopheles himself.

After working on the story for almost a month, I had enough material for a magazine article. I compressed as much as I could into our column. Among other things, I reported that Epstein had quietly settled with Jane Doe 102, who'd claimed that he'd paid her "to be sexually exploited by [his friends] . . . including royalty [and] politicians." We reported that Epstein's pilot had recently been deposed about whether any of Epstein's passengers had witnessed underage girls on the plane. The passengers had included Kevin Spacey, Chris Tucker, Bill Clinton, Britain's Prince Andrew, former Israeli Prime Minister Ehud Barak, and Obama economic adviser Lawrence Summers. We also quoted Epstein's defenders, who said the women's lawyers were dragging his famous friends into the mud as part of a shakedown.

Even with his denials, Epstein's antagonists were thrilled that the story had made it into the paper. But one of them soon bit me in the ass.

Attorneys for Epstein's accusers were having a hard time deposing him. When they managed to sit him down, he'd invoke his Fifth Amendment right against self-incrimination on every question except his name. Once, the lawyer for a fifteen-year-old girl inquired: "Is it true that you have what's been described as an egg-shaped penis?" The lawyer was quoting a police report, but Epstein's lawyer immediately stopped the grilling.

It's no wonder that Brad Edwards, who represented "Jane Doe" and other women, perked up when I told him I'd interviewed Epstein. We'd been swapping information. Edwards asked me if he could get a copy of the tape. I told him no. I said that the interview had been off the record and that Epstein hadn't said anything that would help him anyway. I thought that was the end of it. Next thing I know, I'm being served with a subpoena. Edwards and another attorney, Paul Cassell, had filed a motion in federal court in Florida, demanding that we share the recording.

Edwards argued in his motion that, in one deposition, Epstein had denied ever speaking with me. The recording could prove perjury. It could also prove that Epstein didn't feel remorse, which would support his accusers' damage claims.

Rush & Molloy and the *Daily News* believed it would set a dangerous precedent to turn over the recording of any interview, particularly an off-the-record one. Our tireless attorney, Anne Carroll, moved to quash the subpoena, arguing that we were protected under the First Amendment. Although I had played a few minutes of the recording for three sources, our response stated, the *News* had not published its contents.

"Forcing me to testify and to give up the tape . . . would compromise my reporting by deterring other sources from speaking with me out of fear that they will become involved in third-party litigations," I said in my affidavit.

Edwards and Cassell came back with a motion claiming that the interview was "unique and not otherwise obtainable from other witnesses." They contended that the *News* had waived its protected privilege when I played the recording for his sources. Even if he hadn't, they argued, the privilege didn't apply because Epstein was not a *confidential* source—everyone knew he was the person on the recording.

The Palm Beach papers were reporting on every motion. Anne Carroll could see the case was escalating quickly. Calling in reinforcements, the *News* brought world-class First Amendment litigator Laura Handman up from Washington. Appearing before US District Judge Lawrence M. McKenna in a cavernous Manhattan courtroom, Handman argued that the give-and-take between reporter and source was "critical to news gathering."

"Mr. Rush could find himself testifying in [many] cases just because he had the temerity to do some reporting on a very important story," she said. Handman maintained that I should not have to testify in court. She encouraged Judge McKenna to listen to the recording in his chambers to determine for himself that it held nothing helpful to Jane Doe's case.

US District Judge Lawrence McKenna said he'd listen to it, adding that he hoped the *News* wouldn't defy his decision if he ruled against the paper. Should the *News* refuse to turn the recording over to Jane Doe's team, I could be held in contempt and go to jail.

"I hope you don't have to bring pajamas to the next hearing," McKenna quipped. Ha, ha.

The next day, the *Palm Beach Daily News's* front page asked, "Could *New York Daily News* gossip columnist George Rush be the next Judith Miller?" Reporter Michele Dargan, who'd flown up for the hearing, recalled that *The New York Times's* Miller spent eighty-five days behind bars when she wouldn't give up a confidential source.

Ten days later, Judge McKenna ordered the *News* to fork over the twenty-two-minute recording.

"The court finds that the materials at issue 'are not reasonably obtainable from other available sources,'" McKenna ruled. "The fact that the recording is in Mr. Epstein's own voice is also significant from a trial perspective."

The decision stunned some media law observers. McKenna said he'd keep the recording under seal until the *News* declared whether it would appeal his decision. Our lawyers estimated that approaching the appellate division would cost $50,000 in legal fees.

Mort Zuckerman wasn't happy. He'd set up my interview with his former business partner, and it had turned into an expensive fiasco. He called to ream me. He said, "How did this happen?" I apologized that it had come to this. Obviously, in hindsight, I wished I hadn't mentioned the interview to anybody. But I reminded him that "off the record" meant that the interview couldn't be *published*, not that it couldn't be spoken about or listened to. I had to wonder if McKenna found the allegations against Epstein serious enough to justify trampling a constitutional privilege. Maybe McKenna did hear a "lack of remorse" in the voice of the registered sex offender.

I told Mort we could still win this. The case law was there. I think Mort knew that the media world was watching to see if the *News* would fight for the principle. Despite his anger, Mort stepped up the plate. The *News* took on the appeal. I hope Mort's friend, Epstein, helped him out with the legal bills. He had the most to lose if Jane Doe's lawyers started picking apart the interview.

I still thought I might get fired. It would have undercut the *News's* case to abandon its "Judith Miller." But who knew? Fortunately, something miraculous happened. Perhaps because of the tape, Epstein settled with Jane Doe. She didn't need my recording anymore.

Four years after Sarah Jessica Parker did a reading of Douglas Carter Beane's play about two married gossip columnists, it opened on Broadway. He called it *Mr. and Mrs. Fitch*. Beane took the columnists' names from the song by Cole Porter. Our mutual friend, Cynthia Parsons, used to talk to Beane about Rush & Molloy, which he'd told us he read. But Beane took the Fitches in his own direction. Mr. Fitch, superbly played by John Lithgow, was gay. Mrs. Fitch (the terrific Jennifer Ehle) was his partner in dashing off the sort of society diary that hadn't existed since Cholly Knickerbocker. Despite Beane's torrent of bon mots, the critics executed *Mr. and Mrs. Fitch* within a matter of weeks. The Tony-nominated Beane hadn't seemed interested in the realities of what we did, but he had, in his way, glimpsed our psychic ache. One critic found it preposterous that Mr. Fitch, a gossip columnist, secretly longed to finish his serious political novel. It didn't seem so preposterous to us.

As much as we tried to inject Burma and debt relief into the column, we still had to wallow in a trough of fluff. Our inbox filled up with "urgent" e-blasts about whose slingbacks Beyoncé wore last night. God forbid we missed a development in the romance of *The Hills'* twits Heidi Montag and Spencer Pratt! When we could steal time to read ancient history or modern fiction, it was like reading porn.

The game had changed.

It used to be exciting to unlock the secrets of legends like Marlon Brando and Bob Dylan, guys who'd never dream of hiring a personal publicist. The new instant celebs never had any talent to squander. There'd always been people who were famous just for being famous—like Brenda Frazier, who inspired the word "celebutante" in 1939. But now there were so many of them. Network execs figured out that they could make more money off so-called "reality" shows. The drecky "stars" of these shows hadn't earned one minute of fame, much less fifteen. One of the principles of a good gossip column had always been: it's as much whom you *don't* write about as who you do. The new reality show gang just had to get drunk and scream at each other. The conflicts of the unreal *Housewives of New York City* were usually scripted. What was unscripted was their off-camera rivalry. Whenever Bethenny Frankel or Kelly Killoren-Bensimon screwed up, the others made sure we heard about it. But who cared if they fell from grace? They didn't have far to fall.

The flacks for these runt talents were always trying to get us excited about their fragrance or fashion line. We even designed the Obligatory Celebrity Brand Marketing board game for the column, where you matched the star with what he'd inevitably try to sell you. Paul Newman had started a food line for the sole purpose of raising money for sick children. Kim Kardashian raved about her new stilettos from ShoeDazzle or her new Bebe dress or her CVS Pharmacy toiletries—never mentioning to her twenty million or so Twitter followers that she was reportedly being paid $10,000 a tweet. Rappers and athletes who grew up in poverty showed no mercy on kids still living in the ghetto. NBA All-Star Stephon Marbury did put his name on a fifteen dollar sneaker. But most of their shoes and clothes cost a fortune.

Canny stars like Beyoncé and Rihanna crafted their brand storyline, doling out calculated glimpses of their private lives on social media—depriving even the most worshipful entertainment shows of their exclusives. Celebs tweeted out snaps of themselves half (or fully) naked. Their "selfie" pictures eliminated the need for stars to do deals with favored paparazzi. Social media allowed them to spin their own version of the truth. They didn't have to convince a columnist to run a correction.

At the same time, their lawyers had become more vigilant than ever. Celebrities whose status as public figures prevented them from suing in America now found barristers in the United Kingdom, where the defamation laws were more in their favor. If they could prove that the offending US publication had a few readers in the United Kingdom, even on the Internet, they could file suit there. This was known as "libel tourism." While visiting London, the libel tourist could seek a "super injunction." Once, we got our hands on a book proposal in which celebrity bodyguard Mickey Brett trotted out stories about his former clients Brad Pitt and Angelina Jolie. In checking out the stories, many of which were specious, we discovered that Brad and Angie had obtained one of these super injunctions. Not only did it forbid the British press from repeating Brett's tales, it also barred Fleet Street from reporting that the injunction even existed. Could we in America report that it existed? Our lawyer, Anne Carroll, was tempted to see what a New York court would say. But considering that the experiment could prove expensive, we kept Brangelina's secret.

The online scramble for "unique visitors" also changed how gossip was covered. While we tried to break news, the young staff on our website had to keep up with the twenty-four-seven babble of bloggers. A hip hop site would claim that Beyoncé had bought Jay Z a plane. To us, the story was obviously crap. Jigga was too smart a businessman not to lease, or have his company buy it. But all the other gossip sites would start "aggregating" the claim. So how could the *Daily News* ignore it? Our web writers didn't always have the time or contacts to check the story out—particulary in the middle of the night. And even stories we broke had to answer to SEO—Search Engine Optimization. Our website's headline-writers had to cook a thirty-inch story down to a crack rock that glistened with as many most-searched words as possible. It sometimes led to libel problems, but such was life. An SEO specialist encouraged all reporters to drop trending names and topics into their stories, even if they didn't have much to do with the story. We suggested, "The budget deficit was Kardashian-ingly large." We were told we were thinking in the right direction.

Expense was becoming more and more of a concern at the *Daily News*. Web traffic was soaring. But the *News* depended for revenue on selling ads in the *paper*. Ad rates were linked to circulation, which was plummeting, because people could read the paper online for free. It was the same story for newspapers around the country. Struggling to keep the *News* in the black, Mort Zuckerman told Martin Dunn there had to be job cuts. Rather than lay people off, Mort offered severance based on time served.

We'd both been at the *News* going on eighteen years. But Joanna was already sort of free from gossip. She had the column where she could write about all sorts of things. So she encouraged me to go for it. Considering the amount of water this ship was taking on, we thought someone better swim for help.

It was hard to think about breaking up the act. But it was time. Inheriting Ed Sullivan's column at the *New York Daily News* used to be a career summit. Now *everybody* was a gossip columnist. There used to be a swaggering cat called the "newspaperman." The bloggers had lit a match to that guy. But the Internet had brought us 12.5 million unique visitors every month. We had managed to outlive ten other gossip columnists at the *Daily News*. We asked the guys in our library how many columns we'd written. We couldn't believe it when they said almost four thousand. That was a pretty good run.

We started a sidebar in our last column with: "Today's top item—Rush and Molloy are splitting! Now that we have your attention, let us clarify that, no, we don't need a divorce lawyer. What is true is that Rush & Molloy, the fifteen-year-old column, is going away."

We thanked the readers who had "developed an unhealthy addiction to R&M" and "all you tipsters, snitches, snoops, and spywitnesses. You know who you are."

To our surprise, a few people seemed to care. The *Post*'s Cindy Adams called. Despite our little tiffs over the years, we'd come to appreciate what a pro Cindy was. Now she wanted to know, off the record, "Are you all right?" Yes, we were. Some eulogies followed. The *Village Voice*'s Joe Coscarelli wrote, "You don't have to like it, but you can't knock the hustle. . . . For fifteen years, George Rush and his wife, Joanna Molloy, had a shit-talking, rumor-spreading operation of the highest order." The *New York Observer*'s Zeke Turner did a story on the wake we threw at an Irish bar, where, he wrote, tearful friends said "goodbye to a column, and an era."

I told Zeke: "I do feel that my wife and I have become like the bagel and cream cheese for a lot of people in New York, and we help get them into their day. But sometimes you want to aspire to a more sophisticated cuisine."

In our last column, we'd thanked our indispensable legmen and leggywomen. Unbeknownst to us, one of them, Ben Widdicombe, later took it upon himself to solicit reminiscences from our graduates, who'd gone on to work for *US Weekly*, *People*, CNN, the Huffington Post, TruthDig.com, *Vanity Fair*, and *The New York Times*, among other places. Gawker, usually pitiless in its snark, ran their nostalgic "oral history." Some of the column's survivors claimed they'd actually learned something from us. Ben concluded: "Rush & Molloy taught a generation of reporters that despite all the temptations and excesses and stereotypes, it is possible to write a gossip column with integrity. That is their legacy."

We felt like we were sitting in the back pew at our own funeral. But we were incredibly touched. Joanna went on to deal with everything from gun control to tax reform in her solo column. But she couldn't entirely escape celebrities.

Lindsay Lohan remained the gift that kept on giving. Her life in and out of rehab, club fights, car accidents, and courtrooms kept Joanna's column well-stocked with calamity. But chronicling her downward spiral was heartbreaking. Her father, Michael, told Joanna, "Dina and I caused this and we need to fix it. . . . Linds needs family therapy with us, but Dina won't do it." The next day, Dina admitted that, if she could do it over again, she "might not" have pushed Lindsay into acting.

Even Lindsay came to be eclipsed by Kim Kardashian and her master Machiavellian marketing plans. When the narcissist for the ages filed for divorce from Brooklyn Net Kris Humphries after just seventy-two days of marriage, Joanna asked readers: "Be strong . . . If only the rest of us poor souls trapped in the reality TV universe could get a quickie divorce from all things Kim Kardashian . . . We have the power to make this money-grubbing airhead go away." An enterprising reader launched the online petition BoycottKim.com. It got 277,500 signatures—an excellent sign of hope in our culture. Unfortunately, it was a fraction of Kardashian's millions of Twitter followers.

Jennifer Lopez's selfishness hit closest to home. Joanna had grown up on the same Bronx street as J. Lo. The singer had followed Joanna at Holy Family School on Castle Hill Avenue, where Lopez's mother, Guadalupe, had been a gym teacher. Yet, even though Lopez's worth grew to an estimated $260 million as she promoted her "Jenny from the Block" image, Holy Family's principal, Claire La Tempa, admitted to Joanna, "Jennifer hasn't even sent us a CD."

Lopez had once claimed she wanted to help "children all over the planet." But her own elementary school was filled with minority students whose parents could barely pay for their lunches. Lopez drove right past them when she took Diane Sawyer around the neighborhood in a limo. Later, she was caught using a body double to actually drive around "the block" for her Fiat 500 commercial, saying in a voiceover: "They may be just streets to you, but to me, they're a playground." As it happened, the kids at Holy Family School wish they had a playground–Principal La Tempa has to put orange construction cones on Blackrock Avenue at lunchtime.

Joanna wrote a column about how Lopez had neglected her alma mater. It ended up on the front page with the headline:

JENNY DISSES THE BLOCK

As for me, I figured it was time to get out of the office. Nothing gave me more satisfaction than exploring the world—particularly the third world. My idols were writers like Norman Lewis, Paul Theroux, Pico Iyer, Bruce Chatwin, Redmond O'Hanlon. Now I had the time to roam around Africa for the *Condé Nast Traveler*. I leapfrogged among the islands of Cape Verde, off Senegal. Eamon and I helped build schools on volunteer trips to Ghana and Madagascar. I wrote a *Travel + Leisure* profile about a remarkable Kenyan conservationist, Richard Bonham, known as "the white Maasai." Every once in a while, I ran into someone famous—like Forest Whitaker in the desert of Oman. Nice guy. We did some dune-bashing.

Yes, the party invitations plummeted. Some people I'd confused with friends disappeared now that I couldn't help them. But quite a few well-known people stayed in touch, especially now that they didn't have to begin every sentence with, "This is *not* for publication!"

25

People Will Talk

Our livelihood did cause some people to shun us. But many more asked us to pull up a chair. The intelligentsia liked hearing dirt about people who mattered to them—topsoil, if you will. Hard-drinking polemicist Christopher Hitchens was happy to get on the phone to take on Alexander Cockburn, Henry Kissinger, God, or whomever he was feuding with that day. One of our favorite columns early on concerned novelist Graham Greene's back-channel negotiations with a mystery man representing Salvadoran guerrillas who held a South African ambassador hostage. Greene finally became convinced that the hostage-broker was none other than Nobel Prize winner Gabriel Garcia Marquez. Greene told our source: "Do I have a scoop for you!"

Later on, we gagged on the reality show stars. But throughout the years, we'd talked to enough bona fide legends to make the job palatable—in fact, delectable. People like Nelson Mandela, astronaut Buzz Aldrin, filmmaker Robert Altman, Nobel Peace Prize winner Elie Wiesel, DNA co-discoverer James Watson, and Taliban-defying Latifa, who opened a school for Afghan girls at age sixteen. We were always honored to be roughed up by the crusty Norman Mailer.

Timothy Leary, shortly before his death, shared his recipe for baked sinsemilla and brie. Joanna cherished her chat with Internet co-creator Dr. Robert Kahn. She asked why he didn't choose to profit from his invention. "By profit," said the puzzled visionary, "do you mean making money?" She once asked Isaac Asimov to sign a book; the futurist asked her name, then inscribed, not just his autograph, but a spontaneous limerick: "There once was a girl named Joanna/ For whom sex was appropriate manna/When asked why this was/ She answered, 'Becuz/I think it is fun and I wanna!'" Hell, we even treasured the absurdity of our back-of-his-limo interview with Wishbone, a sprightly Jack Russell terrier who had his own TV show.

We met a surprising number of actors whose egos didn't suffer from edema. We liked talking about the Romani people with gypsyish Johnny Depp. I enjoyed the Godfatherly kisses James Gandolfini planted on my cheeks after I oafishly asked the *Sopranos* star if he was going to watch his show's third season premiere. ("I've seen it," said Gandolfini. "You want me to sit at home and masturbate?") They all demonstrated that interacting with the media didn't have to be a blood sport—that maybe surly Sean Penn didn't have to lash himself to the press torture wheel.

The king of the gents was Tom Hanks. Once, when we fled the crush of *New York Times* columnist Maureen Dowd's 2009 inauguration party, we found Hanks standing outside. Dowd's Georgetown townhouse was packed with senators and stars. But Hanks was content to cool his heels on the sidewalk with other freezing guests. He jovially warned new arrivals, "She's stopped giving out free hot dogs, people!" Joanna asked the two-time Oscar winner how he stayed so down-to-earth. One of his first jobs, he answered, was as a bellhop in an Oakland hotel. The manager told him to drive a beautiful R&B singer—he never learned her name—to the airport. "She talked to me the whole drive, and asked me about myself, and when we arrived, she gave me a big tip," he said. "I never forgot that." It was our luck that Hanks went on to bring our friend Mike McAlary back to life in Nora Ephron's Broadway play *Lucky Guy*. (McAlary also inspired Dan Klores's equally powerful play *The Wood*.)

Why did we bother with the dimmer lights? Why did we write about self-immolating celebs like Charlie Sheen, Britney Spears, and

Lindsay Lohan? And why did people read it? Maybe it was because we were all rubberneckers. Their crack-ups comforted us. We'd escaped their fate. Their money didn't save them. Sometimes, though, their meltdowns were a little too vivid. We still wish that paparazzo hadn't sent those close-ups of Britney's vomit in the back of her limo outside the club where she'd taken off all her clothes.

Our critics saw us as rag pickers, trash compactors, purveyors of prurience. Most major religions condemned our trade. George Harrison cheekily called gossip "the Devil's radio." But we were, in our way, enforcers of old-fashioned decency. Gossip columns—and tabloids in general—are built on upholding threatened values, like fidelity and transparency. Otherwise how could we proclaim so much behavior as SHOCKING! "Scandal is gossip made tedious by morality," said Oscar Wilde, who must have enjoyed a good item. Never mind that few gossip columnists lead lives that recommend them for sainthood. There'd always been a fine line between the dispensers of the gossip and preachers of the gospel, especially those preachers who got busted with boys. What do people ask when they're hungry for some dish? "What's the Good Word?"

It's often been said that our celebrities are like the gods of Olympus. We pass down myths of their exploits and romps. We're chastened when we see them fly too close to the sun. We're awed by the amount of sex they appear to be having. They seem to be forever coupling and recoupling.

President Kennedy, as frisky a satyr as any who gamboled through Arcadia, said, "All history is gossip." Well, maybe not all. But much of it. Cicero accused Mark Antony of being a debauched bisexual. Thomas Jefferson hired a pamphleteer to claim John Adams was "mentally deranged." Franklin Roosevelt told an aide to spread the rumor that Wendell Willkie was having an affair (even as FDR was cheating on his own wife, Eleanor). J. Edgar Hoover amassed the deadliest arsenal of gossip in history. Virtually every presidential campaign has relied on moles to disseminate opposition research on everything from one candidate's $400 haircut to another's possible black love-child. Dish—about illegal nannies, stray pubic hairs, membership in restricted country clubs—has been used to scuttle Supreme Court and cabinet confirmations.

Maybe we crave the personal details of the great stars to try to decipher their talents. Still, we stopped wanting to know more about one of Hollywood's most venerable and bankable actors—a would-be president in his homeland—once a friend told us he'd twice tried to rape her. Americans look for celebs that *appear* to have the strength we need—especially during wars and recessions. Year after year, we hoist Clint Eastwood atop our list of most admired stars, despite his progressive nuttiness. Occasionally, a celeb imparts a genuinely courageous lesson, as Angelina Jolie did when she broke the news of her radical mastectomy on her own terms. For all the bad news we devour about them, we're mostly devoted to our celebs. We name our babies after them. We spend our pay checks on their rank fragrances, hideous jewelry, and sweatshop-made apparel. Why have we made ourselves indentured servants to these "brand ambassadors"? Once only the Queen of England issued royal warrants. Soon we'll see sensual jelly made "By Appointment to Lord Tracy of Morgan."

Celebrity gossip helps us chisel the ice with strangers. Women may get to know each other exchanging the latest on Gwyneth Paltrow's nauseatingly perfect life. Guys may swap dope on whether Barry Bonds's steroid use left his bat a little limp. And don't think guys don't gossip. Rumor is rampant in army barracks, on trading floors, in locker rooms. Only men call it "news." Rumor bonds strangers in a spontaneous conspiracy, like two old cellmates plotting a new heist. Venerable columnist Earl Wilson said, "Gossip is when you hear something you like about someone you don't." Put in those terms, who doesn't like gossip? Except for maybe a devout Hutterite or . . . you, dear reader, when you're the target of it.

Unfortunately, truth doesn't have the properties of Kevlar. Truth won't necessarily make the scandal go away. In fact, today, the scandal never really dies. You used to be able to wrap fish in the scandal. Unless you knew the date, you couldn't even find the scandal in the library. But now it's always online. There are people who know how to push it down the search results. But other people know how to pull it back up. Somewhere, it will remain cached.

Some hypocrites bring gossip on themselves. Senator Larry Craig, Representative David Dreier, and other closeted politicians were asking to be outed when they supported anti-gay legislation. So were Congressmen Dan Burton and Henry Hyde when they voted to impeach Bill Clinton despite their own infidelities.

Sometimes gossip takes too heavy a toll. General David Petraeus's affair with biographer Paula Broadwell made for delicious reading, especially socialite Jill Kelley's claim that Paula had cyberstalked her. But when the commander resigned as director of the CIA, it was a loss for the country. In wartime, "Careless Talk Costs Lives," as the WWII propaganda posters warned. Teenage gossips are scary at times, like child soldiers who've been given AK47s. Their merciless sniping has driven their classmates to take their own lives. Innocent people who haven't sought the spotlight are entitled to their privacy.

But we still think gossip can be a force for good. The shifty celebs may think they won. They do have more control over their images. But more often than not, they shoot themselves in the groin (witness the bodily function bulletins from John Mayer, Katy Perry, Ke$sha, and Jessica Simpson). All their image consultants can't protect them from a nation armed with smart phones. Palm cameras can be used against bullies like Rutgers basketball coach Mike Rice. The night has a thousand eyes.

Rumor consumers have become cannier. They often vote *against* the candidate who waged the smear campaign. They recognize that an actor isn't always the noble hero he plays—not when they've reviewed his arrest report. They know when they're being spun—like when Tom Cruise playfully jumps on *Jay Leno's* couch to try to reverse the image damage he did by jumping on Oprah's.

We may be out of the game but still can't stop gossiping. The urge runs too deep in our DNA. Primatologist Robert M. Sapolsky will tell you that if two high-ranking baboons get into a scrap, a third one will stay to gawk and then spread the news. (Watch for baboons to start posting Instagram pictures.)

"Anyone who has obeyed nature by transmitting a piece of gossip," wrote Primo Levi, "experiences the explosive relief that accompanies the satisfying of a primary need."

Whispers draw people closer. Gossip is a raw, real feeling. It's where we speak our heart, even if by gossping we reveal our heart to be black.

"Secrecy sets barriers between men," observed philosopher George Simmel, "but at the same time offers the seductive temptation to break through the barriers by gossip or confession."

Gossip digs a tunnel under the walls of elites who would exclude us. It dynamites gag orders. It remains the murky wellspring for important exposés like the My Lai massacre, the Watergate break-in, the pedophilia of Penn State coach Jerry Sandusky. So often, after the truth comes out, people realize they should have gossiped more, and earlier. Fishwives can provide a waterfront watch against hoodlums—including hoodlums who arrive on yachts.

The era of the professional gossip is almost obsolete. It was fun while it lasted. We liked being oracles, handing down pronouncements on which celebrities to worship. But we can't help but celebrate the ability everyone now has to be a gossip columnist—to indulge in this most fundamental form of storytelling via blogging, tweeting, Facebooking, or whatever queen-sized platform for social intercourse they think of next. Our advice to would-be gossips is to gossip about something that matters to you. Go after the liars, braggarts, quacks, and hypocrites. Try to give your victims a chance to respond. Your stories will be not only more believable but more dramatic. Retweet not just those who agree with you but those who think you're full of crap. We hereby hand our laurel branches to you. You are now free to carve your own false idols—and to smash them when you please.

Acknowledgments

Several kind people aided, abetted or resisted throwing a monkey wrench during the construction of this book. Skyhorse publisher Tony Lyons and senior editor Jennifer McCartney indulged the delusion that anyone would care about the ravings of two recovering gossip columnists. Jenn showed remarkable intelligence and poise under pressure. Judith Regan, publishing visionary and valkyrie, showed that it is possible for one of our column's unwilling subjects to become a friend. She contributed invaluable pro-bono guidance and butt-kicks.

We're also beholden to resourceful Rush & Molloy reporters Shazia Ahmad, Zoe Alexander, Kasia Anderson, Lisa Arcella, K.C. Baker, Marcus Baram, Sari Botton, Sean Evans, Caitlin Feurey, Morgan Goldberg, Patrick Huguenin, Baird Jones, Cristina Kinon, Rebecca Louie, Marc Malkin, Spencer Morgan, Deborah Newman, Lola Ogunnaike, Jo Piazza, Riana Positano, Michael Riedel, Karen Robinovitz, Chris Rovzar, Suzanne Rozdeba, Lauren Rubin, Dakota Smith, Heather Stein, Leah Sydney and Ben Widdicombe, as well as to our column's editor, Lance Debler. Thank you all for your nerve and your verve.

George Rush and Joanna Molloy